The Streetsmart Guide to

Short Selling

The Streetsmart Guide to

Short Selling

Techniques the Pros Use to Profit in Any Market

Tom Taulli

McGraw-Hill

New York   Chicago   San Francisco   Lisbon   London   Madrid
Mexico City   Milan   New Delhi   San Juan   Seoul
Singapore   Sydney   Toronto

The **McGraw·Hill** Companies

Library of Congress Cataloging-in-Publication Data
Taulli, Tom, 1968–
    The streetsmart guide to short selling : techniques the pros use to
profit in any market / by Tom Taulli.
        p. cm.
    ISBN 0-07-139394-3 (hardcover : alk. paper)
    1. Short selling.   2. Speculation.   I. Title.
HG6041 .T37 2002
332.64—dc21

                                                         2002005824

1 2 3 4 5 6 7 8 9 0 DOC/DOC 0 9 8 7 6 5 4 3 2

ISBN 0-07-139394-3

McGraw-Hill books are available at special discounts to use as premiums
and sales promotions, or for use in corporate training programs. For more
information, please write to the Director of Special Sales, Professional
Publishing, McGraw-Hill, Two Penn Plaza, New York, NY 10121-2298. Or
contact your local bookstore.

 This book is printed on recycled, acid-free paper containing a
minimum of 50% recycled de-inked paper.

Contents

Foreword

"Buy low, sell high."

Most stock market participants recognize the challenge as well as the humor embedded in that simple adage, but many do not realize that they can change the order. "Sell high, buy low" is an often profitable alternative for those willing to learn the techniques and the pitfalls of short selling.

Short selling is not complicated. First, you sell a security you don't own. How is this possible? Working through your broker, you borrow shares and deliver them to the buyer. In the future, you will have to settle this position by buying shares on the open market and using them to repay those you borrowed. If you can buy those replacement shares at a lower price than your original sale, you make a profit. During the period prior to settlement, you are "short." If the price of the stock rises, then your short position loses value. If the price of the underlying security falls, your short position gains in value.

Investors take short positions for two basic reasons, the first of which is obvious. An investor who believes that the price of a security (or even a broad market index) is going down, can "go short" to profit if his or her hunch proves correct. In the less obvious case, an investor holds both long and short positions in the same portfolio, so that one goes up when the other goes down in value. In other words, the short position is a hedge, and is used to reduce portfolio risk.

As director of portfolio management for a family of mutual funds that include short funds—funds that move in the opposite direction of the general market—I am often asked whether short positions aren't in some way harmful to the securities markets. Particularly after the 2001 terrorist attacks, many journalists expressed discomfort that some investors actually profited from those calamitous events. Isn't it admirable, on the other hand, that our markets offer a means to protect those who are unable to withstand the financial consequences of such a calamity? In the best of market conditions, short selling adds liquidity and flexibility to our already dynamic securities markets. During difficult times, we should remember that those who bought flood insurance did not cause the flood. They are entitled to their claims.

As Tom Taulli makes clear on the pages that follow, short selling is a powerful tool. Short selling can expose investors to unlimited risk, but this same technique can be used to virtually eliminate portfolio risk. In other words, the tool itself is not inherently risky, as long as it is in the hands of a prudent and knowledgeable user.

As we move through the third year of a ferocious bear market, more investors are learning the range of choices available as they approach the role of buyer or seller in a securities trade. Those who take time to understand these choices can unlock a whole new world of investment opportunities.

Charles J. Tennes
Director of Portfolio Management
Rydex Global Advisors
July 5, 2002

Acknowledgments

No book is written in isolation. In fact, because there is actually very little written on the subject of short selling, I interviewed a variety of top people in the field. Some of these people run hedge funds and did not want to be mentioned in the book. But thanks anyway!

Others I want to thank include: Will Lyons, who has a great investment newsletter called Short On Value; Howard Schilit, the whiz at finding accounting shenanigans; Gary Smith, who writes a column on technical analysis for thestreet.com; Chuck Tennes, a portfolio manager at the Rydex Funds; Kaye Thomas, an expert at taxes for investors; Shalin Patel, an analyst with Gomez.com; David Tice, a top manager of The Prudent Bear Fund; Whitney Tilson, a top portfolio manager; Jack Ciesielski, who publishes a newsletter on accounting issues; Howard Simons, an expert in single stock futures; Mark Roberts, who has his own short newsletter; Herb Greenberg, the well-known, hard-hitting columnist at thestreet.com; Ed Ketz, a top accounting professor at Penn State; Lynn Turner, a former head of accounting for the SEC.

I also want to thank Kelli Christiansen, my sponsoring editor, and Scott Kurtz, my production editor. Above all, I want to thank my wife, Shauna.

CHAPTER 1

History of Short Selling

Short selling is not a new phenomenon. Its history stretches back centuries to the establishment of stock markets in the Dutch Republic in the late 1500s, when investors realized that they could not only buy a stock long but could also short a stock.

Like many great economic powers, the Dutch Republic had the advantage of access to the seas—making trading easier. To finance the growth of trade, the Dutch Republic had created a stock exchange. One of the hottest companies was the East Indies Company, which was founded in 1602.

Besides short selling, Dutch investors created other newfangled financial instruments, such as options, unit trusts, and debt/equity swaps. One of the most flamboyant short sellers was Isaac le Maire, who basically invented the "bear raid." That is, he would target a company that was faltering and short as many shares as possible, driving the stock price down. After this, he would buy the depressed stock and create rumors to boost the stock value.

The Dutch Republic underwent a tremendous boom. But, like any capitalist wave, it ended—not with a thud, but a thunder. The markets crashed in 1610. Investors wanted someone to blame. Why not short sellers? Don't they profit when stocks fall? Didn't they put selling pressure on the markets?

As has occurred throughout history, the Dutch stock market consequently prohibited short selling. But, as has also been the case through history, the ban did not last long. Investors found ways around it.

For example, in the 1720s, the French market collapsed and short sellers were blamed. Short selling was outlawed. Interestingly enough, Napoleon considered short selling to be treason, because it was more difficult for him to finance his wars when the markets were shaky. The ban was not lifted in France until the late 1880s. Yet during the time of the ban, there was certainly a good amount of short selling.

The Robber Barons

The history of short selling in the United States is similar to that of the Dutch Republic. That is, it did not take long for the United States to outlaw the practice.

Keep in mind that until the 1850s, the United States was essentially a Third World nation. The economic system was quite unstable, as the country underwent extreme boom–bust cycles. To try to mute the speculation, the New York legislature banned short selling in 1812. However, the ban was not very significant. After all, the New York Stock Exchange was small. For example, on March 16, 1830, there was volume of a mere 31 shares. Such low volume days were not at all uncommon.

By the late 1850s, the short selling ban was lifted in the United States, which was good news for the many speculators of the time. Even though the U.S. economy was showing strong growth, the stock market was still small. Thus, it was not difficult for a speculator to move markets.

In fact, new technology was making it easier to trade. The invention of the telegraph in the 1840s made it possible to trade on a national basis. Then in the 1860s, a telegraph cable was laid across the Atlantic Ocean, making it easier for European investors to access U.S. markets. It was also during this time that the ticker tape was invented. As the name implied, this was a machine that streamed current stock quotes from the New York Stock Exchange.

A critical element in the economic growth of the U.S. economy, and in the boom of the stock market, was the rise of railroads. But building railroads required huge amounts of capital. Thus, savvy financiers had to find ways for these railroads to get the much-needed investment dollars.

For the most part, these financiers were fiercely competitive. They would do just about anything to make money. And the top financiers would make fortunes. They were known as robber barons.

One of the first robber barons was Daniel Drew. Although illiterate, he was an expert at short selling. One favorite technique was "the corner." Simply put, it means an investor captures most of the market of available stock. Once this was done, the speculator could dictate the price.

For example, Drew would manipulate a stock, driving up the stock price. It would achieve a very high valuation. Short sellers would see this as a chance to make money from the collapse of the stock. But Drew would control most of the stock; he had cornered it. Thus, when short sellers tried to cover their shorts, there was no stock to do it. It could be ruinous for them. One of Drew's favorite sayings was: "He who sells what isn't his must buy it back or go to prison." This was definitely the Darwinist view of the era.

In 1854, Drew loaned the Erie Railroad $1.5 million and eventually took control of the company. The railroad was poorly managed and its stock price crashed several times. Interestingly enough, he shorted the company's stock, making huge sums of money.

Drew met Jay Gould and Jim Fisk, both of whom also wanted to make a fortune buying and shorting stocks. Gould was a fervid entrepreneur. His first business was a tannery, which quickly became profitable. He parlayed the money from this business into investments in hide futures. By 1818, at the age of 21, he was a multimillionaire.

As for Jim Fisk, before making his splash on Wall Street, he had such disparate jobs as a waiter and a ticket agent for a circus. In fact, he eventually earned the nickname of "Barnum of Wall Street."

When Drew died in 1867, Gould and Fisk took control of the Erie Railroad. For them, the company was a personal piggy bank. Gould and Fisk used the Erie treasury to finance their extravagant tastes.

These so-called robber barons also had strong political connections. For example, Gould was close with Boss Tweed and the Tammany Hall Group that ran New York City. Bribes became an ongoing cost of business. Gould even bought the *New York World* newspaper. It was an ingenious way to hype his business interests.

Besides running a railroad, Gould was a speculator. At one point, he attempted to corner the gold market and made about $10 million.

As a result, several major investment banks went bust. Because of the incident, a New York crowd attacked Gould. It was no surprise that, after this, Gould would always have a bodyguard. By 1872, he had been removed from the railroad. It was also during this year that Fisk died, after being shot by the lover of a former mistress.

No doubt, the eighteenth century was a financial free-for-all. There seemed to be no boundaries. Take, for example, John Gates, who was the president of the American Steel and Wire Company. He announced that business was soft, so he laid off workers and closed down plants. He also shorted the company's stock, which went from the $60s to the $30s. He covered his short and then announced that business was better. He hired back the employees and opened the plants. Of course, he bought the stock in the $30s, making a tidy profit when the stock rose again.

Livermore

By the twentieth century, the stock markets were getting much bigger and, as a result, more difficult for individuals to manipulate prices. Besides, there were more regulations, such as the ban on cornering a stock.

Despite this, there were legendary traders who made fortunes from short selling. One was Jesse Livermore, who was born in Massachusetts in 1877. At age 14, he left home and got a job at Paine Webber. It was not an exciting job; basically, he would post stock prices on a chalkboard. But it turned out to be a great education. He closely watched how stock prices moved and wondered how he could make money from the volatility.

In Livermore's era, there was little information available about stocks. Rather, investors would act mostly on rumors (or, in many cases, create the rumors). The atmosphere was wild.

But Livermore did not believe in rumors. He thought he could use stock movements as a way to make money from the market. He had a photographic memory and incredible math skills. He could remember all the historical price movements of the stocks he followed. From this, he was able to determine profitable trading patterns. Essentially, Livermore was practicing technical analysis (which is explained in detail in Chapter 11).

Livermore had no preference between buying long or shorting a stock. Rather, he would do whatever would make him the most money. Some of his most memorable trades were short sales. In 1906, he shorted Union Pacific Railroad. Within a few months, the San Francisco earthquake hit and the stock crashed. Livermore made about $250,000 on the trade. A year later, Livermore thought the stock market was overvalued and shorted heavily. The stock market crashed in October 1907 and Livermore made about $3 million.

Livermore lived large. He had an estate on Long Island and a 300-foot yacht, which he used to commute every morning to Wall Street. Livermore quickly became famous on Wall Street. In fact, his nickname was the "Boy Plunger." But Livermore had his detractors. Among them was J. P. Morgan, who was angered and (and perhaps envious) that Livermore had made a fortune from the panic of 1907.

Livermore was not always a winner. In his lifetime, he declared bankruptcy four times. For example, in 1915, he made some bad trades and accumulated $2 million in debts. However, after two years, he paid off all the debts using money he earned in the stock market.

He shorted the market in 1929 and made another fortune (some estimates are $100 million). But many people believed that Livermore was the cause of the crash and economic bad times. As a result, Livermore received multiple death threats and had to hire a full-time bodyguard.

Interestingly enough, in 1934 Livermore went bust again. He was able to pay off all his creditors and even start his own financial advisory firm, but in 1940 Livermore committed suicide.

One of Livermore's contributions to investment theory was the book he wrote in 1923, *Reminiscences of a Stock Operator*. Here are some of the many great investing rules from the book:

Profits always take care of themselves but losses never do.

There is only one side to the stock market; and it is not the bull side or the bear side but the right side.

The speculator's chief enemies are always boring from within. It is inseparable from human nature to hope and to fear. In speculation when the market goes against you, hope that every day will be the last day—and you lose more than you should had you not listened to hope—to the same pioneers, big and little. And when the market goes your way you become fearful that the next day will take away your profit, and you get out—too soon. Fear keeps you from making as much money as you ought to. The successful trader has to fight these two deep-seated instincts. He has to reverse what you might call his natural impulses. Instead of hoping he must fear; instead of fearing he must hope. He must fear that his losses may develop into a much bigger loss, and hope that his profit may become a bigger profit. It is absolutely wrong to gamble in stocks the way the average man does.

Never act on tips.

"The Park Bench Statesman"

Another famous short seller was Bernard Baruch. Born in 1870 into a working-class family, he started his career as an office boy on Wall Street after college. He worked hard and eventually became a partner at the Wall Street firm of A. A. Housman & Co, with a seat on the New York Stock Exchange. By age 30, he was a millionaire.

One of Baruch's most famous short sells came in 1901. At the time, Amalgamated Copper Company attempted to monopolize the copper market, driving competition away—and prices up. However, Baruch thought that higher prices would lead to lower demand. He was not convinced that the copper market could be cornered, so he shorted the stock. He was right and made about $700,000 on the trade.

Over time, Baruch collected papers that defended the practice of short selling. In 1913, he published the collection in a book called *Short Sales and the Manipulation of Securities*. Baruch did not use his name on the book because he was often blamed for falling stock prices, as a result of his short selling. Besides, he had to testify before Congress regarding his involvement in short selling.

Baruch thought the book would help reduce the U.S government's pressure to restrict short selling. In the book, Baruch details many real-life examples outside the stock market that parallel short selling. Don't homebuilders sell homes before they are made? Don't farmers enter contracts to sell crops before they are harvested? In other words, short selling was really not all that unusual. In fact, Baruch argued that short selling was a critical part of the financial system.

Ultimately, it was not short selling that Baruch became known for. During World War I, he joined the Council of National Defense and then became the chairman of the War Industries Board. He subsequently became a close adviser to presidents Harding, Coolidge, and Hoover. In this role, he did not have an official title and, consequently, he got the nickname "park bench statesman."

The Roaring Twenties and New Regulations

The 1920s saw a huge surge in the stock market, as the economy grew at a rapid pace. While the railroad was the driving force in the 1800s, it was radio and autos that drove economic growth in the 1920s.

In the 1920s bull market, investors tried to find the best ways to make money. One approach was to form a pool of capital. One of the most notable was organized by William Durant. Interestingly enough, he was also the founder of General Motors.

With his massive pool of capital, Durant could manipulate stocks for profit. One target was International Nickel, a mining company based in Canada. It was a favorite for short sellers because of its erratic performance. As for Durant, he used his pool of capital to drive up the price of the stock 60 points, trying to corner the stock. Then more and more investors shorted the stock. As the stock went higher, the shorts were forced to cover at higher prices. Basically, the short sellers were forced to buy Durant's stock at inflated values.

As stock prices increased more and more, there was a rush to buy stock. Everyone wanted to get rich. It was a mania. And a major factor driving the stock prices upward were the market manipulations of capital pools like Durant's. But by the middle of 1929, the market was starting to falter. Big investors were sensing that the market was overvalued and began to take profits. Then, in October, the stock market crashed.

As usual, short sellers took the blame. Didn't they make money when the stock prices fell? Wasn't it their heavy selling of stock that ended the bull market? Ironically, though, short selling actually was light during the late 1920s compared with previous decades. Savvy investors had already learned that shorting stocks when the market was booming was a quick way to lose money.

When the market fell in 1929, there certainly was no shortage of abuses to point out. One of the most notorious was that of Albert Wiggin. No doubt, he was on the fast track of finance in the first part of the twentieth century. By age 36, he was the youngest vice president of Chase National Bank. By 1911, he was the president of the bank. At one point, he served on 59 boards of directors.

When the markets were falling in October 1929, he helped form a banker's pool, which was supposed to help prop up stock prices. Yet at the same time, for his personal account, he was actually shorting 42,000 shares—of Chase, his own bank! It was a profitable trade, netting him a cool $4 million. He did not even have to pay for the stock he covered; Chase lent him the money to do this. And he did not have to pay taxes on the trade because he used a tax loophole.

The nation was in outrage and as a result, President Herbert Hoover launched a Senate investigation into the practice of short selling. Consequently, Congress passed key legislation that resulted in wide-scale regulation of the securities markets. The Securities Act of 1933 required complete disclosure of any offerings of securities to the public. Then the Securities Exchange Act set up the federal regulatory agency for the securities agency, the Securities and Exchange Commission (SEC). Also, the Federal Reserve was given the power to regulate margin requirements.

The first chairman of the SEC was Joseph Kennedy, who practiced many of the antics of Wall Street during the 1920s. In appointing the Kennedy patriarch and stock market insider, President Franklin Roosevelt chose someone he thought would know "where the bodies lie."

In the Securities Exchange Act of 1934, Congress drafted Section 10(a), which gave the Securities and Exchange Commission wide powers to regulate short selling. To this end, the clause provided a definition of short selling: the sale of a security that the seller does not own or that the seller owns but does not deliver.

When the stock market tumbled again in 1937, the SEC wielded its powers under 10(a) and created clause 10(a)-1. Interestingly enough, this clause has remained virtually intact until today. It is the uptick rule, which briefly states that an investor cannot short a stock if the price has decreased (this is explained in more detail in Chapter 3).

Why the new rule? The SEC believed that short selling could result in undue downward pressure on a stock price. However, if a short sale can only be conducted when the stock is up, then this problem would be avoided.

The SEC and Short Selling Rules

Over the years, the SEC has conducted a variety of studies on the effects of short selling. They include:

- 1963 Study. The report demonstrated the relationship between short selling and price patterns. It showed that short selling volume increased as markets declined and that the uptick rule did not prevent the ill effects on stock prices that Congress intended. The report called for better record keeping of short sales.

- 1976 Report. This study found that data collection on short sales was lacking, making it difficult to study the overall effects of short selling.

   The SEC proposed the temporary suspension of the uptick rule in an effort to determine whether there was indeed a relationship between short selling and falling markets. The SEC received 12 comments from the industry to the proposal and 8 were against. Two of the dissenters were the NYSE and the AMEX

   In 1980, the SEC withdrew its proposal to indefinitely suspend the uptick rule.

- In 1991 the House Committee on Government Operations published a report on short selling. The report said that short selling was confusing to most investors and that the uptick rule was not necessarily helpful for protecting investors.

   Additionally, the report indicated that short selling provided an effective means of providing liquidity to markets and could stabilize volatile situations. Also, the report suggested that investors overemphasized the power of short sellers on affecting prices.

In October 1999, the SEC made yet another attempt at changing the rules of short selling. It did this by publishing a so-called Concept Statement. It was an attempt to get comments from the industry to see if the uptick rule was still viable. While the proposals were extensive, there has been no decision on the implementation of the new rules. You can see the Concept Statement at http://www.sec.gov/rules/concept/34-42037.htm.

Basically, the SEC believes that the uptick rule is from another era, when markets were much smaller. Besides, the markets today are much more sophisticated for investor protection, especially in light of disclosure requirements and online trading technologies that give small investors the same tools that institutional investors have. Furthermore, regulators have sophisticated computer systems that can monitor trading that may be manipulative.

In the Concept Statement, the SEC notes how after-hours trading and decimalization have affected short selling:

After-Hours Trading.   Short selling is allowed in after-hours trading. But there is an important distinction to keep in mind. The tick test is based on trades from the Consolidated Tape, which is a high-speed electronic reporting system that stock exchanges utilize. As the name implies, the Consolidated Tape includes transactions from many different markets for a security. These markets include national and regional exchanges, as well as ECNs. An ECN (electronic communications network) is a private trading system that is not part of the Nasdaq or NYSE. One of the most prominent ECNs is Instinet.

However, for some stocks, the Consolidated Tape may not operate in after-hours trading. This is not a problem for stock exchanges such as the NYSE or Nasdaq because they are allowed to use the last price quoted on their exchange when calculating the uptick rule. Unfortunately, ECNs cannot do this. Rather they must use the last trade from the Consolidated Tape. The SEC believes this greatly reduces short selling activity in after-hours markets.

Decimalization.   Until recently, stocks were quoted in fractions. In 2001, this changed. Now, stock prices are noted in decimals. The SEC believes that a very small price move—even less than a penny—would activate the uptick rule and make it even more difficult for investors to sell short.

In view of the above, the SEC has made the following proposals:

1. The uptick rule would not apply when the stock price is above a threshold price. For example, suppose XYZ stock has increased

from $10 to $20 in three days. During this time, the stock has had many down ticks, making it difficult for short sellers to take a position. The SEC believes that short selling would act as a moderating force to help reduce the volatility of this move of $10 to $20. What would be the benchmark? One idea is that short selling would be allowed so long as the stock price is currently higher than the previous day's close.

2. The tick test should not apply to actively traded securities. The main reason is that it is difficult if not impossible to manipulate these stocks. Can short sellers really drive down the price of GE? Probably not. One proposal is that the uptick rule would not apply to those companies with market valuations of at least $150 million and a minimum of $1 million in daily volume.

3. Short selling should be restricted only during certain market events. The theory is that these times—mergers, tender offers, the expiration of options—may make a stock more subject to manipulative short selling behavior.

4. The short selling rules should not apply to hedging transactions. In fact, hedging is a key element for many portfolio managers because it can help stabilize a portfolio. The uptick rule, however, adds to transaction costs of hedging. The SEC believes that there are so-called bona fide hedges. For example, suppose you own 100 shares of XYZ and then short 100 shares of XYZ. This is a neutral position, as any increase in price is offset by the short position and vice versa.

The Emergence of Hedge Funds

Until the 1950s, short sellers were mostly individuals. After all, mutual funds were not even allowed to short stocks. But in 1949, Alfred Winslow Jones started the first hedge fund, which allowed institutions to engage in short selling strategies.

Jones had a diverse past. A Harvard graduate, his first job was as a purser on a steamer. Next, he became the vice consul at the U.S. Embassy in Berlin when Hitler rose to power. He went back to school and in 1941 obtained a Ph.D. in sociology from Columbia University. His thesis was *Life, Liberty, and Property*. In fact, it became a standard text for sociology.

Jones then became an associate editor of *Fortune* magazine. One of his articles was "Fashions in Forecasting." He realized that he could do a better job at forecasting than the professionals. So, at age 48, he created the world's first hedge fund. He raised $60,000 from wealthy investors and put $40,000 of his personal money into the fund.

Jones's fund was called a hedge fund since he would protect his portfolio by using short positions; that is, he was hedging his portfolio by short selling. Moreover, he would borrow money to buy stocks, as well. He believed that by combining borrowing and short selling, he could construct a portfolio that was actually conservative.

Jones translated his theory into the following formula:

$$\text{Net market exposure percentage} = \frac{(\text{Long exposure} - \text{Short exposure})}{\text{Capital}}$$

In plain English, suppose you have a portfolio that has a value of $100,000. You would take a margin loan of, say, $20,000. With the $120,000, you buy $120,000 in stocks. Then you short $40,000 in stocks. Add up everything and you have a total investment of:

$$\$120,000 + \$40,000 = \$160,000$$

This represents 160 percent of your initial capital of $100,000. But using the Jones formula, your actual exposure to the market is:

$$\frac{(\$120,000 - \$40,000)}{\$100,000} = 80\%$$

Thus, you have a "net long" exposure of 80 percent. That is, you have only 80 percent exposure to a decline in the market, not 160 percent. If the short positions were higher than the long positions, then the portfolio would be a net short. However, Jones always had a net long position, since he thought the markets tended to increase over time. Yet, when the markets did fall, he wanted to lessen the damage.

Jones was innovative in how he structured his hedge fund. It was a limited partnership. As such, it was not subject to federal regulations. Simply put, there was no requirement for the funds to submit filings with the Securities and Exchange Commission. (A hedge fund allows only "accredited investors." That is, you must have income of at least $200,000 per year or a net worth of $1 million. In other words, the federal government assumes that you are either a sophisticated investor or have the resources to hire someone to provide professional management to your portfolio.)

Another key innovation was how Jones created the compensation system for portfolio managers. The managers would get 20 percent of any of the profits generated. In other words, there is a huge incentive for the portfolio managers to make huge returns.

Without any need to report his portfolio performance, Jones was relatively unknown until 1966, when a *Fortune* article profiled the fund. The article showed that his fund had outperformed the top five mutual funds. As a result, there was a surge in new hedge funds. Some of the top new hedge fund managers at the time included George Soros and even Warren Buffett.

Many of these new hedge funds did not use short selling; this would not have been wise anyway during the 1960s and early 1970s, because the stock market was very bullish.

But by 1973, the stock market went into a tailspin and many hedge funds disappeared. It was not until the 1980s that hedge funds made a comeback. Some of the top players often shorted the market, including George Soros.

Soros was born in 1930 in Budapest. Seventeen years later, he immigrated to England, where he attended the prestigious London School of Economics. In 1956, he came to the United States and started his own hedge fund.

Soros proved to be a good short seller. He was not afraid to target well-regarded brand-name stocks. For example, during the 1970s, he shorted Avon when it was trading at $120 per share. His main reason for the trade was his belief that the population was getting older and thus the demand for Avon's products would start to falter. Within two years, the stock was trading at $20. He made about $1 million on the trade.

Use of short selling was helpful during the bear markets of the 1970s. From 1969 to 1974, Soros's hedge fund, Quantum, went from $6.1 million to $18 million. One of his most amazing years was in 1977. While the Dow was down 13 percent, the Quantum fund was up 31.2 percent.

In 1990, Soros retired from the day-to-day management of his funds. Stanley Druckenmiller took his place at the helm, and he took a new direction. He would make macro bets; that is, he would buy long or short a country's currency, interest rate futures, or stocks.

However, Soros still was involved in the major trades. A trade that become legendary was the short of the British pound in 1992, in which he made about a billion. The British were not happy with this, though. Yet Soros was not apologetic, saying, "If I hadn't done it, someone else would have."

But the macro bets certainly carried high risk. This was very much apparent in 1998, when Soros lost $2 billion on his trades in the Russian market.

Another influential hedge fund portfolio manager was Michael Steinhardt. In the 1960s, while still in his 20s, Steinhardt became a hot Wall Street analyst. He covered the hot conglomerates, which were the investment rage of the decade (somewhat like the Net stocks of the late 1990s). Interestingly enough, he was credited with developing the concept of "synergy."

In 1967, he started his hedge fund with an initial capitalization of $7.7 million. It was a good time to start a fund, since the U.S. economy was booming. If a stock had the word "data" in it, the stock was likely to skyrocket. The era was aptly named "the go-go years."

Steinhardt was not only buying stock; he also allowed for short sales. This would certainly help the performance of the fund when the economy soured during the 1970s. Interestingly enough, the high-flier stocks he bought at profits during the 1960s he then sold short in the 1970s. His fund went net short during this period. In other words, the percentage of his short positions was higher than that of the long positions.

Steinhardt also targeted the so-called nifty 50. These were considered "one-decision stocks"; that is, the only decision you would need to make was to buy them, since the companies were "solid." These companies included the mega brands, such as GE, Coca-Cola, and McDonald's. Steinhardt made millions by shorting these stocks.

However, Steinhardt still had bad trades. One of his biggest mistakes was actually the short sale of Occidental Petroleum. He thought the company was overvalued and overhyped and shorted it at the mid $20s. The stock then went to the $30s and he shorted even more shares along the way. Then the company announced a major oil discovery and the stock doubled.

Steinhardt, though, did not predict the 1987 crash. By September 1987, his fund was up a whopping 45 percent. With the crash, he ended the year up only 4 percent. But this did not stop Steinhardt; his fund continued to do extremely well. It was no surprise that the fund was accumulating billions in more assets. Like many other mega hedge funders, he started engaging in macro bets. While these worked in the early 1990s, the trades became unglued in 1994 and his fund was down 30 percent that year.

In the next year, his fund was up 26 percent and Steinhardt decided to retire. Since then, he has devoted his time to philanthropy and wrote his autobiography, *No Bull*.

Short-Only Funds

Hedge funds tend to pursue a blend of both long and short positions. In fact, it is typical for hedge funds to have a larger percentage in the long side. The short positions, in a way, act as a hedge if the market falls.

However, there are some hedge funds that focus only on short sales. These are known as short-only hedge funds. A handful of these funds emerged in the 1980s. One of the most famous was the hedge fund managed by the three Feshbach brothers, Matt, Kurt, and Joe (the last two of whom were twins). Their fund, which they started in 1982, is considered the first short-only hedge fund.

The Feshbach brothers were true bears. In fact, each had a jacket with a logo of a Merrill Lynch bull with a red slash through it.

One of their legendary shorts involved ZZZZ Best. The founder of ZZZZ Best was a teenager named Barry Minkow, who ran a carpet-cleaning operation. The Feshbach brothers did a tremendous amount of research, such as calling competitors, suppliers, and analysts. When ZZZZ Best announced an $8 million carpet-cleaning contract for two buildings, the Feshbach brothers smelled trouble. By their research, there was never a contract as high as this. Shortly after the announcement, the company went into bankruptcy and Minkow was convicted of securities fraud—and the Feshbach brothers profited immensely by shorting the stock.

Between 1985 and 1990, the fund had a phenomenal 40 percent annual compounded rate of return. At the height of its success, the fund had about $1 billion under management. However, the fund quickly deteriorated by short selling during the bull market of the 1990s. And the Feshbach brothers made some bad calls, their biggest mistake being the short of Wells Fargo. The brothers rode the stock from $50 to $200 per share. Consequently, the Feshbach brothers changed the direction of the fund and steered away from short selling. The fund now looks for undervalued stocks that represent strong growth opportunities.

Another top short-only hedge fund is Kynikos Associates, which is managed by famed short seller Jim Chanos. He also had many difficulties in the 1990s, which we discuss in Chapter 3. He shorted high-fliers, such as the Internet stocks, and lost substantial amounts of money for his fund.

The question arises: If top managers cannot win at short selling, how can a regular investor prevail? Remember that the Feshbach brothers and Chanos had funds that were short only. To win consistently in this mode is very difficult. Rather, as we saw earlier with hedge funds, portfolio managers typically have a blend of long and short positions.

Conclusion

The history of short selling is an incomplete one, and the reasons for this are numerous. Many investors do not like to disclose that they are short sellers. It often comes as a surprise when certain investors really short the markets. For example, Roy Neuberger was a successful short seller, even though he was the founder of the Neuberger mutual funds, in which the focus is mostly on buying stocks for the long term.

Neuberger's story began in 1929, when he worked as a clerk at a brokerage firm on Wall Street. That year, he shorted a symbol of American innovation, Radio Corporation of America. The stock hit nearly $600 per share, but Neuberger could not justify the valuation. Everyone he talked to said the company was strong because it represented America's new age. But Neuberger was right and RCA eventually fell to $2 per share. Ironically enough, he got married on the day the Dow Jones hit its all-time low of 41.22 in 1933.

Neuberger continued to selectively short the market. For example, he shorted in 1972 to 1973. Like Steinhardt, he thought the nifty 50 stocks were selling at stratospheric valuations. He also shorted the market before the crash of 1987.

As we have seen, even the greatest traders have been burned on short selling. Short selling is no easy feat and requires homework. In fact, it is a good idea not to have a large percentage of your portfolio in short positions. The risk can be too high. After all, many hedge fund managers remain, for the most part, net long in their portfolios. The belief—as history bears out—is that markets tend to rise over time. However, by having some exposure to short positions, a portfolio can be hedged against the fall.

In the next chapter, we will look at the nuts and bolts of short selling.

CHAPTER 2

The Short Selling Process

You visit your stockbroker to learn more about short selling and to set up an account to handle it. You quickly realize that there is much more involved than you thought. Your broker uses lots of complex jargon, and you are more confused than ever. You wonder if you really know what short selling actually means.

Don't despair! Short selling is not rocket science. However, it can be a valuable tool for serious investors and shouldn't be taken too lightly. Unfortunately, there is a lot of misinformation about the subject. In fact, there's a good chance that even your stockbroker does not have a good understanding of the subject (hence the use of jargon). In this chapter, we will take a step-by-step look at the short selling process—without the jargon.

What Is Short Selling

To many new investors, the concept of short selling sounds strange: to borrow stock and sell it now with an agreement to buy it back in the future. It seems backward and foolish. How can you really make money when a stock goes down? It seems impossible.

Let's take an example of short selling: You've been doing extensive research on Go South Corp. and decide it is an excellent short sale opportunity. The stock is currently selling at $20 per share and you think it will quickly drop to $10.

You borrow 100 shares of Go South from your broker. Borrowing stock from a broker is the most common procedure. Alternately, you could arrange for a private transaction. That is, you might know someone who already owns 100 shares, and you can write a contract to borrow the shares and agree to deliver them in the future. But this latter practice is quite uncommon.

A brokerage firm will usually have its own stock loan department from which its clients borrow stock. In fact, before doing any short sales, it is a good idea to talk to the people who work in the stock loan department. They can provide great insight into the short selling process.

You may ask why a broker would be willing to lend the shares. The $2000, which is set aside in an escrow account that the broker can access if you do not follow through on your legal obligations, is kept in a secure money market account that earns interest. But this interest is not for you; it's for the broker. No doubt, this can be a nice profitable business for the broker.

The next step is that the 100 shares are sold on the open market at the current $20 a share, which gives you gross proceeds of $2000.

To close out the short position—also known as *covering*—you will need to deliver the 100 shares to the broker. If the stock price goes to $30, it will cost you $3000 to buy the 100 shares and cover your short—$1000 more than you paid, losing money on the deal. On the other hand, if the stock does plunge to $10, then you can buy the 100 shares for $1000 and take the $1000 that is in the escrow account.

This is a fairly simple example, but it shows the overall dynamics of the short selling process. In the next section, we will look at the inner workings of opening the necessary accounts to conduct short sales. It is somewhat heavy reading. While you do not need to be an expert in the intricacies of margin accounts, it is still a good idea to have exposure to these issues.

Setting Up the Brokerage Accounts

To sell short, you must open a cash account and a margin account. Margin accounts are quite involved, and we will look at them after discussing the cash account.

The cash account is the most basic brokerage account. That is, it allows you to buy and sell stocks, bonds, mutual funds, and other securities, as long as you have enough cash in the account to make the purchase.

To open a cash account, you must fill out an account application, which will request the following:

- Personal information (address, social security number for tax purposes, other names on the account, martial status, citizenship)

- Type of ownership (joint, tenants in common, trust and so on)

- Financial status (annual income, net worth)

- Employment

- Residence (rent or own)

- Objectives (growth, income, speculation)

- Investment experience

- Whether you are an officer, director, or a 10 percent or more stockholder of a company. If so, you are considered an insider. If you have insider status in a company, you are not allowed to short the stock for profit.

When filling out the account form, be truthful. If you do not have much investment experience or do not have a high net worth, then indicate this on the form. An important reason for doing so is that, if you decide to sue your broker in the future (we will look at certain causes of legal actions in the next chapter), then the account form can be used as evidence. If it shows you are a very savvy investor, then your case will certainly be weakened.

When you submit the application, you will be authorizing the brokerage firm to do a credit check on you. However, you have the right to get the name and address of the credit reporting agency. This is important because credit reports can be wrong. It is a good idea to get a copy of the report and double-check the information on it.

Once your account is approved, you will get an account number and you can start trading.

If you are opening a discount brokerage or online account, the application will likely indicate that the firm will not provide you with any investment advice. Then again, many brokers do not have a strong understanding of short selling and probably will not be of much help with the strategies you would employ. In this case, it is cheaper to use a discount broker anyway.

A brokerage firm may have educational material regarding short selling in a brochure or on its Web site. Unfortunately, the information is usually not very informative. It is up to investors to learn about the intricacies of short selling.

There will be a minimum deposit amount—which can range from $1000 to $10,000. But this need not be in cash. That is, you can deposit or transfer securities from other accounts.

All brokerage firms are members of the Securities Investor Protection Corporation (SIPC). Basically, this organization protects the value of your account if the brokerage firm fails. Along with traditional investments, short sales are covered under SIPC. At a minimum, the protection is up to $500,000, of which no more than $100,000 is allowed to be in cash. For example, suppose you have $600,000 in your account. Of this, there is $200,000 in short sale positions and $200,000 in long positions. You also have $200,000 in cash. In this case, the $200,000 in short and $200,000 in long positions are covered, but only up to $100,000 of the cash is protected.

However, many firms have insurance that exceeds these levels. For example, E*TRADE has coverage of up to $49.5 million, of which $900,000 is cash. Keep in mind: This is insurance against the broker going bust. It is not insurance to protect you if you personally make bad investments.

Be aware that you cannot close your brokerage account if you have any short positions. These positions must be paid in full. The broker can take legal action against you to pay off the debt and can even get legal fees reimbursed. Moreover, the broker has the right to liquidate any securities in the account to pay off the debt. So you could lose your holdings in investments that are not part of the short sale.

Your brokerage firm will mail you written confirmations of your short sale trades within one day after an order has been executed. A confirmation will include: the quantity of shares, the name of the security, proceeds or costs, commissions, fees, taxes, and principal/agency.

It is critical that you read these confirmations. Did they charge the right commission? Did they execute the right quantity of shares? With the volatility in the markets, it is not uncommon to see errors in confirmations. If you have any questions, make sure you contact your broker promptly. Any trade is considered final if it is not objected to—in writing—within 10 days of receipt of the confirmation.

Keep all your confirmations. This will make it easier for you or your accountant to do taxes. Keep them for at least three years. In Chapter 14, we will look at tax strategies for short selling.

Besides confirmations, your broker will send out account statements at least every quarter. Most firms send account statements every month.

Margin Accounts

Debt is a big part of the U.S. economy. Consumers borrow huge amounts—typically with credit cards—to buy the nice things in life. Consumers use mortgages to buy houses. There are car loans, as well as loans to finance furniture and appliances. Such debt really makes the economy hum.

But there is another interesting type of loan—the margin loan. This allows a person to borrow against the value of his brokerage account. For example, suppose you have a diversified portfolio of $100,000 in common stock. Through your brokerage firm, you can set up a margin account and borrow up to $100,000. You could use that $100,000 to buy anything; in fact, you do not have to use this cash to buy stock. You could buy a car, house, boat—or whatever your heart desires.

However, margin borrowing is certainly risky. This is especially the case when your portfolio starts to decline. The market crash of 1929 was a classic example of the dangers of margin borrowing. Many investors borrowed huge sums of money to buy stocks. When the stock prices collapsed, many people lost everything. As a result, Congress passed a variety of laws to regulate margin accounts to help prevent excesses (and even bankruptcies).

The key regulation is Regulation T (or "Reg T" for short). This is part of the Securities Exchange Act of 1934 and gives the Federal Reserve the power to regulate the types of securities that can be traded on margin and the borrowing amount.

- *Types of securities.* These are securities that are listed on the New York Stock Exchange, the American Stock Exchange, regional stock exchanges, and the Nasdaq.

- *Borrowing amount.* Since 1974, the Federal Reserve has set 50 percent as the amount that an investor can borrow (or, margin) against his portfolio. Keep in mind that this is the maximum amount. In fact, it is common for brokerage firms to have a higher percentage for margin accounts.

When you read the margin account guidelines from your broker, they will definitely look daunting. They are written in dense legalese and often in small print. Chances are that even your broker does not understand all of the nuances.

To understand margin accounts, we first need to become familiar with some key concepts:

Street Name.   Every security that is used as collateral for a margin loan must be in "street name." This means that the stock certificates are held by and registered to your brokerage firm. However, you are still considered the owner of these shares (in legal terms, you are known as the "beneficial owner").

Actually as a general rule, it is a good idea to place all of your securities in street name. Benefits include:

- SIPC protection (which is discussed previously)
- The availability of updates and information about the stocks (on a monthly basis if you have a trade during the monthly periods, or quarterly if there are no trades)
- The ability to limit and stop orders on the stocks, which helps get better pricing on your trades (we explain this in more detail in Chapter 3).

In fact, if you do not have stocks in street name and lose the certificates, it can take a month or so to replace them (as well as a fee). For the most part, it is most common to have your shares in street name. Although, sometimes a company will encourage its shareholders not to do this so as to make it harder to short a stock. We will look at this in more detail in Chapter 3 with the example of Microstrategy.

Hypothecation.   Hypothecation means you agree to pledge your securities as collateral for a margin loan.

Rehypothecation.   Rehypothecation allows a brokerage firm to take hypothecated securities and get loans from banks based on the value of these securities.

Interestingly enough, not all accounts can be put in margin accounts. Examples include custodian accounts and IRAs. Thus, you cannot short stock in these types of accounts.

Buying on Margin

To understand margin trading, let's look at margin accounts from the viewpoint of buying stock. This will help build a foundation for understanding how the margin account is then used for short selling, which we describe next.

Suppose you open a margin account and want to buy 2000 shares of Surge Corp., which is currently trading for $10 a share. Your account would look like the following:

TABLE 2.1   Initial Margin Account

Current market value (CMV)	$20,000
Debit balance	$20,000

While you own $20,000 in Surge stock, you also owe the brokerage firm $20,000 for the purchase. This debt is called a debit balance. Your brokerage firm, Charge 'Em, has a margin requirement of 50 percent. Thus, Charge 'Em will issue a Fed margin call (which is what brokers call a margin deposit) and you will need to deposit at least $10,000 to meet the minimum margin requirement. You do this promptly by delivering a check to your broker on the day you open the account. The new account looks like this:

TABLE 2.2   Margin Account After a $10,000 Deposit

CMV	$20,000
Debit balance	$10,000
Equity	$10,000

As you can see, the $10,000 deposit reduced the debit balance by $10,000. Any type of cash deposit reduces a debit balance on a dollar-by-dollar basis.

The debit balance is essentially a loan from the broker. The loan is pledged (hypothecated) by the Surge shares.

The equity is your ownership in the account. This is calculated by subtracting the CMV from the debit balance, which is $10,000. Also, note that a margin account must always have at least $2500 in equity according to the law (a brokerage firm may have a higher requirement). If not, you would need to deposit new securities or cash or close out the account.

A simple rule of thumb for calculating how much you can borrow is defined by this formula:

$$\frac{\text{Amount deposited}}{\text{Margin requirement}} = \text{Amount that can be borrowed}$$

If a brokerage firm has a margin requirement of 50 percent and you deposit $10,000, you can buy this amount of securities:

$$\frac{\$10,000}{50\%} = \$20,000$$

Why do people use margin accounts? There are a variety of reasons. A person may want to borrow money to buy a car or a house. A person may want to use leverage. For instance, suppose you did not use a margin account and instead invested $10,000 in Surge stock. The stock increases 50 percent and you make a tidy profit of $5000. On the other hand, if you used margin, you would have been able to buy twice as many shares or a total of $20,000. A 50 percent increase in your portfolio would be a profit of $10,000. But be careful! Margin can be a high-risk endeavor. If the stock price falls, you can lose much more money. Instead of doubling your gains, you will be doubling your losses. During the bear markets of 1929 and 2000, many investors were wiped out because of heavy use of margin.

Let's imagine that after several months, Surge reports strong earnings and the stock is now trading at $15 per share. Your 2000 shares are now worth $30,000. The updated margin chart will look as follows:

TABLE 2.3   Current Market Value Increases to $30,000

CMV	$30,000
Debit balance	$10,000
Equity	$20,000

The CMV increased by 50 percent to $30,000, but there was no change in the loan amount (you did not deposit more cash to pay down the loan). As a result, the equity is $20,000.

There is another chart to look at called the T chart (this is not called the T chart because of Reg T, but because traditionally it has been written in a T-style format).

TABLE 2.4   T-Chart for a Margin Account

Fed Requirement Amount	Equity
$15,000	$20,000
	− $15,000
	$ 5,000 excess over Fed requirement

The Fed requirement amount is calculated as:

$$\text{CMV} \times \text{Fed requirement}$$
$$\$30,000 \times 50\% = \$15,000$$

As shown above, you subtract the equity from the Fed requirement amount, which gives you $5000 in excess of the requirement. This is known as a *special memorandum account* (SMA). You can keep this extra $5000 in your account; withdraw the cash for your own personal purposes; or use it to buy more securities.

Suppose you decide to purchase more stock. Your buying power is more than the $5000 in the SMA. It is $10,000. Why the bigger amount? The reason is that, according to the margin calculations, the borrowing amount is based on the total amount of the stock being purchased. Here is the formula:

$$\frac{\text{Amount of excess equity}}{\text{Federal requirement}} = \text{buying power}$$

$$\frac{\$5000}{50\%} = \$10,000$$

Your account will now look like this:

TABLE 2.5   Market Value at $40,000

CMV	$40,000
Debit balance	$15,000
Equity	$25,000

If you want to buy more stock, you will need to make a deposit in accordance with the federal requirement. For example: Let's say you purchase $5000 more stock. Your debit balance will increase by $2500, which you will have to provide for your broker. Here is the chart:

TABLE 2.6   A $5000 Purchase of Stock with $2500 Margin Loan

CMV	$45,000
Debit balance	$17,500
Equity	$27,500

Let's say that Surge pays dividends to its shareholders. At the end of the latest quarter, Surge pays $100 in dividends to you. You have these options: withdraw the money for personal purposes; use the cash to reduce the debit balance (which increases the SMA by $100); or keep the cash in the account (which increases the SMA by $100).

Of course, stocks fall in value. This is what eventually happens to Surge. By the end of the year, the company runs into tough times and the stock has gone from $15 to $7.50 per share. What does this do with the SMA? Nothing. Rather, the SMA will be the same amount as it was when the stock was $15 per share.

Do not let this fool you. You cannot borrow any more money. Instead, your account will become "restricted." The CMV of the account will have fallen by 50 percent to $22,500. Here's the new chart:

TABLE 2.7   Stock Falls 50 Percent in Value

CMV	$22,500
Debit balance	$17,500
Equity	$5,000

A *restricted account* is one in which the account's equity is lower than the federal requirement. The federal requirement is now:

$$\$22,500 \times 50\% = \$11,250$$

Since the $5000 in equity is lower than the $11,250 federal requirement, the account is now under restriction.

Actually, having a restricted account is not necessarily a problem. In fact, it is quite common. It is possible to buy more securities in a restricted account so long as the investor makes additional deposits to the debit balance in accordance with the Fed requirement.

If you want to sell stock, then 50 percent of the proceeds must be used to pay down the debit balance. The other 50 percent can be kept in the account, or it can be used to buy stock or withdraw cash. Typically, with a restricted account, the dividends received are used to reduce the debit balance. Keep in mind that withdrawing money from the account is not a taxable event; rather, it is only when you sell stock that you have a taxable event. Chapter 14 goes into much more detail on capital gains taxes.

Let's consider another possible variable in this example. Sometimes a stock can go into a tailspin. The brokerage wants the right to take action if the stock falls below a point where the investor is unable to pay off the debit balance. To this end, the NYSE and the Nasdaq have set up rules called minimum maintenance requirements. Like the federal Reg T requirement, a brokerage firm can have margin account requirements (called *house requirements*) that are higher than the federal minimum.

The basic rule in most brokerages is that an investor's equity must be at least 25 percent of the CMV. Let's continue with our example. Suppose your account is as follows:

TABLE 2.8   Margin Account—Before Big Fall in Stock Price

CMV	$20,000
Debit balance	$10,000
Equity	$10,000

Unfortunately, the stock price collapses and the CMV is now at $11,000. The chart now indicates:

TABLE 2.9   Stock Collapses and Broker Can Make Margin Call

CMV	$11,000
Debit Balance	$10,000
Equity	$ 1,000

The minimum maintenance requirement is:

$$CMV \times 25\%$$
$$\$11,000 \times 25\% = \$2750$$

Since the equity is lower than $2750, the broker will make a margin call to you. You will need to deposit the $1750 ($2750 minus $1000 in equity). If not, the broker will liquidate securities in the account to meet the requirement. There are no fines levied in this situation. Thus, you might want to just have the broker sell out the position.

Margin Account Interest

The amount you borrow in the margin account is not free—whether you buy stocks or short stocks. On any credit that is extended to you, interest will be charged. The interest rate will typically be based on some reference interest rate that is commercially recognized, such as the Treasury bond rate. As interest rates change, so will the rates on your margin account. No prior notice is required for any changes in the interest rate. The base rate is what the broker uses as the reference. Generally, the higher the amount borrowed, the better your rate. The rates are usually tiered. Here's a hypothetical example:

TABLE 2.10 Tiered Rates for a Margin Account

Average Debit Balance	Margin Interest Rate
Less than $50,000	2.00% above base rate
$50,000 to $249,999.99	0.75% above base rate
$250,000 and above	0.50% below base rate

Short Selling in a Margin Account

So far we have been looking at margin accounts in terms of buying stocks. So why are these accounts helpful tools for short selling? Remember that in a short sale the investor is borrowing shares from the brokerage firm. Of course, these shares have value and the brokerage firm wants to make sure that it does not give away these shares for free. By requiring a margin account, the short seller is really putting up a good faith deposit against the borrowed shares.

It is interesting to note that before widespread use of computers, brokerage firms would separate a margin account into two accounts: long and short. This was done to make it easier for bookkeeping. Of course, this is no longer needed, yet some firms still use the terminology. Regardless of the terminology, the account is still a margin account; it's not a special account.

Let's continue with the example from the section above. Imagine that you believe that Surge is ready to plunge and decide to short 1000 shares of the stock. The stock is currently selling at $20. The broker uses the 50 percent Reg T requirement for this transaction.

You decide to borrow 1000 shares from your broker. Where do these shares come from? Interestingly enough, these are from the pool of shares that people have purchased on margin. Think back to the guidelines of the hypothecation agreement. The brokerage firm also has the authority to lend its own shares to customers for short selling or shares from customer accounts. There is no prior notice required for the broker to do this. At any time, a broker can use shares from margin accounts for short selling purposes.

Next, the brokerage firm will sell the 1000 shares in the open market at $20, generating total proceeds of $20,000. This amount is credited to your margin account. Remember, you do not have access to the

$20,000. Instead, it is in an escrow account that protects the broker for its loan. Here is what the margin account looks like:

TABLE 2.11   Investor Shorts $20,000 in Stock in Margin Account

Proceeds	$20,000
Short market value (SMV)	$20,000
Credit balance	$10,000

To do the $20,000 short sale, you must put up 50 percent of the SMV as a deposit in your margin account, which is $10,000.

In addition to its ability to call the margin, the broker has an added protection. It is called *mark to the market*. This means that the amount in the escrow account will always cover the debt. The mark to the market concept does not apply when you buy stock in your margin account; it only applies to short selling.

If the stock prices increases 10 percent, it will cost you $22,000 to buy Surge to cover the short position. The account chart looks like this:

TABLE 2.12   Stock Bought Short Rises 10 Percent

Proceeds	$20,000
SMV	$22,000
Credit balance	$10,000

The amount in the escrow account only covers $20,000 of the $22,000 in the account. In this case, the broker will require that you deposit an additional $2000 to increase the escrow account to $22,000. Thus, the account has been marked to the market. As seen below, $2000 is placed in the proceeds section, which is in escrow.

TABLE 2.13   Account Is Marked to the Market

Proceeds	$22,000
SMV	$22,000
Credit balance	$ 8,000

Also, notice that the credit balance has fallen to $8000. Basically, to mark to the market, you did not have to write a check for $2000, but instead you were able to use the amount in the credit balance.

Now, let's say the value of the stock you bought short falls to $18,000.

TABLE 2.14   The Stock Bought Short Falls

Proceeds	$22,000
SMV	$18,000
Credit balance	$ 8,000

The stock price fell, thus increasing the value of the account to $22,000. There is $4000 more than needed in the escrow account to back the short account. There will be a reverse mark to market. That is, $4000 is taken out of the proceeds section and placed in the credit balance. Here is what it looks like:

TABLE 2.15   Reverse Mark to the Market When Price Falls

Proceeds	$18,000
SMV	$18,000
Credit balance	$12,000

The account now has an SMA of $3000, which is calculated in two steps. First the Fed requirement is found:

$$SMV \times 50\% = \text{Fed requirement}$$
$$\$18,000 \times 50\% = \$9000$$

Second, subtract the federal requirement amount from the credit balance:

$$\$12,000 - \$9000 = \$3000$$

You can use the SMA to buy or short more stock, or you can withdraw cash or keep the credit in the account (or any combination of these transactions).

Let's suppose that you decide to buy more stock. Your buying power is:

$$\frac{\$3000}{50\%} = \$6000$$

You buy $6000 of stock for your account. The margin account looks like this:

TABLE 2.16 Investor Purchases Stock

Proceeds	$18,000
SMV	$18,000
CMV	$ 6,000
Credit balance	$ 6,000
Equity	$12,000

The proceeds and SMV do not change. There is enough in the escrow account to cover the short trade. But the credit balance has been subtracted by the amount of the stock purchase, which was $6000. Earlier in the chapter, we stated that equity is calculated by subtracting the CMV from the debit balance:

CMV – Debit balance = Equity

With short sales, we need to modify the formula to:

CMV – Debit balance + Credit balance = Equity

While a debit balance is money owed to the broker, the credit balance is money that a broker owes you. So, the equity in your account in the previous transaction is $12,000 ($6000 + $6000). (Note: You will receive interest for the credit balance.)

Now, you decide you want to take some profits. So, you cover half of your short position. By covering the short, the proceeds fall by the same amount as the SMV. The new margin chart will look like this:

TABLE 2.17   Short Position Covered

Proceeds	$ 9,000
SMV	$ 9,000
CMV	$ 6,000
Credit Balance	$ 6,000
Equity	$12,000

Minimum Maintenance Requirements

Like buying stock in a margin account, short sale positions are subject to minimum maintenance requirements. If the short positions fall below the minimum levels, the brokerage firm will issue a margin call to deposit more money or to liquidate assets in your account to meet the deficiency.

The minimum maintenance rules for short selling, though, are based on the stock price. The reason is that low-priced stocks tend to have less volume and can be subject to increased volatility. There can also be a higher risk of a short squeeze. A short squeeze is when many short sellers try to cover their positions at the same time, adding tremendous buying pressure on the stock price. In fact, it is not uncommon for a low-priced stock to double or triple on good news. However, this can mean substantial losses for a short seller.

So, the rules for low-priced stocks are as follows:

- Rule 1: For stocks selling below $5, the minimum maintenance requirement is $2.50 per share or 100 percent of the CMV, whichever is greater.

- Rule 2: For stocks selling at $5 or above, the minimum maintenance requirement is $5 per share or 30 percent of the CMV, whichever is greater.

What does all this mean? We need to look at some examples. Suppose you have a short position of 100 shares of Surge, which is trading at $4. In accordance with Rule 1, two calculations are made to find the minimum maintenance:

TABLE 2.18   Minimum Maintenance for a Stock Trading at $4

$2.50 per share	$2.50 × 100 = $250
100% of CMV	$4 × 100 = $400

You must use the higher number, which is $400. This is the minimum maintenance requirement in accordance with Rule 1.

Suppose that the stock price is $8. Since the stock price is above $5, you use Rule 2:

TABLE 2.19   Minimum Maintenance for a Stock Trading at $8

$5.00 per share	$5 × 100 = $500
30% of the CMV	30% × $800 = $240

In accordance with Rule 2, you use the higher amount, or $500.

These are examples that show what happens if your account has only one short sale position. But this is unlikely. You probably have an account of a variety of long and short positions. Let's see how the minimum maintenance rules apply in this situation. Suppose this is what your portfolio looks like:

Long Positions

2500 shares of ABC at $10 = $5000

50 shares of XYZ at $10 = $2500

250 shares of Z at $10 = $2500

CMV = $5000 + $2500 + $2500 = $10,000

Your debit balance is $7000 (what you owe).

TABLE 2.20   Long Positions in a Margin Account

CMV	$10,000
Debit balance	$ 7,000
Equity	$ 3,000

Short Portfolio

100 shares of Y at $20 = $2000

300 shares of J at $1 = $300

200 shares of K at $7 = $1400

SMV = $2000 + $300 + $1400 = $3700

Credit balance = $3700

To see if a minimum maintenance requirement is needed, you must first calculate the minimum requirement for the long positions, which is $2500 ($10,000 × 25%).

For the short positions, you must apply the short sale minimum maintenance rules to each of the short positions. For stock Y, the stock price is over $5, so we use Rule 2:

TABLE 2.21   Minimum Maintenance for Short Position in Y

$5.00 per share	$5 × 100 = $500
30% of the CMV	30% × $2000 = $600

In accordance with rule 2, the higher amount is used, which is $600. Next, we use Rule 1 for position J since the stock price is below $5:

TABLE 2.22   Minimum Maintenance for Short Position in J

$2.50 per share	$2.50 × 300 = $750
100% of CMV	$1 × 300 = $300

In accordance with rule 1, the minimum maintenance is the larger amount, $750.

Finally, we use Rule 2 for the K stock short position. The amount is $1000.

TABLE 2.23   Minimum Maintenance for Short Position K

$5.00 per share	$5 × 200 = $1000
30% of the CMV	30% × $1400 = $420

In accordance with rule 2, the minimum maintenance for position K is $1000.

Next, add up all the long and short requirements:

$$\$2500 + \$1000 + \$750 + \$600 = \$4850$$

You then subtract this from the total equity:

$$\$4850 - \$3000 = \$1850$$

This is the amount that you must deposit in your account to meet the margin call.

A final word on margin requirements: Without prior notice, a firm can change the margin requirements on your account. This could mean you need to immediately deposit more money or shares in your account. And there are no limits on what a brokerage firm can impose. Moreover, the broker does not even have to notify you if it decides to liquidate and close your account because you have not met your margin requirements.

Special Margin Rules for Day Traders

In the summer of 2001, both the New York Stock Exchange and the Nasdaq implemented new margin rules for so-called pattern day traders. If you are classified a day trader, then the minimum account balance goes from $2000 to $25,000.

What is a day trader? The rule applies to those who make at least four day trades (trades that are opened and closed in a day's session) per week. This is the case as long as these trades comprise more than 6 percent of all the trades during this time period.

Moreover, the trades in the account must not exceed four times the equity in the account for a given day.

If you are classified as a pattern day trader, you will need to keep funds in the margin account for at least two days. If you fall into the pattern day trader category and fall below the $25,000 limit, you have 5 days to meet the deficiency. If not, your account is restricted for 90 days until the call is met. However, you can still liquidate the account at any time.

Conclusion

As stated earlier, you do not need to have an intimate understanding of the accounting rules for margin to short sell a stock. However, you should be constantly asking your broker questions and reviewing all your confirmations and account statements. By doing this, your knowledge will get stronger and stronger—making these arcane rules more understandable over time.

In the next chapter, we will look at the many pitfalls a short seller needs to be aware of.

CHAPTER 3

What Your Broker Won't Tell You (or Doesn't Know) About Short Selling

You have done your homework and decided that Big Drop Corp. is a great short sell candidate. So, you call your broker and try to place the order. However, your broker is resistant. She says, "At our firm, we try to promote asset allocation and conservative principles. Short selling is a dangerous game. Do you really know the risks?"

Actually, this is a good stockbroker. She is certainly looking after your interests. Short selling is a risky game and before you do it, you should have a good understanding of the fundamentals. In Chapter 2, we looked at the basic mechanics of short selling. In this chapter, we will look deeper at the risks of short selling. And there are some big ones. We will also look deeper into the practice to better understand what short selling is.

Marginable Stocks and Street Name

Let's continue with the Big Drop Corp. example. A year ago, the stock was trading at a nosebleed level of $150 per share. Now, the stock is at $5. It is still a good short, since there is really no value to the firm. It is on the verge of bankruptcy.

You think to yourself, if the company is close to bankruptcy, why is the stock price still at $5? This is a common situation. By the time a stock has collapsed to these levels, most professional institutional investors are out of the stock and there is no more selling pressure from them. Rather, there are probably a handful of small investors speculating on the stock. This explains why the volume of the stock is so low.

You think this is a great time to short. You call your broker and try to place a trade. But you are denied. Why? There are several possibilities:

- No brokerage firm allows margin on the stock, because the stock is considered to be too risky (and the brokerage firm wants to prevent a possible lawsuit).

- No investors have shares in margin accounts (we will learn why below).

- No investors have shares in "street name." If shares are in street name, a broker can lend these out to short sellers without permission. If not, brokers cannot lend these shares.

In some cases, a company will try to take steps to prevent short sellers from borrowing shares. One example is the case of Microstrategy, an enterprise software company. As the company's stock was plunging, the company's CEO, Michael Saylor, wrote a letter to stockholders and gave advice on how to make it difficult for short sellers. At the time, the stock price was $7.

The first part of the letter talked about the various deals that the company was pursuing that would help boost its stock price. Then, Saylor went after the short sellers, writing: "However, there is something that you might be able to do to help us, and in the process, help yourself."

He described the short selling process. According to Saylor: "By selling first and buying later, short sellers benefit from stock prices going down instead of up. This makes their interest in our company directly opposite from what most of our stockholders want—i.e., for the price of our stock to increase." This is no doubt true.

Then again, short sellers had some very good reasons for believing the stock price would fall. In March 2000, the company announced that it would have to restate its earnings for 1997, 1998, and 1999. The company's results were far below what was originally reported. Earnings during this period had propelled the stock to over $300. However, when earnings were restated, it was shown that instead of generating

$205.3 million in sales for 1999, the real figure was $151 million. The company also showed a loss of 43 cents per share; they originally had shown a gain of 15 cents per share. Moreover, the company warned that its next quarter would be less than expected. At the same time he restated earnings, Saylor also slashed the workforce by one-third (for the stock performance, see Figure 3.1).

Next, in his letter to shareholders, Saylor wrote: "If there is a lot of short selling, supply of our shares may exceed demand for our shares, causing the stock price to go down. In other words, short sellers can make money by selling enough stock short to artificially increase the volume of selling and drive down the market price."

This is true. To understand this, let's look at an example. Suppose Small Corp. has only two shareholders of record, Jack and Jill, each owning 500 shares, for a total of 1000 shares outstanding. The stock price is $10 per share and the company has a market value—also known as a market capitalization—of $10,000 (1000 shares × $10).

Silly Short decides to short 500 shares. To do this, he borrows on margin the 500 shares that Jill has and then sells them on the open market to Howard for $5000. As a result, according to the company's shareholder list, the shareholders of record include Jack with 500 shares and Howard with 500 shares. Since it has only issued 1000 shares, it cannot have more than this amount on its shareholder record.

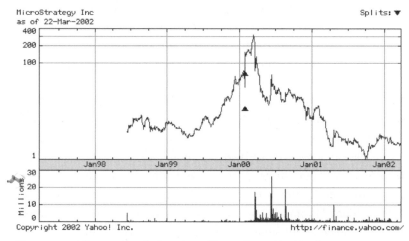

Figure 3.1 Microstrategy's Attack on Shorts Does Not Work.

Despite this, doesn't Jill still have 500 shares in her account? That's correct. While she is not a shareholder of record, she nonetheless has a beneficial interest in the 500 shares, because the short seller has agreed to deliver them back to her in the future. In short seller's parlance, she has 500 artificial shares in Small Corp.

In all, Jack has 500 shares, Howard has 500 shares and Jill has 500 shares. As Saylor said, the company has increased the supply of shares from 1000 to 1500. The market capitalization is $15,000. But has it really increased by $5000 in real value? No. Only the company's supply of shares has increased. Theoretically, the stock price should fall until it reaches the $10,000 valuation, in effect forcing the stock price down to $6.60. This is why Saylor believes short selling reduces the stock price.

Another interesting consequence of the increase in supply of stock is dividends. Jack, Howard, and Jill believe they each own 500 shares, but the company considers the owners to be Jack and Howard. The company will pay dividends to Jack and Howard. Silly Short will then have to pay the dividends to Jill.

What happens with a shareholder vote? In this case, only shareholders of record can vote. So, Jill cannot vote her 500 shares. But, Saylor did not mention a piece of crucial information in his letters to shareholders: Eventually, short sellers will need to cover their positions (that is, to buy back the shares). In other words, there are 5 million shares that will need to be bought back. This represents a potentially large future demand for the stock. Later in this chapter, we will look at the dreaded short squeeze and see how this future demand can dramatically increase the stock price.

Despite this, Saylor continues to blame short sellers for the stock's fall. He writes: "Where do the traders get the stock to borrow? Ironically, whether you know it or not, they probably have been borrowing shares from stockholders like you. If your shares are registered in your broker's name instead of yours or are held in a margin account, your broker may have lent your MicroStrategy shares out to these 'short sellers.'"

Consequently, Saylor made the following recommendation to his shareholders: "Promptly call your brokers and have your MicroStrategy stock taken out of street name or put into a cash account."

Saylor did mention there are some headaches for making the switch. There is some paperwork and perhaps even a fee. Then again,

Saylor writes that: "We think this is a small price to pay for relieving the heavy short selling pressure on our stock."

But, he did not mention that in addition to paperwork and fees, it also can be a headache to sell a stock when it is not in street name.

Some companies will go even further than Microstrategy. For example, a company may even take out advertisements in the *Wall Street Journal* to attack short sellers.

If you see companies take such actions, it is certainly a warning sign. If a company is truly executing on its business model, why should it be worried about short sellers?

The "Borrow"

The borrow is a common phrase in short selling. If you try to short a stock and the broker says there is no borrow, then you cannot short the stock (at least from this broker). Simply put, the broker cannot find any shares to borrow. You are out of luck.

There may be a variety of reasons for not getting a borrow, such as no shares are on margin or in street name. However, there is another potential reason: The broker may really have the shares, but does not want to lend them to you. Why? It is similar to how IPOs work. If you are an investor with a small account, a brokerage is likely not to allocate shares to you of a red hot IPO. Instead, the brokerage will focus on the big clients who can bring in more money in large commission dollars.

This motivation is also the case with short selling. Having a borrow on a stock is valuable to a brokerage firm, as well as investors—especially if shares are hard to get. The temptation is to lend to big time clients. However, if you are an investor with a small account (under $50,000), you do increase your chances of getting a borrow if you open accounts with a variety of brokers.

Unlimited Losses

A professor in finance who is also a hedge fund manager and short seller has a story about short selling called "The Stock Genie." The Stock Genie comes to you and says that there is a stock selling for $100 per share. He knows the stock, Great Drop Corp., will go bankrupt and the stock price will go to zero. This will happen in the next two years. However, he does not tell you when it will happen.

Great short? Some in the professor's class believe so and have said they would bet the farm on the trade.

Before you do, it is important to keep in mind that short selling involves potentially unlimited losses. Of course, this is the most common complaint against short selling. To understand the concept, let's continue with Great Drop Corp. You short 100 shares at $100 per share. If the stock does go to zero, you will make a cool $10,000.

The problem is what if the stock price soars to $200. Or suppose the stock goes to $400 or even $500. True, this sounds outlandish, but even questionable companies can soar to absurd values. A classic example was the dot-com surge in the late 1990s when stock prices easily reached $200 or $300 per share with little evidence that a company was turning any profit (a classic example is Amazon.com, as seen in Figure 3.2). There was also a big surge in biotech stocks in the early 1990s.

Being on the wrong side of these mega waves can be very damaging. If Great Drop goes to $400 per share, it will cost you $30,000 to cover the transaction. Besides, your broker will be sending you margin calls. If you do not put up more cash, your account will be liquidated. Because of this, you could literally go broke—even if the stock eventually does fall to zero.

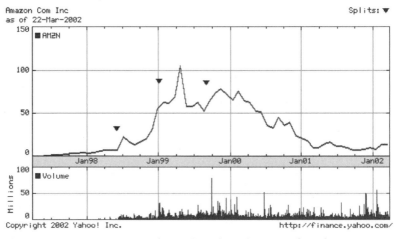

Figure 3.2   Amazon.com Stock Continued to Rise Even Though Unprofitable.

The Buy-In

You short 100 shares of Great Drop Corp. at $100 per share. The stock hits $110, but you are not worried. You still believe the stock is poised for a fall. However, the next day, you get a confirmation from your brokerage firm. It says that you covered the stock at $11 and sustained a $100 loss. What happened?

This is called a *buy-in*. In your margin agreement, the broker has the right for a buy-in. That is, the broker can require that you cover your short.

Basically, this happens when the lender of the stock decides to either sell the stock or take physical delivery of the certificates. If the broker cannot find new shares to back the short sale, he will have to call for a buy-in.

This can be a rude awakening to the investor but it does happen—especially for thinly traded stocks. A thinly traded stock is when there is low volume.

Let's continue the example. Suppose you have 100 shares short and another client at the brokerage firm has 100 shares short. The broker can only borrow 100 shares but must buy-in either you or the other client. Who gets the buy-in? This is arbitrary. But, there is a temptation from the broker's viewpoint to buy-in a smaller client versus a bigger client.

Short Interest

Short interest is the total number of shares that have been shorted but not yet covered. On a monthly basis, both the NYSE and the Nasdaq publish short interest data. You also can find this data on popular finance sites, such as finance.yahoo.com. For example, if you pull up the quote for the online supersite Priceline.com, the short interest might be 4.94 million shares on a particular date.

Monitoring short interest can be a good tool for uncovering shorting opportunities. For example, if you see a surge in short interest, then investors may be getting skittish about the prospects of a company. However, this does not necessarily mean this is a good short sale candidate. The many reasons for short interest include:

Hedge.   Some investors that are long-term bullish on the stock may be hedging a part of their position. Hedging is a way to protect a current position or portfolio from a fall in price.

Arbitrage.   This is when an investor profits in the difference between the price of a single security that is traded on more than one market. A classic example is the following: Let's say gold is trading for $300 per ounce in the United States and is trading for $320 in Europe. This is an arbitrage opportunity. You would buy the gold in the United States for $300 and sell it for $320 in Europe. Investors who engage in this activity are called *arbs,* and they typically use sophisticated computer systems to facilitate their trades.

How might this apply to short selling? Consider this example: Big Corp. agrees to buy Small Corp. The stock price of the former is $50 and the stock price of the latter is $10. In the deal, Big Corp. agrees to buy Small Corp. for $25 per share. After the announcement, the stock of Small Corp. goes to $24. Why the $1 difference? The reason is that there is a possibility the deal could collapse. The difference between the market price and the buyout price is called *the spread.*

In the deal, Big Corp. offers to exchange one-half of a share of its stock in exchange for one share of Small Corp. That is, Big Corp. is using its stock as currency to buy Small Corp. In this situation, if an arb believes the deal between the two companies will indeed happen, he will short 0.50 shares of Big Corp. stock for every share bought of Small Corp. So, let's say the arb buys 1 million shares of Small Corp. for $24, which costs $24 million. Then he shorts 500,000 shares of Big Corp., which nets him $25 million. Currently, he has a profit of $1 million. If the deal happens, the arb will receive 500,000 shares of Big Corp. in the share exchange. Next, the arb will deliver these 500,000 shares to cover the short and he pockets the $1 million.

However, if the deal breaks down, the arb could potentially lose money on both the long position and the short decision. For example, when the deal falls, the stock of Big Corp. goes up $5 and the arb losses $2.5 million on this trade (the stock went up because Wall Street thought it was smart to break the deal). The stock price of Small Corp. falls $3 (the shareholders are unhappy that they will not get a premium for their shares). The arb loses $3 million on this trade. In other words, there is a degree of risk with merger arbitrage.

But keep this in mind: The reason for selling short the stock of Big Corp. was not the arbs' opinion that the company was bad. Rather, the arb thought there was a price discrepancy in the market place and saw an opportunity for a quick profit.

Making Markets.   Brokerage firms, specialists, and market makers will take short positions in stocks. If one of these firms cannot get stock for customers, they will borrow it to get supply. This is very common. Basically, these financial firms are providing liquidity to the market-place to make it run more smoothly.

Short Squeeze

As we learned above, there is the potential for unlimited losses when shorting a stock or acting as an arb. To combat this risk, when a stock begins to skyrocket, it is common for short sellers to cover their positions. Unfortunately, this can result in the dreaded "short squeeze."

Here's how it works: Suppose that Big Drop Corp. has many short sellers with significant positions. However, the company surprises analysts and posts a profit. The stock goes from $50 to $70 on the news.

Some of the shorts want to cut their losses and cover their positions. Others panic and cover. There may be some margin calls and these shorts cover. Or, there may be buy-ins and shorts who are forced to cover. The covering means that the short sellers are buying more and more stock—fueling the rise in the stock price. It goes from $70 to $80. The shorts are being squeezed.

Here are two ways to see if there is a potential short squeeze with a company: by calculating the short-interest ratio and the float.

Short-Interest Ratio.   The ratio shows the number of days it would take to cover all the shorts. It is calculated as follows:

$$\frac{\text{Short interest}}{\text{Average daily volume}} = \text{Short-interest ratio}$$

If the short interest is 1 million shares and the daily volume is 200,000 shares, then it would take 5 days to clear all the stock.

If the ratio shows it would take more than a week to cover all the shorts, then be careful. The shorts can be squeezed if the stock surges.

If the ratio is less than a week, the chances of a squeeze are diminished. It is likely easier to get shares to cover a position.

Float.   People often confuse outstanding shares with the float. But there is an important difference. Outstanding shares are the shares owned by all shareholders. That is, these are all the shareholders of record for the company. However, in most cases, a big percentage of the stock is restricted from trading. For example, there may be a contract that prevents trading for a period of time (called a *lockup*). There may be governmental regulations that put restrictions on selling (called *Rule 144*).

As for the float, it is equal to all the shares that can be traded. The formula for the float is:

$$\text{Float} = \text{Outstanding Shares} - \text{Restricted Shares}$$

If the stock has a small float, then it could be difficult to buy stock to cover a short. If the short interest represents 10 percent or more of the float, you could be in danger of potential short squeeze.

Shorting Against the Box

Shorting against the box means that you short and buy long the same amount of stock. It can be at the same price or not. For example, let's say Great Drop Corp. is selling for $50 per share. You buy 100 shares long. You wait a few months and the stock goes to $60. Then, you short 100 shares of the stock. In market parlance, you have boxed the stock.

You have locked-in (or boxed) a gain of $10 per share or $1000. Thus, if the stock price increases $1, the short position will be down $100 and the long position will be up $100. In other words, there is no change. By shorting against the box, you cannot lose any money (but you can't earn any money either). It is a perfect hedge.

Until 1997, shorting against the box was a great way to lock in profits without paying the IRS any taxes. This changed when Congress passed new tax legislation in 1997. This is explained in more detail in Chapter 14.

However, there is another approach to shorting against the box. Let's continue the above example. Suppose you buy 100 shares and then immediately short 100 shares of Great Drop Corp. at $50. In this case, there is no way to make money. You locked in a price of $50 per share.

Why would you do this? This can be a good way to get a borrow on a stock. As a stock starts to fall, there tends to be more and more short sellers who come into the stock. As the short interest increases, it can be more difficult to borrow the stock.

Let's say that a few months earlier you thought the stock might be a good potential short, but you were not convinced. So, you shorted against the box to get a borrow on the stock. Then, as you did more research, you sold your long position and went completely short on the stock.

Uptick Rule

Another roadblock to short selling is the so-called uptick rule. The SEC passed this rule in 1937 (it is known as Rule 10a-1) in response to the wild markets of the 1920s. During that point in history, it was not uncommon for some traders or pools to launch "bear raids" against a company. This was done by short selling huge amounts of stock at successively lower prices. With the uptick rule, this would be much harder.

Keep in mind that the uptick rule was originally meant for the New York Stock Exchange (NYSE), the American Stock Exchange (AMEX), and regional stock exchanges. However, the uptick rule would eventually apply to Nasdaq (but with a different variation).

The uptick rule states that short selling is allowed only when done on an uptick or a zero plus tick. A *tick* is either an upward or downward move in a stock price. As the name implies, an *uptick* is when the last reported stock price was an increase. If you look at a stock quote, an uptick would show a + sign. A zero plus tick, on the other hand, is when the current stock price is the same as the previous one, but is higher than the last different price. Example: Suppose Big Drop Corp.'s stock price is $50. Then the stock increases to $51. The next trade is at $51. This would be a zero plus tick.

In 1986, the Nasdaq adopted its own form of the uptick rule (known as NASD Rule 3350). The rule states that short sales are prohibited at or below the current best bid (which is called the inside bid) when that bid is lower than the previous inside bid.

What does this mean? Let's take a look at a Nasdaq quote for Microsoft:

TABLE 3.1   Microsoft Stock Quote

Bid	Ask
$60.00	$60.20

In this example, the last trade for Microsoft shows a bid of $60 and an ask for $60.20. *The bid* is the price at which you sell the stock. If you want to short a stock on the Nasdaq, the price you need to look at for the uptick rule is the bid. *The ask*, on the other hand, is the price you get when you cover the short sale (there is no restriction when covering your short).

To see if you can short Microsoft, we need to look at the previous trade, which was:

TABLE 3.2   Microsoft Quote for Previous Trade

Bid	Ask
$60.10	$60.30

In this case, the current bid is lower than the prior bid. Thus, if you want to short the stock (Microsoft, in this case), you must place a trade that is higher than $60 per share. This can be a matter of just one cent or $60.01.

Finally, the uptick rule does not apply to the OTC Bulletin Board (OTCBB). OTC stands for over the counter. Basically, an OTC security is not listed on the Nasdaq, NYSE or AMEX. The OTCBB is a regulated quotation service that provides real-time quotes for OTC stocks. The Web site is located at www.otcbb.com.

Before 1990, the OTCBB was a wild marketplace. In fact, it was not uncommon to see stock manipulation and fraud. As a result, Congress passed the Penny Stock Reform Act of 1990, which gave the SEC the power to establish an electronic system for OTC stocks.

In January 1999, the SEC approved the OTCBB Eligibility Rule. The rule requires that any company listed on the OTCBB report its current financial information to the SEC. While these regulations have made it more difficult to promote frauds, the OTCBB still has many question-able companies. And, given the fact that there is no uptick rule for this market, the OTCBB is an attractive venue for short sellers. Further, because of the potential for manipulation of stock prices, there tends to be a higher probability of short squeezes. This makes the OTCBB an exceptionally dangerous market for short sellers—although potentially lucrative as well.

Types of Orders.   When you place a short sale order in the NYSE or Nasdaq, you must abide by the uptick rule. But you do have some options when placing the order. Let's look at an example. Big Drop Corp. is trading on an uptick at $50. You want to short 100 shares. Since you are selling the stock, you want to get a high price. There are two approaches you could take: You could place a market order or a limit order.

Market Order.   Placing a market order means you will get your order filled at the current price, which is $50 per share. The advantage is that you are nearly guaranteed to get execution on the order. Moreover, the order will be quick and the commission is likely to be lower (as com-pared to placing a limit order, which we discuss next).

However, market orders do have some disadvantages. For instance, you might not get a good price on the trade. In fact, for an order beyond 100 shares, you are likely to get different prices. For example, in a 200-share trade, 100 shares might be at $50 and another 100 shares might be for $49.50. The reason is that markets can be volatile. If there is a big block of stock being sold, this might alert buyers. They may sense they can get a better deal by trying to get a lower price. And, remember, the short seller wants to get a high price when selling the stock.

Limit Order.   While you are a price taker when making a market order, you are essentially haggling when placing a limit order. With the limit order, you will only get execution of your trade at a price you specify or above for a sale. For example, you can place a limit order for $50.50. Thus, you will get the short sale executed at a price no lower than $50.50. A big advantage is if the stock suddenly collapses, say to $45.00. In this case, your trade will not be executed.

One disadvantage is that you might miss out on a great trade. Example: You place a limit order for $50.50. The stock goes to $50.45, so your trade is not filled. Then, in the next few days, the stock collapses to $45. You missed an opportunity for a $5 short sale profit on the trade.

Both market and limit orders are assumed to be "day orders." That is, the order is good for the trading day. These orders do not extend into after-hours trading. However, you can place a good-till-cancelled (GTC) order. As the name implies, this means the order will be open until you cancel it or it is executed. A brokerage firm may place a limit on how long a GTC order can be open. The advantage of a GTC order is that it allows you to wait for a few days—or even a few weeks—to try to get a good price on the trade.

Cover Orders

We have seen that when placing orders, there are strategies you can use to improve your position. In terms of covering your short position, you also have a variety of ways of placing orders:

Market Order.   As shown above, your order will be bought (or covered) at the current price. With this order, you will get immediate execution, which can be important if the market is increasing quickly. Again, as discussed above, you are basically a price taker. If the stock spikes, you will be covered at a high price.

Buy Stop Order.   This can help protect a profit in the short sale. For example, let's say you shorted 100 shares of Big Drop Corp. at $10 and the stock is now at $5. You have a paper profit of $500. You place a buy stop order at $5.50. If the stock hits $5.50 or above, a market order is issued, and you could make $450 on the trade (assuming you got $5.50 on the cover).

Or, a buy stop can be used to try to set a cap for further losses. Let's take the Big Drop Corp. example. You short 100 shares at $10. If the stock price goes to $12, you want out of the trade. So, you set a buy stop order at $12, which limits your loss on the trade to $200 (again, assuming you do get $12 on the trade).

One disadvantage of a buy stop order is that you might be stopped out of a trade due to temporary price fluctuations. From the example above, suppose the stock goes to $12.02 and you cover the short, but then the stock collapses to $5. You essentially would have lost an opportunity to make $500 on the trade. Even worse, if the stock goes to zero, you would have made $1000.

Remember: When the stop order is triggered, a market order is sent. Suppose Big Drop goes to $12.02 and a market order is sent. Then news is released and the stock goes to $13. You just covered your short at $13. Your loss is $300.

Stop-Limit Order.   You can prevent the above example from happening by using a stop-limit order. By placing a stop-limit order, if the stock goes to $12 or higher, a limit order to buy at $12 will be placed. You will only be filled on the trade if the stock is $12 or lower. The most you can lose on the trade is $200. Then again, if the stock spikes to $15, the order is not filled and you have an existing short position that—on paper—has a loss of $500.

It is important to note that you cannot place buy stop orders on stocks in the OTC Bulletin Board.

Using Stockbrokers

To place short sale trades, you will need the services of a broker. As suggested in the last chapter, a discount broker is a good idea. However, you still might want the comfort of having a full-service broker. But be choosy. Interview the broker and see if he has a good understanding of short selling.

It is also a good idea to do a background check on your prospective stockbroker. The broker may have many complaints or even been sanctioned by regulatory authorities.

Every broker is a member of the NASD (National Association of Securities Dealers), which is a self-regulatory agency for the securities agency. The NASD has a site at www.nasdr.com, where you can get a background summary on the broker. The information includes:

- Examination history (such as the Securities 7, which is the license for stockbrokers)
- Employment history
- Criminal convictions or indictments
- Civil judgments and arbitration decisions

- Pending disciplinary actions from the NASD or other regulatory agencies

- Personal bankruptcies filed in the last 10 years

- Outstanding liens

- Pending written complaints for damages of $5000 or more

- Settlements of $10,000 or more for arbitrations or civil suits

- Final disciplinary actions by state, federal, and foreign securities regulators

A request for a background report is anonymous. Moreover, you may be able to get more information from your state securities regulator (call 202-737-0900 or visit *www.nasaa.org*).

In addition to investigating your broker's background, it is important to note that some brokers can be sloppy with paperwork, which can damage the potential for profitable trades. For example, a confirmation from your broker must indicate that the trade was a short sale. Sometimes a broker will mistakenly call a short sale a long sale, which is false, and obviously undermines your trading strategy. A broker can be fined for such actions, but that doesn't change the fact that the wrong trade was made on your behalf. Moreover, a broker may violate uptick rules or make trades in a cash account. Again, fines can be levied for these actions and you can file complaints with the SEC and exchanges against the broker.

Also, a broker must make a determination that securities are available to borrow for a short sale. Unfortunately, some brokers assume that this is the case and short the stock anyway. If this happens, you can get damages for any lost profits on the trade. This is a gross violation of a broker's duties.

If you see these violations, it obviously is a good idea to get another broker. Also, you may have legal recourse, as well. But the first step should not be to sue. Instead, see if you can resolve the dispute directly with your brokerage firm.

First, write a complaint to your broker and send it to the branch manager. This should be done promptly. Request that you get a response in a timely manner (say a week). If there is no response, then write a complaint letter to the firm's Compliance Officer. He is in charge of legal compliance issues with the NASD, SEC, and federal securities laws. Also, ask for a response.

If you do not get a satisfactory response, then you may file a complaint with the NASD and the SEC. You might also want to file a request for arbitration. Nearly every new account form has an arbitration clause. This means that you cannot bring your case to court, but must use arbitration as an alternative.

ARBITRATION

The NASD supervises arbitrations and you must file a written complaint to one of its directors of arbitration at one of their six regional offices (New York, Los Angeles, Chicago, Washington, DC, San Francisco, and Boca Raton). Your filing will set the damages sought. You should definitely ask for money lost. But you can also ask for forgone profits (for example, the amount you would have made if you were invested in conservative securities) and attorneys fees.

Your broker will be represented by an attorney. You should be, too. If you lose an arbitration case, you cannot appeal it.

Don't Do It!

Some short sellers will try to manufacture news to drive down a company's stock price. In fact, with small cap companies, it can be easy to use such techniques to drive down the stock price. Simply put, there is likely to not be much volume in the stock. A few thousand shares in new volume can have a significant impact on the stock price. In this section, we'll look at examples of this kind of dangerous activity.

The lesson: Don't do it. Besides being illegal, chances are good you will be caught. The SEC has been investing resources in taking enforcement actions against securities violations for stock manipulation. In fact, the SEC gets valuable leads from investors. If you have substantial evidence that a company you are following is a fraud, you can make a report to the SEC, which has a division called the CyberForce at this URL: *http://www.sec.gov/divisions/enforce/internetenforce.htm.* The site states:

> What used to require a network of professional promoters and brokers, banks of telephones, and months to accomplish can

now be done in minutes by a single person using the Internet and a home computer. Thinly traded microcap stocks are particularly susceptible to online manipulations. That's why we have made this area one of our highest enforcement priorities. Ultimately, however, the best way for investors to protect themselves against all forms of Internet fraud, including pump-and-dump schemes, is to do their homework and to be highly skeptical of information they receive from strangers on Internet websites, message boards, and chat rooms.

A famous case of short selling manipulation involved Mark Jakob. In his early twenties, Jakob lost about $97,000 in the stock market. He worked at a company called Internet Wire, which published press releases for companies. His experience led him to believe he could profit from is ability to write press releases, and Jakob wrote a release about a highflier tech company, Emulex. In the press release, which was posted on the Internet, Jakob said the CEO of Emulex quit and that the company would have to restate earnings. It was a bombshell on Wall Street, as the stock plunged immediately. Before this, he shorted the stock, making $241,000 within minutes.

But Jakob's fortunes were not to last. Within less than a week, the SEC implicated Jakob in the scheme and brought charges. He had to repay the profits, plus $97,000 in interest and a $102,642 penalty. Although Jakob ended up losing more than $440,000, it was investors who paid the real price. In fact, the SEC estimated that the scheme cost investors $110 million.

Certainly, Jakob's was a grandiose plan. However, some short sellers may engage in less spectacular plans to manipulate stock. One common approach to manipulating stock prices is to post messages on financial chat boards.

While there is nothing illegal about posting messages on bulletin boards or in chat rooms, it is illegal to purposely spread lies about a company. Such postings could be libelous, and, of course, smart short sellers will refrain from posting any messages about a company if they are not basing their opinions on fact. In fact, if you are posting information for the sole purpose of driving the stock down, you may be subject to actions from the SEC or lawsuits from the company.

Clearly, savvy short sellers will make fair trades, and avoid schemes that unjustly affect stock price. More often than not, the penalties for such actions are costly, and, in some cases, ruinous.

Expectations

Clearly it seems that short sellers cook up such schemes as Jakob did out of the desire to turn a quick profit. While short selling certainly can be profitable, it also is a risky endeavor with potential for painful losses. The key is in balancing expectations.

It would definitely be great to short Enron at $80 and see it fall below a buck. In reality, however, this is a rare event. In fact, stocks generally go up—even bad ones. That's why long-term investing in the stock market is generally profitable for investors. It is also why it is important to be thorough in your analysis before shorting a stock.

As with any type of investing, short sellers need to have realistic expectations. Do not expect to make huge amounts when short selling.

For starters, do not chase stocks. Just as you can average down on a long, you can also average up on a short. For example, let's say you think XYZ is the next Enron and is poised to fall. You short 100 shares at $100. A few days later, the stock pops to $110 and you short another 100. The stock then goes to $130. More than ever now, you think XYZ is a great short and you place another order for 100 at $130.

Then the stock shoots to $200 in a few days. The pain is unbearable and you cover your short in a panic. In all, you shorted 400 shares for $47,000. To cover the trade at $200 means you must buy $80,000 in stock. In all, you lost $33,000.

As you can see, you were getting deeper and deeper into a bad trade. While averaging down may have validity for long positions, it is usually a bad idea for shorting. After all, on these positions, you have margin that you are responsible for, which is not the case for long positions. And, as we discussed earlier in this chapter, the stock could go up and up and up—adding more pain to your portfolio.

As a result, savvy short sellers will diversify their short sale positions. They will also not have any position represent a substantial part of their portfolio. Paul McEntire is one such short seller who manages several hedge funds for Skye Investment Advisers, which focuses on short selling. He has been running the funds since 1985.

He is truly a "rocket scientist," having worked on the Apollo space program. He has also published a variety of scholarly articles on computers. He has used this technical knowledge for short selling.

One of McEntire's key management principles is to have no stock more than 1 percent short in his portfolio. The risk of a stock doubling or tripling is too high. If the stock does this, a good short seller quickly gets out of the position.

The Right Time to Short

History indicates that stock prices tend to increase. This is why professional hedge fund managers have more long positions than short positions. Short positions represent a hedge if the market falters. But there are times when the markets get excessive—which can make it particularly difficult for short sellers. This was certainly the case during the 1990s, when the market underwent an explosive drive during what many called the greatest bull market in history (see Figure 3.3). There were only a few dips and huge gains. Even companies that apparently lacked business models, revenues, or profits had no problems achieving extremely high valuations.

Needless to say, it was a terrible time for short sellers. Even if short sellers spotted bad companies, this was often not enough. Investors

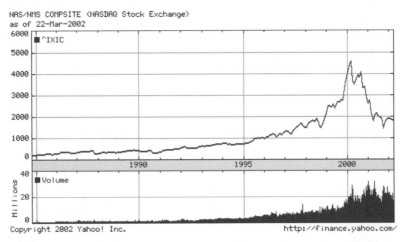

Figure 3.3 Short Sellers Had a Difficult Time in the Roaring 1990s Bull Market.

would buy seemingly anything, driving prices up, thwarting short selling opportunities.

Even the top short sellers of the 1980s had difficulties making profitable trades. The Feshbach Brothers, which posted annual returns of over 40 percent from 1982 to 1990, changed the direction of its short-only firm and began to *buy* undervalued stocks (they said it was still a contrarian approach).

One of the best hedge fund managers, George Soros, also had many difficulties. He shorted many tech stocks at the wrong time, losing millions of dollars in the process.

Famed short-seller Jim Chanos saw his short-only Ursus fund fall 75 percent from 1991 to 1999. One particularly bad short was America Online. Chanos admits that he did not realize how significant the online world would eventually be. To reduce the risk level of his overall portfolio of funds, Chanos started another hedge fund called Beta Hedge. Basically, for every dollar Chanos shorted there would be an equal long-position in the Beta Hedge fund.

Short selling requires in-depth investigation. Doing your homework is key. As these examples show, it certainly is important to have a feel for the overall market environment when shorting stocks. If you short stocks when the market is in the beginning or middle stages of a bull market, it could prove very damaging. No doubt, the best time to short is when the market has hit a speculative high. Of course, knowing when this happens is no easy feat. The 1990s market showed that it would have been terrible to short when those markets dipped. Those dips were really corrections in a long-term bull market. However, keep in mind that the high-flying market of the 1990s was rare. Markets do not typically have this type of sustained advance.

Short sellers make their most lucrative profits in down markets. While no system is perfect, there are a few techniques that may help spot the beginning of a bear market:

DON'T FIGHT THE FED

One of well-known market timer Marty Zweig's favorite sayings is "Don't fight the Fed." Zweig called the stock market crash of 1987. When the market plunged 22.6 percent in one day, his portfolio was up 9 percent. Zweig has developed a variety of useful indicators to help investors not to go against Fed policy.

Zweig looks at the prime interest rate to sense the direction of the Fed. As the name implies, the prime rate is the interest that a bank charges its best customers. If a borrower is considered risky, a loan will typically be based on a rate that is higher than the prime rate (you will hear bankers say "prime plus 2 percent," for example).

Zweig likes using the prime rate for two reasons:

1. It does not change much during the year. Thus, it is easier to determine overall trends.

2. A change in the prime rate tends to lag moves by the Fed. For example, suppose the Fed begins to increase the money supply. A month later, the prime rate decreases from 7.5 to 6.5 percent. The lag is important, since it takes some time for monetary policy to have an impact on the stock market.

Zweig considers any increase in the prime above 8 percent to be bearish. If the prime rate is less than 8 percent, he considers two hikes or a 1 percent increase to be bearish.

CASH ON HAND

The influence of mutual funds on the stock market has been substantial since the early 1980s. It is not uncommon to see funds with more than $1 billion in assets under management. Since the 1950s, the Investment Company Institute has published mutual fund activity, including the ratio of cash to assets in all mutual funds. If mutual funds have low amounts of cash, their firepower is muted. It is harder to push stocks higher because there is not enough cash to do so. Besides, the fact that most mutual funds are fully invested indicates that there is tremendous bullish sentiment in the market. A ratio of 5 percent cash to stocks or lower is a good benchmark to use to determine market sentiment.

INVESTMENT ADVISER INDICATOR

Developed by Zweig, this indicator tracks the bullishness or bearishness of financial newsletters. If there is an extreme, he goes against it.

In calculating the indicator, Zweig only counts those investment newsletters that have bull and bear calls. He does not count neutral advisers. For example, suppose there are 120 newsletters and 20 of them are neutral. Of these, there are 70 that are bullish and 30 that are bearish. The ratio would be 70 percent bullish (70/100). For Zweig, if the bullish ratio is 75 percent or above, this is a danger sign, signaling that the market may be poised for a fall.

Conclusion

Short squeezes, buy-ins, the "borrow"—there are many dangers that lurk in the world of short selling. It is not for the faint of heart. To be successful, you need to fully understand what short selling really is. From trusting your broker to using indicators to determine when to short, there are many guidelines to follow in order to have the best chance to turn a profit. This chapter has provided a foundation for understanding the mechanics of short selling.

In the next chapter, we will look at alternatives to short selling, such as with put options, index futures, and a new product, single stock futures. We will also compare these alternatives to short selling.

CHAPTER 4

Short Sale Alternatives: Futures and Options

et's say you've been short selling for a few months and have had success on several trades. Then you hear someone talk about options and how you can use puts to bet on the downside of a stock. Then, when reading an article in a financial magazine, you hear about a new financial instrument, single stock futures (SSFs), and wonder if you should consider these.

No doubt, the U.S. financial system is dynamic. It seems there is always something new for investors to put their hard-earned money into. In this chapter, we will take a look at two alternatives to short selling: stock options and futures.

Stock Options

In terms of the entire investing landscape, options are fairly new. It was not until 1973 that individual investors could invest in them. Over time, they've become very popular. However, there is much confusion about options. Some people believe that *all* options are high risk. This is not the case. Some option strategies are quite conservative.

An option is a contract that gives you the right to buy or sell 100 shares for a certain price over a period of time. Keep in mind that this is a *right*; you are not required to buy the stock. There are two types of options:

Calls. These give you the right to buy 100 shares.

Puts. These give you the right to sell 100 shares.

Let's consider an example: Suppose Fall Corp. is selling for $20 per share. The quote for the call might look something like Table 4-1, which is for a call option that expires in 3 months. You can also pull up charts for options that expire longer than that (say, 6 months). But options typically last for 3 months. You can find options quotes at any major financial site, such as quote.yahoo.com or cbs.marketwatch.com.

TABLE 4.1   Call Options for Fall Corp

Premium	Volume	Strike Price
$15.50	1,425	$10.00
$7.60	12,230	$15.00
$2.90	22,320	$20.00
$1.75	30,240	$25.00

The premium is how much an option costs. This is done by taking the price of the option and multiplying it by 100 shares. So, in the table, the first contract has a premium of $1550 ($15.50 × 100).

The volume shows how many options are traded for the day.

The strike price is what the call option gives you the right to buy the stock at. These are usually expressed in ranges (in this case, the range is between $10 and $25 per share).

There are two parties to the call option:

- *Call buyer.* The call buyer pays the premium to buy the option. Thus, if he buys the first option in Table 4.1, he has the right 100 shares at $10 each for the next 3 months. For this right, he pays $1550.

- *Call seller.* This is the person who is selling the right to buy 100 shares. For this, he receives the premium. If within the next 3 months the call buyer decides to exercise his option to buy the 100 shares, the call seller must deliver 100 shares.

An option has two components in its value:

- Intrinsic value. This is the current stock price minus the strike price. In our example, this would be $10 ($20 – $10).

  If an option has intrinsic value, it is called an *in-the-money option*. If the strike price is above $20, then the value will be negative and there is no intrinsic value. This is known as an *out-of-the-money option*.

- *Time value.* The time value is the difference between the premium and the intrinsic value. Taking a look at the same example:

  $15.50 premium – $10 intrinsic value = $5.50 time value

Generally, the closer an option gets to expiration, the smaller the time value. In fact, at the time of expiration, the time value goes to zero. There can only be intrinsic value.

Moreover, time value tends to be less for out-of-the money options compared to in-the-money options. Why? There is less risk that the option will expire worthless, since it already has intrinsic value.

Also, if a stock is volatile, this tends to increase the premium of an option.

The call buyer makes money when the stock price increases. If Fall Corp. increases from $20 to $40 at expiration, then the intrinsic value is $30 per share or $3000 for the contract. This is a pretty nice return, since the initial investment was $1550.

Then again, suppose the stock goes to the strike price of the option or below ($10). This means there is no intrinsic value. There is also no time value. So the contract is worthless.

A rule to remember in options is that the most you can lose when buying calls is your initial investment. Moreover, before expiration, you can sell your option (you are not required to hold it until expiration).

The option seller, on the other hand, is actually considered a short seller. That is, this person is currently agreeing to sell the stock now and deliver the shares in the future.

Thus, the option seller does not want the stock to increase in value. Example: Suppose you own 100 shares of Fall Corp. and sell a call for 100 shares for $1550. If the stock soars to $32 and the option is exercised, you must deliver the 100 shares to the call buyer. For this, you get the exercise price or $10 per share or $1000. You also keep the premium of $1550. In all, you make $2550. If you did not sell this call, your shares would have been worth $3200.

This is what would happen if you owned the 100 shares. If you did not, you are considered a naked-call seller. This can be very dangerous—especially if the stock soars.

To continue our example, to deliver the 100 shares, you will need to buy them on the open market for $3200 and deliver them to the call buyer. The call buyer then pays you the $1000 and you keep the premium.

Let's now look at put options. Like a call option, there are two parties to the transaction:

- *Put buyer.* The put buyer pays the premium to buy the option. For this, the put buyer has the right to sell 100 shares at the strike price.

- *Put seller.* This is the person who is selling the right to buy 100 shares. For this, the put seller receives the premium. If within the next 3 months the put buyer decides to exercise his option to sell the 100 shares, the put seller must buy back the 100 shares.

Example: You decide to buy a put on Fall Corp. Currently, the stock price is $50 and you think it will collapse. You buy a put with a strike price of $50 for a premium of $400.

Let's say you are right and in the next 3 months, Fall Corp. plunges to $25 per share. You buy 100 shares for $2500 and then sell them to the put seller for $50 each or $5000. The total cost of the transaction was the $400 premium plus the amount of the purchase of the 100 shares—which is total of $2500. Your profit is $2100.

How does this compare to a short sale transaction? Let's take a look. If you shorted 100 shares of Fall Corp., you would have generated proceeds of $5000 ($50 times 100 shares). To do this, you needed to have margin of at least $2500. You cover the short when it hits $25 for $2500 and you keep $2500 (keep in mind you had to pay some interest on the margin loan). Basically, the return was much higher on the put option, because you only had to invest $400.

However, the problem with the put option is if the stock does not fall. If the stock stays at $50 when it expires in 3 months, the put option is worthless. On the other hand, suppose the stock goes to $25 a month later. In this case, you would have made money from the short position, but not the put position. In other words, the big disadvantage to put options is time. With short selling, you can stay with a trade as long as there is no buy-in or margin call you cannot meet.

Thus, buying puts is very risky. Just like calls, most puts expire worthless. It's really a speculator's game.

Then again, selling calls is a fairly low-risk strategy—assuming you own the underlying shares for the option you sold. Interestingly enough, most calls expire worthless. Thus, chances are you will keep the 100 shares plus the premium.

Futures

Interestingly enough, the futures markets have been in existence for hundreds of years. Traditionally, futures were for agricultural markets. After all, it can take months for a crop to grow. But an investor may want to speculate on the price. Or a farmer may want to hedge the value of his crop in the event the crop is destroyed because of bad weather.

The futures markets were chaotic during the nineteenth century. As trade exploded, it became more and more difficult to transact these types of agreements. During the century, there were more than 1600 futures exchanges established

Now there are but a handful of exchanges. Here are the main ones:

Chicago Board of Trade (CBOT).   This was founded in 1848. Now, the CBOT is the biggest marketplace for derivatives. The exchange has more than 3600 members and trades 48 types of futures contracts. In 2000, the CBOT had trading volume of 233 million contracts.

Since its inception, the exchange has been an open auction system, in which traders transact face-to-face on a trading floor. Interestingly enough, each trading area is called a pit. However, the CBOT has an extensive computer system to handle trades, as well.

Chicago Mercantile Exchange (CME).   This exchange was originally known as the Chicago Butter and Egg Board and was founded in 1898 (the name was changed to the CME in 1919). The exchange has been an innovator. In 1961, it introduced the frozen pork belly futures contract and the first financial futures contract in 1972 (based on seven foreign currencies).

In 2000, there were more than 231 million contracts traded. This represented a staggering $155 trillion.

New York Mercantile Exchange (NYMEX). This exchange was known as the Butter and Cheese Exchange when it was founded in 1872. When the egg market grew, the exchange was renamed as the Butter, Cheese, and Egg Exchange. However, to make things simpler, the exchange was renamed yet again in 1882 to the NYMEX.

Now, because of a merger in 1994, there are two divisions: the NYMEX trades crude oil, heating oil, gasoline, natural gas, platinum. and propane, whereas the COMEX (Commodity Exchange) trades gold, silver, and copper.

In the latter half of the twentieth century, the futures markets expanded greatly. Today, the futures market is no longer a market only for commodities; you can trade currencies, bonds, and stock market indexes.

With a futures contract, you can either be long or short. While many stock market investors only invest long, this is not the case with futures traders. Most futures traders feel comfortable trading from both sides.

People often confuse options with futures. In fact, they are quite different. An option gives a person the right to buy or sell something for a 3-month period at a fixed price. There is no obligation to buy or sell the security. This is not the case with a futures contract. Rather, you have an obligation to buy or sell the underlying asset of the contract when it expires (usually in 3 months).

This can be a surprise to some investors. For example, suppose you buy a futures contract on pork bellies that are delivered in 3 months. If you do not close out your transaction before then, these pork bellies will be delivered to you. So be careful!

Some investors use futures as a way to protect their portfolios. Example: You have a portfolio of stock that has a value of $100,000. You think the stock market will fall within the next 3 months, but you do not want to sell all your stock. To protect your position, you could short an S&P 500 futures contract.

For smaller portfolios (those under $500,000), an investor would purchase a mini S&P 500 futures contract. The value of the contract is calculated as $50 times the futures price. If the S&P is at 2000, then the futures price would be $100,000, which would cover your portfolio.

The futures contract will track the performance of the S&P 500 futures contract fairly closely. The changes in value are expressed in ticks, which represent 0.10 points in the index. This amounts to a minimum $25 increment or decrement in value.

To follow your futures trades, you need to understand how they are quoted. See Table 4.2.

TABLE 4.2   Example of a Futures Quote

Month	Open	High	Low	Settlement	Vol	Open Interest	Change
Dec 01	2100.01	2280.02	2099.02	2170.03	240230	342030	+25
Mar 02	2070.03	2240.33	2010.03	2110.02	210350	310302	+50

Here is an explanation of the terms in Table 4.2:

Month: The first contract expires in December 2001 and the other expires in March 2002.

Open: This is the average price of the first bids when trading starts.

High: The highest bid price for the day.

Low: The lowest bid price for the day.

Settlement: This is the closing price.

Vol: The volume or number of contracts traded.

Open Interest: At the end of the trading day, this is the number of outstanding futures contracts that have not been closed out by delivery or an offsetting futures contract.

Net Change: The difference between yesterday's close and today's current price.

When you buy the futures contract, you must deposit margin against the transaction, which could run 3 to 5 percent of the value of the contract. In our example, you might have to deposit $5000. After each day of trading, each futures contract is marked to the market. See Chapter 2 for more information about margin.

To continue with the example above, let's assume that the S&P falls by 10 percent and your portfolio declines by 12 percent. Without the hedge, your portfolio is now worth $88,000.

With your short hedge, the value of your S&P contract will have appreciated by 10 percent or $10,000. Thus, your overall loss on your entire portfolio would be $2000; that is to say, your portfolio would be worth $98,000.

You also can use futures to speculate on the market. Remember, however, that any speculation involves high amounts of risk. Taking the example above, suppose you did not have a portfolio of $100,000, but instead went long on the S&P futures. The move in the market would have meant that you would have lost $12,000. If your margin was initially 5 percent or $5000, then you certainly took a major hit.

Single Stock Futures

So far in this chapter, we have looked at futures that are based on stock indexes. Why not trade futures on a single stock? This certainly makes sense, but it was not possible because of a law passed in the early 1980s called the Johnson Act.

In December 2000, Congress passed the Commodity Futures Modernization Act. It allowed for single stock futures (SSFs). A big reason is that SSFs were being traded in Europe successfully (there are 15 overseas exchanges that trade these instruments).

So far, there are two exchanges where SSFs will be traded:

Nasdaq Liffe Markets (http://www.nqlx.com). This is a joint venture between Nasdaq and the London International Futures and Options Exchange (LIFFE).

OneChicago (http://www.onechicago.com). This is a joint venture involving the Chicago Board Options Exchange (CBOE), the Chicago Mercantile Exchange (CME), and the Chicago Board of Trade (CBOT).

Single stock futures are slated to begin trading in March 2002. As of the writing of this book, there is not enough information to determine the ramifications of SSFs. However, there are many issues that must be worked out. One difficulty is that SSFs are regulated by both the SEC and the CTFC, which regulates the futures markets. Some of the issues:

- Margin. Traders want the low margin requirements of futures markets, which can range from 1 to 6 percent (depending on the volatility of the market and the contract size). While this may not be the case, the margin rules are likely to be lower than the Reg. T 50 percent requirement for short selling individual stocks.

- Settlement. Futures settle every day, but stock settle on the third business day.

- Fungability. In market trading, *fungability* means "interchange-ability." For SSFs, this looks at the standardization among different exchanges. Since there are two exchanges for SSFs, the issue is if the SSF contracts will have the same parameters, such as tick size.

- Taxes. It is expected that SSFs will be taxed as short-term capital gains. The wash rule is likely to apply, as well. However, it looks like a sale of a future against a long stock position will not be considered a constructive sale unless the stock is delivered.

Besides potentially lower margin requirements, there are other advantages SSFs have compared to traditional short selling:

- There is no uptick rule.

- There is no need to borrow stock; thus, there are no short squeezes.

- You do not have to pay dividends on the underlying stock of an SSF.

There is certainly much excitement regarding SSFs. According to Peter Borish, the senior managing director of business development for OneChicago, SSFs will be as revolutionary as the debt futures were. He says this will be the first time that equities, options, and futures markets will be linked. "This should create many new trading opportunities for investors," says Borish.

On the face of it, trading in SSFs looks better than traditional short selling. This may be true. However, only time will tell. Also, at least at the start, only a few stocks will be traded as SSFs. If interest does not catch on, these investment vehicles could go into the dustbin of financial history.

Conclusion

Table 4.3 compares short selling, options, and SSFs:

TABLE 4.3 Short Selling, Options, and Futures

Issue	Short Selling	Options	SSFs
Margin	Yes	No	Yes (but likely to be lower than for short selling)
Unlimited losses	Yes	No (unless you do trade naked calls)	Yes
Borrow stock	Yes	No	No
Uptick rule	Yes	No	No
Buy-in	Yes	No	No
Short squeeze	Yes	No	No
Pay dividends	Yes	No	No

In the first three chapters, we have built a foundation of knowledge for short selling. No doubt, it can be complex. Short selling certainly has special rules and requires different thinking compared to buying stock long.

With this foundation, we are now ready to look at how to spot good short selling techniques. As you will see, there is much a short seller needs to look at: the dynamics of the industry, business models, management, and financial statements. Again, the analysis requires lots of work. But in the end, it is worth it.

CHAPTER 5

Making the Case for a Short Sale

Danger Signs and Trigger Events

Imagine that over the past few months, you have been tracking Plunge Corp. The stock has seen a tremendous run-up in the past few years, becoming a Wall Street darling. But, there has been some recent bad news. Last quarter, the company reported a loss that was unexpected. You also notice that the company's management has been selling many shares of their personal holdings. The company has been in a fast-growth industry. But is it the end of the fad?

Short sellers try to look at all types of information when making their decisions. It is not surprising that short sellers are often called information junkies. The process can range from studying overall industry trends to even having a discussion with a customer of a company.

For a short seller, there are two types of information. First, there is information that shows that a business is having problems—these are known as "danger signs." While this sounds very simple, short sellers try to delve very deeply into a company's internal workings. They constantly question the business model, the industry, the management, and so on. Short sellers want to find the weak links.

However, these weak links may not necessarily be apparent to institutions, analysts, or individual investors. Perhaps the danger signs are too opaque. In some cases, it seems investors do not want to see bad news. They have an inherent interest for the stock to go up. So they often will try to rationalize the danger signs. It is no surprise that a seemingly weak company can continue to see its stock price rise more and more. As we see in the story of the "Stock Genie," in Chapter 3, short selling requires very good timing. The question for short sellers is, when will the stock fall? It is not uncommon for it to take several years—despite many danger signs—for a company's stock to fall. Or in some cases, a company may even be bought out, preventing you from profiting from the short sale.

If the danger signs continue to pile up, a short seller may decide to take a risk and start shorting a stock. However, it is likely that the short seller will not take a big position at first.

Short sellers will look at another type of information: "trigger events." A *trigger event* is some type of bad news that makes investors skittish. They begin to wonder: Is the stock headed for a fall? Are there more problems in the offing? In many cases, the trigger event is the first time the stock price has fallen based on bad news.

Chances are good that the initial bad news will not be the end of the bad news. Short sellers call this the "cockroach theory." If you see one cockroach, there are likely to be many more.

In this chapter, we will first look at common danger signs. These danger signs will alert you to a potentially good short sale candidate. Next, we will look at trigger events. This provides some validation that the danger signs are, in fact, real. Now, just like anything in investing, there is not always a clear-cut difference between a danger sign and a trigger event. Actually, as you spend more time analyzing potential short sale candidates, you will start to develop your own system.

Keep in mind that danger signs are often found in a company's financial statements. Financial statement analysis is covered in detail in Chapters 6 through 9.

Danger Sign 1: Fads

Fads in the financial markets recur and typically last a few years. Inevitably, people lose interest in the fad. When this happens, the fad can quickly turn into a bust.

For a short seller, this is very good news. However, sometimes the mania is not a fad, but a true long-term trend. When McDonald grew in popularity in the 1960s, many investors thought it was a mere fad. Of course, the company continued to climb as it established itself as the leader in the emerging industry of fast food. The challenge is in separating hype and fads from reality.

There are certain industries that are prone to fads. Here's a look:

Restaurants.   The restaurant industry is extremely competitive. People's tastes can change quickly and a once-hot restaurant can become a dud almost overnight.

Restaurants will often be based on a theme that hopefully will resonate with customers. A classic example of a theme restaurant is Planet Hollywood. No question, the restaurant had tremendous glitz. Owners included such high-profile stars as Demi Moore, Bruce Willis, and Arnold Schwarzenegger.

The Planet Hollywood IPO was strong. In 1996, the stock went from $18 to $28. However, the food was not great and people soon grew tired of the theme. The company eventually went bust, filing for bankruptcy in 1999.

Another fad was bagel mania. During the mid-1990s, Americans could not get enough of this snack food. In 1996, Einstein's Bagels went from $17 to $36. But the bagel mania fizzled and so did the stock. The stock was selling for 5 cents per share in 2001.

Toys.   Kids drive fads. Fads can be intense and then evaporate at lightning speed. In fact, it is rare for a toy not to be a fad. There are, after all, few Barbies in the toy world.

A classic fad was the Cabbage Patch doll from Coleco. It seemed that every kid in America wanted at least one. The company had difficulties manufacturing enough to satisfy the demand, which only served to turn up the heat on the frenzy. But when kids moved on to newer toys, the fad disappeared, and Coleco quickly went into bankruptcy in 1988.

Let's also consider Happiness Express. More than 80 percent of its revenues came from the red-hot Mighty Morphin Power Rangers, based on the popular children's cartoon. Even though the company saw a surge in demand, it was still losing about $1 million per month. The fad fizzled and so did the company, which filed for bankruptcy in 1996.

Technology.   Remember the Betamax? It was cutting-edge technology, but was overtaken by VHS technology.

Technology companies are subject to short swings in product cycles. After launching a hit product, it is very difficult to come up with an encore. For example, in the early 1980s, Lotus grew fast because of its innovative spreadsheet software called 123. But it could not follow this up with another blockbuster product, and the stock price languished. Eventually, the company sold out to IBM in 1995 because the competition was too intense.

The Internet has proved to be very fruitful for fads. In the mid-1990s, the conventional wisdom was that we would all shop online. But even this was not an entirely new idea. During the mid-1980s, the conventional wisdom was that everyone would shop from their TVs. As a result, Home Shopping Network soared in value. From 1986 to 1987, the stock zoomed more than 1500 percent. But by late October 1987 the company had troubles and the fad was wearing off. The stock fell to $5 as the number of people shopping via television dropped.

A symbol of the dot-com e-tailing frenzy was eToys (Figure 5.1).

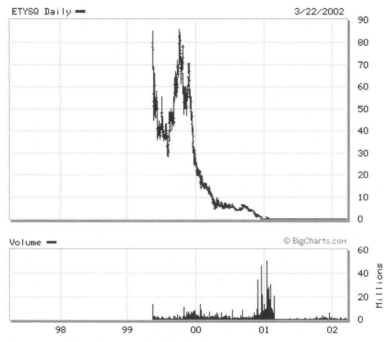

Figure 5.1 The eToys.com Fad Fizzled.

In 1999, eToys stock went from $20 to $86. It even had a bigger market value than stalwart toy seller Toys "R" Us. But eToys could not sustain this sky-high valuation for long. Every quarter, the company's losses mounted. Simply put, the company was selling its goods below cost; it would never make money. By March 2001, the company had lost all its value (see Figure 5.1).

What are the danger signs that indicate a fad is losing momentum? While there is no exact science to it, there are some signs to look for:

- The company is dropping its prices. This indicates that demand is falling off. Increased inventory and receivables also indicate falling demand.

- Competition is entering the industry. This is what happened to Snapple. Although the all-natural ingredients approach was fresh at the time, it did not take long until the major soft drink companies entered the marketplace, increasing competition and reducing Snapple's market share.

- Earnings start to drop.

Danger Sign 2: No More Big Growth

One common strategy for growth is acquisitions. This is especially the case for a maturing industry. In this situation, a company is motivated to buy other companies to try to continue its growth rate.

This mergers and acquisitions strategy can work for several years. But eventually the successful acquirer will start to see its growth slow, as it becomes the leader in the industry.

Let's consider this example: Dominance Corp. is in the drug store industry. This is a mature industry and it is growing—but slowly. Currently, Dominance has 10 percent of the market with $1 billion in sales and $100 million in profits. In the next five years, Dominance buys five competitors and expands its sales to $7 billion and profits to $600 million. Now, the company has 70 percent of the market.

While the company is currently very profitable and has a dominant market position, where will new growth come from? True, Dominance could try to buy the rest of the industry, but, of course, this could be difficult because of antitrust concerns. Or, the company could diversify into other markets, but this is a risky strategy that could damage the company's overall vision.

Dominance is in a tough position. As a result of its strong showing over the years, Wall Street will have become accustomed to strong growth. It will expect it to continue and Dominance stock will be priced for this expectation.

If, however, Dominance starts to see its revenue fall, Wall Street likely will no longer see it as a darling. But one quarter of slow growth isn't enough for short sellers to act. The trigger event is when there are several quarters in which the revenue and profit growth rates disappoint Wall Street.

Danger Sign 3:
Intensifying Competition

Adam Smith, the father of capitalism, wrote about his ideas in the late 1700s in his classic work *The Wealth of Nations*. He believed that self-interest would lead to competition and stronger economic growth. If one company offered a product at $10 and made profits, another company may see an opportunity to make a better product and sell it for, say $8, and still make a profit. It was a virtuous cycle. Prices would fall, which benefits consumers, and products would get better.

Despite this, companies do not like competition. While some competition is healthy, too much takes a bite out of the business. Falling prices result in lower profits. Besides, a new competitor could disrupt the market and take away market share.

Thus, companies prefer to have monopolies, not competitive markets. During the 1800s, titans of industry such as John D. Rockefeller and JP Morgan established monopolies over huge markets in order to maintain their profits.

With antitrust laws and the emergence of global markets, it is hard for companies to battle against competitors. It is common to see a company rise to greatness and quickly fail as a new company overtakes it. As we will see in Chapter 12, one of the toughest things for technology companies to do, for example, is to make the transition from one generation of a product to the next generation. Basically, though, just about any leader in a given marketplace is vulnerable to this.

As a short seller, you need to be mindful of competition. It will inevitably come and could expose leading companies to danger—which means good short sale candidates. Indications that competition is gaining the upper hand include: discounting; pleading for help from Congress and other governmental agencies; lawsuits against competitors; falling profit margins; and several quarters of failing to meet Wall Street expectations.

Another factor to pay close attention to is when the government deregulates an industry. That is, an industry that was once a monopoly must now allow new competitors. Keep in mind that the industry has been accustomed to no competition. Now, competition will be part of a new environment that the industry is not likely to be able to handle very well.

Deregulation happened in the savings and loan industry in the early 1980s. The result was increased competition. Many savings and loans ultimately lost money and went broke. Less than a decade later, the federal government had to bail out the industry. Short sellers like Jim Chanos made lots of money shorting savings and loans.

Yet there are ways for companies to beat the competition. One approach is to use patents as a way to push back competitors. But this approach is not asfoolproof as some investors think.

For example, a truly revolutionary medical procedure is LASIK surgery. As many have experienced, the surgery means you will no longer need to wear glasses. While this is bad news for makers of glasses and contact lenses, it is good news for companies that provide the necessary technology for the surgery.

The pioneer of LASIK technology is VISX. During the late 1990s, the stock was a highflier, reaching about $100 per share. This was not an irrational surge. After all, the company was very profitable and had more than 100 patents on its technology. Essentially, a patent provides exclusive use of a certain type of technology. The federal government issues patents in order to encourage companies to invest in new innovations.

A patent can be a barrier to the entry of competition. If a company uses the same technology, then it will be liable for patent infringement. A company like VISX can sue the infringer. Or the infringer may agree to license the technology for a fee, and such licensing revenue can be substantial.

Despite all this, VISX's stock began to collapse. Why? Competing companies were building better technologies and, as a result, were not infringing on existing patents of VISX or paying hefty licensing fees. VISX's revenues were drying up.

It can take time for competition to eat into a leading company—say, several years. But throughout history, this danger has been very common. Therefore, short sellers will be very focused on the competitive environment.

Danger Sign 4:
Flawed Business Model

A company can have top management and lots of cash but still fail because its business model is flawed. Essentially, the core of any company is its business model. A solid business plan provides a company with the vision—and the means—to generate profits. While this seems obvious, there are many companies that have convinced investors to buy stock even though their business model does not work.

Enron is a classic example of a faulty business model. In fact, short seller Jim Chanos found that the more he read about the company, the less he understood about their business model. And, in reality, the chairman and CEO actually had an increasingly harder time articulating their business model in their annual letters to shareholders (see Chapter 6 for more on this).

The question is: If a company cannot understand its own business model, how will its customers understand it? A confusing, ill-stated, unclear, or unfocused business model is a clear sign that a company could be in trouble.

Moreover, another clear danger sign is when a company shifts from one business model to the next. In fact, this was the case with Enron. While Enron may be the poster child *du jour* for businesses with faulty business models, it is by no means the only company to have built itself up on a shaky foundation.

According to Mark Roberts, who publishes the *Off Wall Street* report, the Internet boom provides a wealth of classic examples of many companies with flawed business models.

Roberts considers the case of Chemdex as a textbook example. Chemdex started as a business-to-business Internet site for the biotech industry. On the face of it, the model was simple. The company would take a small fee for every transaction that went through its online trading exchange. The problem was that there were not enough transactions to hit critical mass for profitability. So Chemdex went into other industries. The company even changed its name to Ventro. Despite all this, there were still not enough transactions to make money.

Could an investor have figured this out? Roberts thinks so. It was a simple matter of using math. Even with the optimistic estimates of potential market share, the market size was still relatively small. Besides, there were literally hundreds of similar companies—all with substantial amounts of cash—trying to get into the same market.

Another situation is that the market may be large enough, but the cost structure does not work. This was the case with online stamp purchasing companies, such as Stamps.com and E-Stamp. True, the companies had patent protection on their technology, which prevented others from entering the industry. Unfortunately, it was simply too costly to sell stamps online—regardless of how many stamps were sold.

Finally, a company may try to compare itself to another type of industry business model. This is what we have learned to be the case with Enron. In 1998, Enron claimed it was a brick-and-mortar natural gas company. A year later, the company said it was a New Economy trading company.

In light of its new model as a trading firm, short seller Jim Chanos compared Enron to the brokerage industry. For the most part, these types of companies sold at two times book value. Enron was selling at about six times book value. Taking the company at face value, it was very overvalued according to Chanos.

Danger Sign 5:
Management Problems

Success or failure for a company hinges a great deal on the management team. What if Microsoft did not have Bill Gates? Chances are the company would not be as successful as it is today.

When researching a company, it is important to look at the management team and perform your own background check. One good approach is to do a Web search for information on the firm, using search engines such as www.google.com. Look for:

- Past run-ins with regulators (A danger sign would be lawsuits from the SEC or fines that had to be paid because of SEC investigations.)
- Prior company failures, such as bankruptcies
- Experience (Does the management have strong industry experience?)

Danger Sign 6: Hype

All companies want to get good press. It helps drive the price of the stock, tends to encourage employees to work harder (to make their stock holdings and options worth more), and attracts customers. However, some companies spend too much time hyping their companies and not enough time refining their product. To generate press, the CEO will attend many conferences, he will be frequently quoted, and he will appear on television often. The company will try to generate its own PR. While certainly most companies have PR departments, if a company issues several releases each day and there is use of flamboyant language (e.g., "the product will revolutionize..."), then it is an indication that the company is hyping its operations.

By generating its own PR, a company may be trying to compensate for internal weaknesses. In fact, a company may go so far as to hire a firm to write glowing research reports on itself. These reports will nearly always say, "Strong Buy." And the write-up will be extremely upbeat.

It is typically small firms—known as investor relations (IR) firms—that publish these reports. Visit the IR firm's Web site and see the other companies they have followed (this could give you more ideas for short sale candidates). How have the stocks performed? Often, the stock will jump when the report is published, but then fall quickly back to where it was.

An IR firm is supposed to provide a disclosure on the report indicating that the report was paid for. When you call the company to get the reports, ask if they were paid for. If they say it was not paid for, yet the report indicates it was, then this is another danger sign.

IR firms usually get paid in both cash and stock. When the stock soars, the IR firm will typically sell its holdings. The stock holdings must be disclosed in the report.

A credible company will not pay for its own research reports. Rather, it will want independent analysts to cover it.

Of course, hyped companies can really be truly great companies that deserve attention. However, this can result in a stock being "priced for perfection." In other words, this is when a company has become a darling of Wall Street. The company never misses a quarter; the company is in a fast-growing market; the company is put on lists as the most admired in the nation or the world.

The stock continues to go up and the hype intensifies. Of course, if the company fails to meet expectations, the consequences can be huge. Wall Street will sell off the stock and focus on other darlings. A good indication that a company is reaching excessive levels of hype is when the CEO appears on the cover of a major publication.

One example was the front cover of *BusinessWeek* on May 8, 2000. On it was the flamboyant founder of Oracle, Larry Ellison, who was wearing sun glasses. The cover said: "Oracle: Why It's Cool Again."

Oracle is a leading developer of database software. According to the article, Oracle's databases were "all the rage." A key reason was that the databases were essential for advanced Web sites. In fact, Ellison said his company was the Internet.

Despite the glowing praise for Oracle, the article did have some important warning signs. Oracle was running against more competition, and its new eBusiness product line was a year late in terms of being finished and ready for the marketplace.

At the time of the article, Oracle's stock was trading for $37 (adjusted for a 2-for-1 split). The cover page very likely helped boost the stock price in the short term. Within a few months of the Ellison cover, the stock was at $46. By 2001, the stock was at $11.

In some cases, a company will start to believe the hype in the press, which can be a major danger sign. The saying "pride goeth before the fall" is apropos for short selling candidates. How do you find examples of corporate hubris? Of course, there is no surefire way, but here are some danger signs:

- A company pays to have its name on a stadium: PSINet paid $105 million to have its name on the Baltimore stadium. The company went bust. Enron paid the Houston Astros to have its name on the stadium (after Enron went bankrupt, the stadium became Astros Field again).

• Entering new unrelated markets: Management will say that they are somehow leveraging their talents and technology. But does management really understand the market?

• The CEO writes articles talking about his company's "new new thing." Or the CEO writes a book about his accomplishments. One example was Al Dunlap's book *Mean Business: How I Save Bad Companies and Make Good Companies Great.* As you can see by the title, the book certainly mentioned many of his successes. But the last company of which he was CEO went bust (it was Sunbeam).

• Grandiose Statements: At an energy conference in 1999, the chairman of Enron, Ken Lay, talked about how his company grew its market capitalization 900 percent to $40 billion. He said Enron would do it again in the next decade.

Danger Sign 6: Mergers

You are watching CNBC one morning and a newscaster interviews the CEOs of two companies that have decided to merge. The CEOs are upbeat and describe the cost efficiencies and synergies. The merger will be accretive (that is, increase the overall earnings of the new entity). The stock prices of the companies increase.

But have you checked the stock of the new company a year later? Chances are it is lower. Mergers are not easy to manage and integrate—especially big mergers. In fact, most mergers and acquisitions are failures for shareholders.

Examples of headline-grabbing, problem-filled mergers include: Daimler Benz and Chrysler; AOL and Time-Warner; and Cendant and CUC.

Perhaps the biggest danger sign that a merger is doomed is when a buyer overpays for the acquisition. For example, be concerned if the price is at a 50 percent or more premium to the current market value. No seller accepts a price because it is a bargain. They sell because the offering price is too good to pass up. Other warning signs include:

- The acquisition is large (perhaps 50 percent or more of the size of the buyer)

- A deal is not for cash, but mostly stock

- A company engages in many acquisitions (more than 10 per year), which increases the chances of a bad deal. (And one bad deal alone can be a killer.)

A striking example is Mattel's purchase of the educational software company, The Learning Company. The purchase was made in May 1999 for $3.5 billion. But there was great difficulty in integrating the two organizations. The apparent synergies were not being realized. In late 2000, Mattel sold The Learning Company for no money down to an investment group called Gores Capital. In the deal, Mattel would get a percentage of the profits of Gores Capital.

Danger Sign 7:
Skepticism from the Public

Some short sellers are known as "tire kickers." That is, they will go beyond the financial statements and interview management, talk to customers and suppliers, use and test the products, and so on. What is the tenor of the comments? Is there skepticism?

One hedge-fund portfolio manager based in SomeTown is an avid tire kicker. For example, if he is analyzing a retail store, he will visit a variety of stores and help people with their shopping bags as he interviews them about the level of service.

For many years, he has been a tutor to inner-city kids. At one point, he was analyzing a company called FILA, which manufactures sportswear. He told the kids to ask their friends about FILA. The response? There was no interest in the new shoes from the company. Next, he called FILA and asked management what it would do if it saw a fall in sales. The company said it could cut prices. So he asked the kids if they would buy the shoes if they were cheaper. Funny enough, fewer kids would buy them because there would be a perception that the shoes were of lower quality. He shorted the stock at $70 and covered it at $7, making millions on the trade. Talking with customers paid off.

Another good source to get an early sign of negative sentiment is to read local newspapers. Often, a local paper will be the first to hear any rumors of troubles on the horizon. For example, Jim Chanos first was alerted to the potential troubles of Enron in early 2001, months before most people had an idea that the company was in trouble, by reading a story from the Houston edition of the *Wall Street Journal*.

Another tool for short sellers is discussion boards. Chat rooms and discussion boards are online systems that allow investors to communicate their ideas about stocks and the markets. The most popular discussion boards include:

MotleyFool.com

Ragingbull.com

Siliconinvestor.com

Yahoo.com

While some information can be helpful, there are definitely problems with discussion boards. A 16-year-old kid could be posting messages. Or it might be someone who was laid off from a company and wants to denigrate his former employer. If you see messages such as, "I just talked to the CEO," or "I know the stock is a fraud," and so on, disregard the messages. In some cases, the posters will get into flaming wars, making personal attacks on each other.

Despite the problems, it can be a good idea to glance at the posts. You might be alerted to a press release you have not seen or an interesting angle on the investment prospects of a company.

Trigger Event 1: Fall in Price

As you pile up the danger signs, you will be building a case for a short sale. No doubt, the more danger signs the better. But as we learned at the beginning of the chapter, this does not mean the stock will fall. Rather, it usually takes a trigger event to knock the stock down.

Of course, one of the most common trigger events for short sellers is a fall in price. For example, let's say you have been following a toy company called Big Fall Corp. for about one year. During this time, you have been looking at the danger signs.

The company has a strong management and the business model is not flawed. The market is growing at a rapid pace. From your judgment, however, it looks as though the company is in the middle of a fad (danger sign 1). If it is indeed the end of the fad, then the market will have little growth opportunities, which means the company is exhibiting characteristics of danger sign 2.

There has been a good deal of hype surrounding Big Fall Corp. and the CEO recently appeared on the front page of the *Wall Street Journal* (danger sign 5). In the article, the CEO made grandiose statements (danger sign 6). Further, the company has made several acquisitions in recent quarters—one of which was a major purchase (danger sign 7). And, finally, you have talked to some customers, including kids, and they are getting tired of the toys (danger sign 8).

Then, for no apparent reason, the stock falls by 25 percent over the course of a few weeks. Is this a correction? It might be, but a 25 percent drop is significant. In fact, this is a trigger event for some short sellers. Investors are learning about the problems of the company and are starting to sell. The price is preceding the news.

With the danger signs in place, trigger event 1 is a 25 percent fall in the stock price when there is no news to account for it. While trigger events are certainly not foolproof, a drop of 25 percent or more is cause for closer scrutiny. As has been the case with many shorts, a stock that loses momentum can quickly unwind. The 25 percent drop can easily turn into a 50 percent drop or more when bad news is released. And, according to the cockroach theory, things could continue to get worse, as the company releases more and more bad news.

Trigger Event 2: Resignations

If the CEO or CFO resigns, then take notice. This is especially the case if the company is doing well. Why would a top executive leave if the future still looked bright for the company?

A bigger concern is if there is no replacement. For example, suppose the CEO of Great Fall resigns. In the press release, the former CEO says he wants to "pursue other interests." The press release also mentions that there is no permanent replacement for the former CEO. Rather, the company has named the president as the interim CEO.

This usually indicates trouble at the company and you will typically see a fall in the stock price. The implication is that the company is trying to take swift actions to remedy problems that have only recently surfaced.

An auditor's resignation from a company's account is also a trigger event. Was the company putting pressure on the auditor to do something too aggressive?

Trigger Event 3: Trading Halts And Suspensions

The SEC has the authority to suspend trading in a stock for up to 10 trading days. This is done when the SEC believes that a public company is not providing current or accurate information to shareholders.

After a suspension is lifted and trading resumes, the SEC will not announce the legal status of the company. It could take several months of more investigation to determine if the company has violated securities laws.

Thus, it is not uncommon to see a stock that has been suspended from trading to continue to fall in value as the SEC eventually brings official charges.

The lifting of a suspension means that a stock will begin trading if it is listed on the NYSE or Nasdaq. But this may not be the case with the OTC Bulletin Board or the Pink Sheets. If these markets believe that information about the company is still not accurate, then it might not continue to publish quotes on the company.

Keep in mind, of course, that a trading suspension is a severe action. The SEC does not do it unless it feels strongly there is evidence of wrongdoing. Moreover, the suspension acts as a way to prevent future investors from being victimized by company fraud.

The SEC keeps a list of all trading suspensions at http://www.sec.gov/litigation/suspensions.shtml.

The NYSE, AMEX, and the Nasdaq can also suspend trading, even without SEC action, which is known as a trading halt. Usually, a trading halt lasts for an hour or so. A trading halt, however, does not carry the same level of warning as a suspension and is not a red flag. Rather, it is a way for a company to better disseminate important announcements (such as a merger) so as not to create order imbalances.

Trigger Event 4: Unexpected Loss/Restatement of Earnings

If a company reports earnings that fall below Wall Street expectations, it is usually not a fluke. However, of course, a company will try to interpret the results as being "one time" and that the company will continue to grow strongly for the rest of the year.

Despite such efforts, earnings disappointments tend not to be one-time events. In fact, one earnings disappointment usually leads to other earnings disappointments. According to Tom Chanos, who manages an independent short sale research firm, a company has much leeway in managing its earnings. If a company expects to fall short, it can typically use its reserve to find earnings. If, however, there is not enough in the reserves, then the company will have to report a disappointment. This can be a telltale sign that the company is headed for more trouble in the next few quarters. In Chapter 8, we will take a further look at how companies can use reserves to manage earnings.

A more prominent trigger occurs when a company announces that it will restate earnings. In most cases, a company's stock will fall on the news (if not plunge).

In most cases, this is the result of problems with prior accounting. For example, a company may have been recognizing revenues too soon. For a short seller, this can be validation that the company has been too aggressive or even fraudulent and that its stock price will drop.

A famous case of an earnings restatement was Microstrategy, an enterprise software developer. The company announced that it was too aggressive in the way it recognized revenues. When the restatement was announced in March 2000, the stock plunged from $140 to $86.75. Even after that precipitous drop it would have still been a good short, since the stock eventually went below $3 per share.

Trigger Event 5: Delayed News

By law, public companies are required to make quarterly reports to shareholders no later than 45 days after the end of the quarter. Annual reports must be filed no more than 90 days after year end. Investors eagerly await these reports to see if the company is progressing or not.

A warning sign is if a company routinely files its reports on the last few days of the filing deadlines. The company likely is trying to suppress as much information as possible.

But the worst situation is when a company does not meet a filing deadline. In many cases, you can expect bad news. For example, there may be an unexpected shortfall in revenues or there could be a tremendous amount of disorganization in the company.

Consider this example: In February 2001, the online advertising company, 24/7 Media, announced that it would delay its fourth-quarter earnings report. The press release indicated the delay would last for at least a month, and that the company was looking for much-needed cash. At the time, the stock was at $1.03. By September, it was trading at 15 cents.

Trigger Event 6: Reverse Splits

A typical stock split is when a company increases the number of shares outstanding. For example, suppose Big Time Corp. is selling for $100 per share. To buy 100 shares would mean a $10,000 investment. This is difficult for smaller investors. Big Time decides to do a 2 for 1 split. This means that for every share an investor owns, he will have two. But since there has been no change in the fundamentals of the company, the stock price will fall by half. Instead of having 100 shares at $100 each, you now have 200 shares at $50 each.

As the name implies, a reverse split is the opposite. This means that a company will reduce the amount of shares in circulation, and, in turn, the price of the stock will increase. For example, let's say that Big Trouble Corp. is at $1 per share and management thinks this makes the company look as if it is in trouble. They announce a 1 for 4 reverse split. For every four shares owned, the company will take away three. The stock price will now be four times higher or $4 per share.

A reverse split is a trigger event. In reality, it is a PR move to make the company look better by engineering the amount of stock in the marketplace. It could be a sign that management has no clear ideas for improving the operations of the company.

An example is PopMail.com, an online marketing company. In August 2000, the company announced a 1 for 10 reverse stock split, which took the stock to $3.40. For a short seller, the announcement of the reverse split would have been a trigger event. By 2001, the stock was delisted and now trades at 9 cents per share.

Stock splits are also used to avoid the $1 Nasdaq Rule. That is, if a stock is below $1 for 30 days, the Nasdaq may delist the stock. The stock will then be traded on the OTC Bulletin board, which is a much less liquid marketplace.

Professor Rodney Boeme of Sam Houston State University conducted a study on reverse splits in January 2000. The study covered the period between 1970 and 1992, and involved a sample of 683 firms. He found that stocks, on average, would fall more than a third within 3 years of the reverse split. He also found that the fall was steeper for Nasdaq companies compared to NYSE companies.

Trigger Event 7: Dividend Cuts

A company's board of directors decides whether a company will pay a dividend or not. If a company cuts its dividend, it is a trigger event. The company probably expects hard times and wants to conserve its cash position.

There is a technique to help predict dividend cuts. Compare the total dividends for the year to the earnings per share (EPS). For example, if a company has EPS of $2 and has a $2 dividend, then the company will have a difficult time maintaining the dividend if the EPS falls.

Trigger Event 8: Regulatory Actions

For the most part, the United States tries to restrain from intervening in the marketplace. But sometimes a company is too aggressive. For example, a company may be engaging in price fixing or may have a monopoly or may be engaging in misleading marketing practices. Or the government may reject a new product from the market (as has happened, for example, to certain biotech companies) or may require that a company take its product off the market because it has now been found to be unsafe.

These regulatory events usually have an adverse effect on the stock price. Yet it could just be the beginning. Often, investors do not adequately forecast the implications of regulatory actions.

Let's take another hypothetical example: Mislead Corp. has seen its earnings grow very rapidly over the past 10 years. Then the federal government fines the company for misleading marketing practices. What's more, the regulator imposes restrictions on the practices. As a result, the stock price falls. This is a trigger event.

However, keep in mind that the company is not allowed to continue the sales practice. Thus, it will be harder for the company to continue its rapid growth rate. Future quarters are likely to be adversely affected. Besides, since Mislead is under the watch of the regulator, it may be much more conservative in its marketing practices so as to not instigate more actions.

Conclusion

Understanding danger signs and trigger events can help short sellers focus on potential shorting candidates. For each stock, it is a good idea to keep a file with articles, press releases and any other relevant information. Next, list the danger signs and trigger events. How many danger signs are there? If you see the list grow and grow, this means you are probably on to a short sale candidate.

However, it is important to realize that when learning any new investment technique or strategy, it is common to have unrealistic expectations. This is certainly a temptation to those investors who are just learning about short selling. It will take time to find danger signs and trigger events. Yet to be a successful short seller, you need to be good at finding these.

No doubt, it's inevitable that you will make mistakes along the way. So do not be too aggressive. It is a good idea to ease into short selling.

In many cases, it may be helpful to start out with short selling without actually doing any real short selling; instead practice by doing paper trading. For example, you start out with a hypothetical amount and then select a variety of short sale candidates. Before executing shorts in the real world, track these candidates on paper and monitor your performance. Once you have built your confidence and have a number of successful paper trades, then you can dip your toes into the water.

In the next four chapters, we will take a deep look at financial statement analysis—covering the balance sheet, income statement, and cash flow statement. Short sellers spend quite a bit of time analyzing these statements, and we will look at the analytical tools they use.

CHAPTER 6

Accounting Rules for Short Sellers

I magine you get a tip from a friend that Disaster Corp. is a good short sale candidate. He tells you that he shorted 10,000 shares at $5 per share. While you are not that confident, you want to investigate further. You go to the company's Web site and are not impressed. You read the press releases, and it appears the company is good at hyping, but not delivering. You look at the financials but are confused. You do not have a finance or accounting background and the statements are quite intimidating. You really do not know what to focus on.

Reading financial statements is no easy task. Even the professionals have difficulties. Jim Chanos, who is a veritable accounting whiz, had difficulties deciphering the financials of Enron. In fact, this was the case for just about anyone—that is, anyone who took the time to read the financials.

Short sellers like confusion in the financials. It's a hint that the company is trying to hide something.

If you short a stock, but have not read the company's financials, you are treading on dangerous ground. Reading the financials is mandatory. Actually, many top short sellers—such as Chanos—place most of their emphasis on the financials.

For most of us, reading the financials is not fun. They can be hundreds of pages long and written in hard-to-understand legalese. There are also many footnotes to these financials. In fact, it is temping to skip the footnotes, even if you suspect there could be important information in them. This is a big mistake. In the short sale game, footnotes often have the juiciest information. This is where companies often like to bury critical information.

For most investors, it will take some time to begin to understand financials. While many top short sellers have gone to top finance schools and received the Certified Financial Analyst (CFA) designation, most individual investors do not have that background. Understanding financial reports, however, does not mean you need to go to Harvard or get your CFA to be proficient in financial statement analysis. The more you read financials, the easier it will get. It's a good habit to start.

In this chapter, we will look at general information regarding financials. Then, in Chapters 7 through 9, we will cover the most critical statements: the balance sheet, income statement, and statement of cash flows. These chapters will help you identify what short sellers look for in financial reports.

Where Do You Get the Financials?

A look back at history sets the stage for financial reporting. While there was a strong bull market in the 1920s, there were also many abuses. Manipulation of stock was a common occurrence. When the stock market crashed in 1929 and the United States plunged into an economic depression, there was a big push for regulation of the securities markets.

The result was the formation of the Securities and Exchange Commission (SEC), as discussed in Chapter 1. The SEC enforces the securities laws and requires that companies make certain disclosures. The main goal of the SEC is to protect investors. The SEC does not recommend securities. Instead, the SEC wants to make sure that investors get the necessary information to make their own decisions. The main required financial reports include:

- *10-K.* This is a comprehensive financial document that includes the financial activities of a company for the year. In it, you will find the income statement, balance sheet, and statement of cash flows. There are also footnotes that can provide useful information. The 10-K must be filed within 90 days of the company's fiscal year end.

- *Annual Report.* While the 10-K is a dry document, the annual report is typically a glossy publication. It is meant to showcase the company to shareholders. In some cases, the annual report can be quite a production, with fancy graphics and pictures. Some short sellers see this as a sign of excessiveness in a company. The annual report also has a letter from the chairman, which is discussed later in the chapter.

- *Quarterly Reports.* As the name implies, these are the financials for the last quarter. The documents are usually not long.

- *10-Q.* There are three filed for each year (the fourth is the 10-K). These documents have much more information than quarterly reports and are published about 30 days after the quarterly report is filed.

- *Proxy Statement.* This is a document sent to all shareholders for important votes, such as for salaries, election of directors, and mergers.

- *Prospectus.* These are called *S-1 filings.* These are what a company files when it is raising money through an IPO or a secondary offering. We will talk more about IPOs in Chapter 12.

- *8-K.* This is filed when there is a significant event, such as a merger, a new director, or even a bankruptcy. This must be filed within 15 days of the event (for special events, it can be 5 days).

As you can see, some of the financial statements are published during certain times of the year. This is known as the *accounting period.*

A company bases its financials on its fiscal year (FY), which is of course a 12-month period of time, but fiscal year does not necessarily coincide with a calendar year. For example, many retail businesses will start their fiscal year on October 1 and end it on September 30.

You can get hard copies of these reports by contacting a company's investors relations department and requesting that your name be placed on the mailing list. Also, many companies publish their filings on their Web sites. Finally, there are a variety of financial sites that have a company's financials, like edgar-online.com.

The ABCs of Accounting

Financial accounting has been in existence for hundreds of years. Essentially, accounting is the process of collecting and expressing information about a company's assets, liabilities, revenues, and expenses. Despite its long history, however, financial accounting is far from perfect. It can only measure things in monetary terms. But what if a company has a valuable patent? How much is this worth? This is one of the many questions that accountants tackle.

Also, accounting may be based on estimates. After all, in valuing a stock option, how does a company know what a stock will be worth in several years? What will a pension fund have in assets in the next 20 years? What will the liabilities be?

There is a certain degree of guesswork with accounting. Thus, do not be deceived by financial statements. They can be misleading. Some companies will capitalize on this and use aggressive accounting techniques to inflate their value. In fact, there are numerous examples of accounting meltdowns, such as Boston Market, Cendant, Micro-Strategy, Rite Aid, and, of course, Enron, which has the distinction of being the largest bankruptcy in corporate history.

These companies, of course, can be excellent short sale candidates. How can investors trust the company anymore? Were there other problems that have yet to be disclosed but not discovered in the investigation? Will customers lose confidence in the company? Will the suppliers have doubts?

There are two main approaches to pushing the envelope on accounting:

- *Aggressive Accounting.* A company will use existing accounting standards that delve into gray areas. While it is not untruthful, it is nonetheless not an accurate picture of the company. Short sellers say that the "quality of earnings" is low. Chanos, for example, refers to this as "opaque" accounting. Basically, a company is using gobbledygook to hide the true status of the company.

- *Fraudulent Accounting* (a more colorful phrase is "cooking the books"). As the name implies, this is when a company flat-out lies about its status. It may go as far as creating fictitious sales or not disclosing expenses. The Enron debacle of 2002 appears to be a case of fraudulent accounting.

For public companies, it is certainly tempting to engage in aggressive accounting. After all, Wall Street analysts are very demanding. They want to put their money into companies that show strong growth. If there is a fall-off, Wall Street will punish the stock price. So, many companies will try to do everything possible to show strong growth.

Also, Wall Street likes stable growth. They do not want to see a company surge 40 percent in sales during one quarter and then go down 10 percent the next. Consequently, companies will try to "smooth" their earnings. What's more, for most companies, management's compensation is based heavily on the stock price. So, there is a big incentive to make Wall Street happy.

Interestingly enough, Enron made aggressive accounting an integral part of its culture. The company would have frequent seminars on how to handle contracts and customers to show stronger financial reports. One seminar talked about how to structure deals so they would not even need to be disclosed in the footnotes of the financials.

Despite headline-making stories of bad accounting practices, there is, in fact, a standard set of rules and procedures for accounting known as Generally Accepted Accounting Principles, or GAAP. For our purposes, it is not necessary to read or understand all these rules (it consists of thousands of pages of rulings). Rather, in the next few chapters, we will look at the main components of GAAP. We will also look at pro forma earnings, which is when a company does not use GAAP for its financial statements. Whether a company uses pro forma earnings or not, it always must publish financials that conform to GAAP standards.

GAAP rules originate from a variety of sources:

- *Financial Accounting Standards Board (FASB).* Started in 1972, this private organization establishes the GAAP standards for accounting and financial reporting. When the FASB establishes a new standard, it is recognized by both the AICPA and the SEC, which are discussed below.

- *American Institute of Certified Public Accountants (AICPA).* Established in 1887, this is the trade organization for the accounting profession. In 1938, the AICPA started to publish its own rulings on accounting, which are guidelines for GAAP.

- *SEC.* The commission has authority to make pronouncements for GAAP and has done so on several occasions. These are known as SEC Accounting Releases. However, for the most part, the SEC relies on the pronouncements of the FASB.

- *Internal Revenue Service (IRS).* The IRS can have a big impact on GAAP. For example, the IRS may have its own interpretation on how to amortize software or to account for an oil lease, and so on.

Keep in mind that the accounting profession is quite conservative. The profession does not want to make many significant changes to the rules. Such changes would make it difficult to compare financial statements or rely on future statements.

Then again, such conservatism can have negative effects. As we will see in the discussion of balance sheets in Chapter 7, the Enron debacle involved so-called special purpose entities (SPEs) which are allowed under GAAP to transfer debts from its balance sheet. There was considerable ambiguity in the rule governing SPEs, though. One uncertainty was whether a parent company, like Enron, could invest up to 97 percent of the value of the SPE and still not have the debts be reflected on its balance sheet. Typically, if a company owned this substantial amount of another entity, the debts would not be considered off-balance-sheet debts.

In 1990, the SEC and FASB studied the matter and made two drafts on its opinion, but nothing was decided in terms of adjusting the rule (such as lowering the percentage). In the meantime, companies like Enron used these SPEs aggressively.

The Accounting Process

A company's financial statements are the result of a long process. While it is not important that you be an accountant to be proficient at financial statement analysis, it is still a good idea to have a general understanding of the process.

A company will usually have a bookkeeping department. The department is responsible for the collection of financial data. This can come in many forms. It may be from printed receipts and invoices, as well as electronic transactions. To deal more efficiently with the tremendous amount of information, many companies will install sophisticated accounting computer systems. Good companies will have systems in place to make sure the data collection is correct. These are known as *internal controls.*

With the data, a company's financial or accounting department will prepare the necessary financial statements. Outside accountants may be involved to some extent in the process, but it is usually the company that compiles the financial statements. However, an outside accounting firm is needed to audit the statements. Auditing is discussed later in the chapter.

All public companies are required to use *accrual accounting,* which means that revenues are reported when they are earned and expenses reported when they are incurred. Thus, you might sign a sales contract for $1 million, but no cash is collected. Instead, you will collect the cash a month later. Despite this, you recognize the revenue now, because you earned it now.

If you sign an agreement to acquire new supplies for $10,000, you recognized that expense now, even though you do not plan to write a check for 15 days.

Public companies also use the *double-entry bookkeeping principle.* It was the Italian mathematician Luca Pacioli who developed the system in the late 1400s. The essence of his system can be expressed in the following formula:

$$Assets = Liabilities + Equity$$

Let's define the elements of the formula:

Assets. This is anything that the company owns, such as cash, inventory, land, equipment, and even patents.

Liabilities. This is what a company owes. The debts can be accounts payables, notes, bonds, unpaid taxes, and so on.

Equity. This is the difference between the assets and liabilities or Equity = Assets – Liabilities.

Thus, if assets are $10 million and liabilities are $5 million, the company has equity of $5 million. This is what the shareholders own.

The formula is the basis of a company's balance sheet (which is explained in much detail in Chapter 7). On the left side of the balance sheet are the assets and on the right side the liabilities and equity. See Table 6.1 for an example.

You will notice that the formula and the balance sheet are the same, that is, the assets equal the liabilities plus equity, or $190,000 = $90,000 + $100,000. This is always true. Both sides of the balance sheet must be equal (hence the name *balance*).

To make sure everything balances, double entry is required. Whatever is done to the left side of the balance sheet must be done equally on the right side. For example, if a company pays the light bill for $1000, then the cash will be reduced by $1000 and the accounts payable will also be reduced by $1000 (accounts payable is what a company owes).

Then again, the entries need not be on different sides of the balance sheet. Suppose a company buys equipment for $5000. The cash will be reduced by $5000 and equipment will be increased by $5000.

Actually, there are nine types of transactions that affect a company's financials:

- *Increase in Assets; Decrease in Assets.* A company is constantly buying new assets. If a company buys a new computer for $1000, then equipment will be increased by $1000 and cash will be decreased by $1000.

TABLE 6.1   Balance Sheet

ABC Corp. Balance Sheet March 31, 2002			
Assets		**Liabilities**	
Cash	$10,000	Accounts payable	$50,000
Accounts receivable	$20,000	Notes payable	$20,000
Equipment	$50,000	Notes	$20,000
Land	$90,000	Total liabilities	$90,000
Patent	$20,000	Equity	$100,000
Total Assets	$190,000	Total liabilities and equity	$190,000

- *Increase in Assets; Increase in Liabilities.* Often a company will not use cash to buy assets; rather, it will incur a debt. Thus, the $1000 computer would increase equipment assets by $1000 and increase accounts payable by $1000.

- *Decrease in Assets; Decrease in Liabilities.* This is the complete opposite of the above. A company decides to reduce is cash by $1000 and use this to pay down $1000 of the accounts payable.

- *Increase in Assets; Increase in Equity.* Investors contribute $10,000 to buy stock in the company. This increases cash by $10,000 and equity by $10,000.

- *Decrease in Assets; Decrease in Equity.* The company manufactured large amounts of inventory. However, it was unable to sell $5000 of it and wrote it down to zero. The inventory is reduced by $5000 and equity falls by $5000. This would also be the case if the company was unable to collect on the money owed to them. But instead of inventory being reduced, the accounts receivable would be reduced.

- *Increase in Liabilities; Decrease in Liabilities.* This is when debt is exchanged for another form of debt. For example, a company issues a note payable for $1000 (which must be paid off in 2 years) in exchange for an accounts payable of $1000.

- *Decrease in Liabilities; Increase in Equity.* Let's say that a company estimated a debt from a lawsuit at $10,000. But, instead the payout was only $5000. The debt would be reduced by $5000 and the equity would increase by $5000.

- *Increase in Liabilities; Decrease in Equity.* Or, a company is hit with a lawsuit and must pay $20,000. The debt will increase by $20,000 and equity will fall by $20,000.

- *Increase in Equity; Decrease in Equity.* This is switching one form of equity for another. A company might buy back $10,000 in common stock and replace it with $10,000 in preferred stock.

A growing business will show growth in its equity. How does this happen? Through profits. You will find a company's profits from the income statement. Table 6.2 is an example.

TABLE 6.2   Income Statement

ABC Corp. Income Statement Year Ended December 31, 2001	
Revenues	$100,000
Expenses	
Cost of goods sold	$40,000
Selling, administration, and general	$20,000
Interest	$10,000
Total	$70,000
Income before taxes	$30,000
Taxes	$10,000
Net income	$20,000

The company generated a profit of $20,000 (known as *net income*). The $20,000 is added to cash and to equity. This part of the equity is called *retained earnings*. Of course, if the company had a net loss, this would have reduced cash and retained earnings.

Look at the top of the income statement. It says that it is for the year ended December 31, 2001. In other words, the income statement covers changes over a period of time. The balance sheet, however, looks at assets, liabilities, and equity at a certain time. This is why the balance sheet is often referred to as a *snapshot*.

Auditing

The federal government requires that all annual financial statements be audited by an independent accounting firm. The rationale is that an independent audit firm will be able to provide investors assurance that the financial statements are reliable. The result is strong investor confidence.

While this is a worthy goal, it is virtually impossible to verify the complete financials of a company. So, an audit firm will do samples. For example, it may check inventory in a certain department and see if it matches the items on the financial statements. Or it may track several sales and see if the invoices were documented properly.

Unfortunately, auditors have not been foolproof. For example, auditors did not uncover the accounting irregularities at such major firms as Sunbeam, Cendant, and Waste Management. As a result, these companies saw their stock prices collapse, and there was a loss of credibility on Wall Street.

Interestingly enough, there are several reasons for serious oversights in company audits. Here is a look at some of the reasons:

- Congress passed legislation in 1995 that put caps on liability for auditing firms. Because of this, an auditor may be tempted to be somewhat lax on its audits—since an adverse legal judgment will not be unlimited.

- There is more reliance on using computer modeling systems to perform audits. True, this saves money, but may result in a poor audit. Some companies will build their own computer programs that anticipate questions that an audit firm's computer program would spot. Thus, an auditor's computer sample will not uncover the red flags because a company's own computer system is basically outsmarting the auditor's.

- A company may not like an auditor's conclusions and may change auditors. In the competitive world of auditing, an auditor does not like to lose business. And so the auditor may be more amenable to accept company demands in terms of engaging in aggressive accounting practices.

In 2002, Congress began looking seriously at bringing about reforms in the accounting profession. Many proposals have been put on the table. One proposal is to create a new federal agency that would have the power to fine accountants for ethical violations. There are also proposals to place restrictions on 401(k) investments, as well as the accounting treatment of off-balance-sheet debts and employee stock options.

Annual Reports

As discussed above, the annual report is not a comprehensive document in terms of finding useful information for short selling. The annual report is very much a PR document—a written commercial. Often, companies will hire an experienced PR firm to develop an annual report that is very attractive to the reader. In a way, it is meant not only to keep existing shareholders but to entice new ones.

Yet this does not mean you should avoid the document. In fact, the annual report can be a helpful indication of the general direction of the company.

An annual report can be helpful in understanding the company's operations. There may be charts and easy-to-understand descriptions. Then again, after reading the annual report, if you are confused about the company, then this is a red flag. It could be an indication of a good short.

Perhaps the most important part of the annual report is the chairman's letter. In keeping with the PR angle, you will typically see a picture of the chairman, who is smiling and looking confident. See Figure 6.1, which shows the smiling face of Enron's chairman for its 2000 annual report, the year before the company went bankrupt.

In the chairman's letter, the direction of the company will be spelled out, along with a summary of the past year and a look at the future. Keep in mind that the chairman usually has much help in crafting the letter. The attorneys will make sure there are no problems with

TO OUR SHAREHOLDERS

Enron's performance in 2000 was a success by any measure, as we continued to

outdistance the competition

and solidify our leadership in each of our major businesses. In our largest business, wholesale services, we experienced an enormous increase of 59 percent in physical energy deliveries. Our retail energy business achieved its highest level ever of total contract value. Our newest business, broadband services, significantly accelerated transaction activity, and our oldest business, the interstate pipelines, registered increased earnings. The company's net income reached a record $1.3 billion in 2000.

FIGURE 6.1. Optimism and Smiling Faces for the Cover of the Shareholder Letter.

the securities laws; the CFO will help with explaining the financials; the sales and marketing vice presidents will give their input. And, of course, a PR representative will try to take this information and make it as optimistic as possible.

So when reading the letter, you must look for nuances. It is important to ask whether the vision outlined in the letter makes sense. Look at past chairmen's letters. Did the present chairman talk about a new venture several years ago and but is not mentioning it now? Look for ominous language. Does the chairman talk about "challenges"? This can be a warning sign of more bad things to come. Or has the chairman changed direction often over the years? Also, is the chairman complaining about "unfair practices" of foreign competitors and asking for government intervention?

In fact, looking at the annual reports between 1998 to 2000 was very instructive in the case of Enron. CEO and Chairman Kenneth Lay and COO Jeffrey Skilling wrote the chairman's letter. In the 1998 annual report, Enron's letter, like many corporate letters, was very upbeat. The company talked about the substantial growth in sales and profits in its business. The vision was that the company was a "global energy franchise." Moreover, the focus was on natural gas and electricity—which the company considered to offer huge growth opportunities because of deregulation. The company also talked mostly about its traditional "brick and mortar" operations, such as for exploration and production, transportation and distribution, and services. However, the letter did mention that Enron was building a digital marketplace for its energy assets.

Basically, this was a fairly standard annual report. There were no red flags that would alert a short seller. But this would change with the following annual report.

The letter in the 1999 report had a new coauthor, Joseph Sutton, the vice chairman. And the letter got much longer and more complex. In fact, it was difficult to understand what business Enron was really in. Ironically, the company even stated in the first sentence: "Enron is moving so fast that sometimes others have trouble defining us." It was a glaring red flag.

What was the company's own definition of itself? See if you can understand it:

> We are clearly a knowledge-based company, and the skills and resources we used to transform the energy business are proving to be equally valuable in other businesses. Yes, we will remain the world's leading energy company, but we also will use the skills and talents to gain leadership in fields where the right opportunities beckon.

There was little talk of the brick-and-mortar assets. Rather, there was lots of "New Economy" language. According to the letter:

> The value of products bought and sold on our new eCommerce platform, EnronOnline, is destined to exceed the value transacted on any current eCommerce web site.
> What you own is not as important as what you know.
> When you define a New Economy company, you define Enron.

In fact, the letter bragged that it sold off some of its brick-and-mortar assets. Suddenly, Enron was now a sleek Internet company.

Enron's 2000 Annual Report, written by Lay and Skilling, raised even more red flags. Major bells would be ringing for a short seller. This letter was several pages longer than the 1999 letter and was even more confusing in terms of the vision. What was this company really doing? According to the letter:

> Enron hardly resembles the company we were in the early days. During our 15-year history, we have stretched ourselves beyond our own expectations. We have metamorphosed from an asset-based pipeline and power generating company to a marketing and logistics company whose biggest assets are its well-established business approach and its innovative people.

The chairman's letter talked about how the Enron model could be "transitioned" to other industries. One was broadband services. The letter stated that the "opportunities are increasing commensurately."

When short seller Jim Chanos noticed this, he was skeptical. He had already made lots of money by successfully shorting broadband stocks. Wasn't the industry in dire straights? Oddly enough, Enron's letter did mention that the broadband industry was experiencing "overcapacity." So in light of this, how could this be a high-growth business for Enron? The red flags were waving brightly.

Chanos was not the only short seller who saw these red flags. There were several others. And these were red flags that did not require intensive analysis of a company's financials and footnotes. Any investor who received these annual reports—and compared them—would have seen this.

Interestingly enough, an analyst at Merrill Lynch, Thatcher Thomas, conducted a study on annual reports based on size. The larger the annual report, the worse a stock price performs. That is, he went to edgar-online, which has a Microsoft Word version. The Web site shows the file size. He would look at the 10-K and if it was more than 500 kilobytes, the stock would have troubles.

Conference Calls

So far, we have looked at printed information. As shown above, a company will spend much time crafting these documents. However, short sellers have an opportunity to listen to management discuss their company. This is done through quarterly conference calls (these calls are made when a company releases it quarterly results).

In these calls, analysts and even some short sellers ask management a variety of questions, such as: how is a new product line performing? What is the outlook for profits in the next quarter? How will a new product from a competitor impact on the company?

With changes in disclosure regulations, all investors have access to conference calls that were once limited to companies and institutional investors. Today, investors can either dial a 1-800 number or visit a Web site to obtain the information provided in the quarterly conference calls. Truth be told, conference calls can be long and boring. The CEO may not necessarily be dynamic and may drone on and on. However, some CEOs do present very well, such as Oracle's Larry Ellison or Apple's Steve Jobs. Martha Stewart also has great conference calls. If you are thinking of shorting a stock, it is critical that you listen to the conference calls. The information can be invaluable and may help explain the financials.

During the conference call, much may be said that seems complicated or confusing. There is also much use of jargon. Common terms include:

- *Guidance.* This is what the company is projecting for the next few quarters. This can have a big impact on the stock.

- *Sequential growth.* Typically, a company's financials will compare the current quarter against the same quarter a year ago. However, some companies may compare the current quarter to the previous quarter. If sales increased over this time, it is known as "sequential growth."

- *Visibility.* This describes the confidence a company has in its projects. If there is a lack of visibility, investors get concerned. A key question is whether there is a big drop in sales in the offing.

- *Granularity.* An analyst may say something like, "Can you provide more granularity on that issue?" This means the analyst is looking for more detail ("granular" refers to the texture of something and is often applied in science). Essentially, an analyst wants to learn more about, say, a company's new customer or a new product release and so on. This can be valuable information. In fact, if the company is evasive, this may indicate that the company is trying to hide something (for example, the product may be having problems).

What is particularly useful over the course of the conference call is the question and answer session with analysts. The questions can be penetrating and add new light on the company, covering such topics as new management members, penetration of new markets, a recent patent, etc. In fact, always be mindful of a company that complains about short sellers. This may indicate that a company is not blaming itself for its problems, but trying to find a scapegoat.

Conclusion

When looking for short sale candidates, you might find one that is almost too good to be true. You might scratch your head and say to yourself, "Why isn't anyone else seeing this problem?" This certainly happens to short sellers. For example, there are cases when the financial statements were not adequately proofread, in which there are spelling or grammar errors or even wrong dates. Or the financial numbers may not even add up properly. These are glaring red flags and can make great short sale candidates.

But this is rare. Rather, when you are doing your analysis, you will be finding red flags. In a sense, you will be like a detective who is looking for clues and trying to build a case. The case will hopefully get stronger and stronger. But in the short selling game, there are ultimately no guarantees.

In fact, you will look at some companies that, on the surface, appear to be obvious shorts. Perhaps you find one that does not have any products or revenues. It's a great short, right? But be wary. A growth company may look weak in its early years, but then become very profitable. This is often the case with biotech companies.

For a short seller, analyzing financial reports and deciphering the true meaning in conference calls means hard work. And also making mistakes, but it is from those mistakes that lessons can be learned.

In Chapters 7 through 9, we will look much more deeply at the financials and the red flags and buying opportunities they can illuminate.

CHAPTER 7

Balance Sheets:
What Is a Company Worth?

You hear a company's CEO claim that the firm has a strong balance sheet (most CEOs say this, of course). That is, there are likely to be heavy amounts of assets and not much debt. In fact, however, not just companies have balance sheets; actually, everyone has a personal balance sheet. You have assets, liabilities, and equity in the assets you own. If you have more assets than liabilities, then you have a positive net worth. Just as you get richer if your personal net worth goes up, so does a company. It's really that simple.

However, companies can be quite creative in making a balance sheet look stronger than it really is. Let's take a look at the major areas where short sellers find good opportunities for short sales.

Cash Per Share

Current assets are resources that will be consumed or used up within a year. The current assets are listed on the basis of liquidity—from the most liquid to the least. Current assets include cash and marketable securities; accounts receivable; inventory; restricted cash; and prepaid expenses.

Let's look at the most liquid part of the current assets: cash and marketable securities. Of course, cash includes bank accounts, petty cash, and deposits. As for marketable securities, these are short-term liquid assets, such as Treasury bills or commercial paper.

From this, a short seller may look at the cash per share, which is calculated as follows:

$$\frac{(\text{Cash} + \text{Marketable securities})}{\text{Shares outstanding}} = \text{Cash per share}$$

Suppose that Cash Cow Inc. has $100 million in cash and 10 million shares outstanding. The cash per share would be $10 per share.

A short seller likes to see this relatively low compared to the industry standard. This means there is less margin for error if a company falters. Simply put, if a company cannot pay its bills, it will either need to raise more money (usually at an expensive rate) or file for bankruptcy. Both alternatives are terrible for the share price.

Moreover, you would track cash per share over time. If you see significant reductions (30 percent or more during the last few quarters), this indicates the company is perhaps experiencing a worsening of its core business.

However, keep in mind that cash per share can decline even though actual cash is increasing. Example: One of Cash Cow's competitors, Low Cash Inc., has $1 million in cash in the bank and 1 million shares outstanding, giving it a cash flow per share of $1. The company issues 500,000 new shares to institutional investors to raise $250,000 (the company had to sell the stock at a cheap 50 cents per share so as to get the interest of the investors). The company now has $1.25 million in cash and a cash flow per share of 83 cents. Thus, when analyzing cash per share, make sure the number of shares has not increased. If not, you could be mislead into believing the company is showing less cash over time.

Accounts Receivable

Accounts receivable are sales that are recognized yet no cash has been collected yet. In other words, credit was extended for these sales and the accounts receivable is what customers owe the company. This is an asset of the company.

A short seller will focus intensely on accounts receivable. It can be a leading indicator that a company is headed for troubles. Here are some of the techniques that short sellers use:

Divergence in Sales and Accounts Receivable.   If a company's sales increase, so should the accounts receivable. This is a normal relationship. A short seller is looking for a significant divergence between the two. Example: Disaster Corp. grew its sales by 100 percent over the past year and earnings are up 150 percent . On the face of it, this looks good.

However, a short seller will look at the quality of these earnings. Are they real? The short seller looks at the accounts receivable during this period and they are up 200 percent. For a short seller, if accounts receivable are increasing much faster than sales, the company could be a good short.

The divergence may be the result of a number of factors:

- The company is having trouble collecting the accounts receivable from its customers. Ultimately, if a significant amount of these accounts cannot be collected, then the company's sales and earnings will have been overstated. It is not uncommon for a company to eventually report much lower than expected in earnings.

- The company may be engaging in aggressive sales practices. For example, it may be shipping goods to customers even though there has been no final sales agreement.

- The company is providing liberal credit terms to customers in order to encourage growth in sales.

- The company has poor collection policies.

Allowances for Doubtful Accounts.   Accounts receivable will usually be expressed as "net of allowances for doubtful accounts." Unfortunately, some customers do not pay their bills. As a result, a company will try to estimate what percentage of the accounts receivable will not be collected (called *allowances for doubtful accounts*). The estimate is just that. In other words, it can be wrong.

For the most part, a company will look to the past trends in customer behavior and use this for its forecast. If a company is underestimating this amount, then things will look healthier than they really are. For example, suppose that ABC has an allowance for doubtful accounts of 5 percent and its sales for the last quarter—net of the allowance—was $1 million. But if the estimate is wrong and it is really 10 percent, then the sales should have been $950,000 (5 percent lower).

It is not easy for a short seller to determine whether an allowance is too optimistic. However, short sellers will compare the percentage to the rest of the industry. If it is lower than the rest, then the company may be too aggressive.

Moreover, short sellers will look for companies that lower the percentage even while accounts receivables are increasing much faster than sales.

Another analytic technique is to look at a company's customer base. Is that industry having problems? Let's take a look at Lucent. In the fourth quarter of 1998, the allowance was 5.32 percent. This fell to 3.16 percent by the third quarter of 2000. Interestingly enough, during this time, accounts receivable increased significantly. Also, the customer base was deteriorating. Lucent had many customers that were upstart dot-coms.

Days Sales Outstanding (DSO).   This is a favorite ratio of short sellers in analyzing a company's receivables. The calculation has two steps. First, you must calculate the average accounts receivable , which is:

$$\frac{(\text{Accounts Receivable for first period} + \text{Accounts Receivable for second period})}{2}$$

For example, suppose Disaster Corp. has sales for the last year of $1 million. At the start of the year, the accounts receivable were $300,000 and at the end of the year, they were $200,000. The average receivables would be:

$$\frac{(\$200,000 + \$300,000)}{2} = \$250,000$$

In step two, you calculate the DSO:

$$\frac{\text{Average accounts receivable}}{(\text{Sales for period divided by days in period})} = \text{DSO}$$

$$\frac{\$250,000}{(\$1,000,000/365)} = 91 \text{ days}$$

Basically, the DSO shows how many days it takes to convert accounts receivable into cash. If you see the number of days increase significantly, this is an indication that a company is having troubles collecting its receivables. For a short seller, this may mean a company is experiencing major problems and its stock price could be ready for a fall.

Inventory

Short sellers look at inventory as an early-warning sign that a company may eventually report bad numbers. Essentially, inventory is the value of a company's raw materials, work in progress, supplies to make products, and finished products. The value of inventory will have an impact on a company's gross profit. See Table 7.1.

TABLE 7.1   Inventory and Profits

	Year 2002	Year 2003
Sales	$100,000	$120,000
Beginning inventory	$20,000	$10,000
Plus purchases	$30,000	$50,000
Goods for sale	$50,000	$60,000
Less ending inventory	$10,000	$15,000
Cost of goods sold	$40,000	$45,000
Gross profit	$60,000	$75,000

To calculate the cost of goods sold (COGS), you add the inventory for the beginning of the year and the inventory purchased. From this, you subtract the value of the inventory that is still on hand. By subtracting the COGS from the sales, you get the company's gross profit, which is $60,000 or a gross profit margin of 60 percent ($60,000 divided $100,000).

The key is the value of the ending inventory. If it was $20,000, then the company's gross profit would increase to $70,000 or 70 percent. But the $20,000 will be carried forward to the next year. This will decrease the gross profit margin to $65,000. Basically, the ending inventory has an effect on two years of a company's gross profits.

Thus, a short seller wants to see if a company has changed the way it accounts for determining the value of its inventory. If this is the case, it may mean the company has been artificially inflating its gross profits. You can learn of these changes in the footnotes of the 10-K or 10-Q.

The two main techniques for calculating inventory include FIFO (first in, first out) and LIFO (last in, first out). To understand these two concepts, let's take an example: Disaster Corp. has purchased inventory two times in the past year. The first purchase was 100 units of its product for $200. The next purchase was for 120 units at $250. During this time, the company sold 180 units at $350.

Using FIFO, the value of the inventory would look at the inventory that was purchased first. This would mean 100 units for $200 and then 80 units at $250. The total cost of the inventory is:

$$100 \text{ units} \times \$200 = \$20,000$$
$$20 \text{ units} \times \$250 = \$5,000$$
$$\text{Total inventory cost} = \$25,000$$

As for LIFO, you do the reverse. The company uses 100 units at $200 and 80 units at $250. The total cost of the inventory is $27,000.

$$80 \text{ units} \times \$250 = \$20,000$$
$$40 \text{ units} \times \$200 = \$8,000$$
$$\text{Total inventory cost} = \$28,000$$

The above example shows that if inventory costs are increasing—as they did in this case, from $200 to $250—then the FIFO method results in lower expenses and thus higher profits. So if a company anticipates higher inventory costs, it may be tempted to change its inventory method from LIFO to FIFO.

Besides a change in valuing inventory, there are other things that a short seller looks at in terms of inventory:

Inventory Turnover.   Inventory is expensive. A company must buy materials, manufacture finished goods, and warehouse the finished goods. The longer inventory sits, the bigger the expense for a company.

Short sellers will look at the inventory turnover ratio, which is calculated as follows:

$$\frac{\text{Cost of goods sold}}{\text{Average inventory}} = \text{Inventory turnover}$$

This ratio shows how many days it takes to convert inventory into cash. Compare this ratio to the industry and also track it quarter by quarter. A short seller wants to see the turnover ratio increase significantly.

Increases in Inventory.   Like accounts receivable, an increase in sales is typically associated with an increase in inventories. If inventories are increasing significantly faster than sales, this is a sign the company is having problems selling its goods or is cutting prices.

But not all jumps in inventory are bad. For instance, a company will typically stock large amounts of inventory of new product releases.

Raw Materials Growth.   If you see strong growth in raw materials, but not in finished goods, a company may be having problems manufacturing its product.

Industries Prone to Inventory Problems

Inventory problems can plague any company. One industry that is subject to inventory problems is retail. An example is Tommy Hilfiger. His company had a pulse on the fashion trends of the early to mid-1990s. But fashion can be fickle and Tommy Hilfiger was no exception. In late 1999, inventory started to pile up. In April 2001, the company announced that its profits would fall 30 to 40 percent. The stock went into a free fall, going from the $40s to $9 per share.

The tech industry often also has difficulties with inventory. One example was Cisco. It was forecasting high amounts of growth for 2000–2001. But that growth did not materialize and Cisco had to take charges against earnings. The stock price collapsed from $80 to $12 in 2 years.

When faced with a pileup of inventory, a company has the following options (none of which cure the problem):

Discount. A company will slash the prices to get rid of the inventory. This will definitely mean lower sales and profits.

Write-off. This is an admission from the company that the inventory is basically worthless.

Stuffing the channel. This is when a company sends products to distributors, even though it is well known that demand has fallen off.

Ultimately, the distributors will return the goods. Then the goods must be written off. (We analyze this in more detail in Chapter 8.)

Restricted Cash and Marketable Securities

Restricted cash is money that is meant for a specific purpose, such as to fulfill an existing contract. Thus, do not consider this part of a company's cash on hand when calculating ratios, such as liquidity ratios, which we will look at below.

Also, look for any footnotes regarding a company's marketable securities. Keep in mind that a marketable security can be a stock that a company plans to liquidate in the next 12 months. But what stocks are these? There were some companies that had huge positions in dot-com stocks. Unfortunately, these stocks were not very liquid and were plunging. Thus, a short seller would consider these types of marketable securities to be of low quality and should be discounted (perhaps by 30 percent or more). Also, a short seller would be alerted if the quantity of marketable securities—especially if they consist mostly of stocks—is rising significantly as a percentage of the company's overall cash position (say 30 percent or more).

Prepaid Expenses

Prepaid expenses are those expenses that a company has paid in advance. Examples include rent, insurance, interest, advertising, and supplies. This is normal part of business. But a company may try to hide current expenses in assets. This is called *capitalizing expenses.*

What does this mean? Let's take an example. Disaster Corp. has spent $10 million in marketing for the year. If the company can reduce this by $2 million, then the company will increase its profits by $2 million. However, Disaster Corp. needs the advertising.

One way to lower this current expense is to capitalize the $2 million and call it a prepaid expense. Instead of being a current expense, it is now an asset. True, this $2 million asset will be expensed—but in following years. Basically, Disaster Corp. is shifting current expenses from the current year to later.

There are legitimate reasons for capitalizing expenses, such as for leases or insurance. However, capitalizing advertising is another matter. Typically, advertising is a current expense and turning it into a capitalized expense is a questionable practice.

Another questionable use of capitalizing expenses is for store openings. No doubt, establishing a new store typically requires a lot of expenses, such as rent, promotion, labor, utilities, and training. It is tempting to be aggressive by capitalizing many of these expenses. Thus, if you see a significant increase of store openings, as well as prepaid expenses, this may indicate that a company is being aggressive with its accounting and inflating its earnings.

Moreover, if you see that a company has not been increasing its advertising, yet its prepaid expenses are increasing significantly, then the company may be capitalizing its advertising.

Finally, a company may refer to prepaid expenses as "other current assets," "software development costs" or "other noncurrent assets." These are known as "soft" asset accounts, because it is not altogether clear how tangible the assets are. Thus, look to see if these assets are rising significantly compared to advertising.

Liquidity Ratios

By looking at current assets and current liabilities, you can get a sense of the overall liquidity of a company (that is, the company can pay its bills). Short sellers look at the two measures: the current ratio and the quick ratio. Here is the first formula:

$$\frac{\text{Current assets}}{\text{Current liabilities}} = \text{Current ratio}$$

As a rule of thumb, a current ratio of 2:1 or better means the company is fairly liquid. Then again, a stable blue chip company does not necessarily need a high current ratio. Such a company should have no problems with generating sufficient cash to pay its current obligations. On the other hand, smaller companies do not have this luxury. A few bad quarters could sink a company. A short seller is alerted if the current ratio falls below 1.50 or so.

Short sellers will also look at the quick ratio. It is calculated as follows:

$$\frac{(\text{Current assets} - \text{Inventory})}{\text{Current liabilities}} = \text{Quick ratio}$$

Inventory is excluded because it could be reduced in value or even written off. If the ratio dips below 1.0, then a short seller would be alerted.

Property, Plant, and Equipment

PP&E is shorthand for property, plant, and equipment. These are long-term assets because they have a use that extends beyond one year.

Over time, PP&E assets wear out or become obsolete. A computer, for example, may last a few years whereas a manufacturing plant could last 20 years.

This reduction in the value of an asset is called *depreciation* and is an expense that impacts on the income statement.

Let's take an example: Suppose that Print Press Inc. buys a printing press for $1 million. Typically, the machine has a useful life of 10 years. If the company took the $1 million as an expense, this would be misleading. While in the first year the impact will be significant, there will be no impact over the next 10 years. Thus, accountants will spread the cost (i.e., through depreciation of the asset over the 10 years). This more accurately represents the cost of the asset to the company.

There are two main ways to depreciate an asset:

- *Straight line.* As the name implies, this takes an equal expense over the life of the asset. Since the asset lasts 10 years, the cost will be depreciated 10 percent annually or $100,000.

- *Accelerated depreciation.* This means that a higher percentage of the cost is depreciated in the first few years of the life of the asset.

Look at the footnotes in the 10-Q or 10-K and see if there has been a change in depreciation. Suppose that Print Press expands the useful life of the asset to 20 years. This means the annual expense is now only $50,000. This cuts the depreciation expense in half, and this will have a favorable impact on the company's bottom line. This would be good news for the short seller since it looks like the company is trying to artificially boost its profits to hide underlying problems with the business.

Intangible Assets and Amortization

Intangible assets certainly have value, but it is something that is not physical. In the Information Age, some of the most valuable companies have few physical assets but large amounts of intangible assets. An example is Microsoft. Its value comes from its intellectual property in software development.

Examples of intangible assets include patents, copyrights, trademarks, trade names, and goodwill.

Goodwill is a special item that results from an acquisition. It is essentially the premium paid for another company. Example: Big Corp. decides to buy Small Corp. for $10 million. Small Corp. currently has a net worth of $5 million. The extra $5 million in value is goodwill and becomes an asset of Big Corp.

Intangible assets do not last forever. Patents will expire. Trademarks may lose their brand value. Software may become obsolete.

To account for this, a company will expense the value of its intangible assets over time. The process is called *amortization*. The intangible assets are expensed in equal amounts over the life of the asset. GAAP considers the life to be no less than 5 years and no more than 40 years.

Like depreciation, a company can reduce its overall annual expenses by increasing the length of its amortization period. Short sellers like seeing this. It's a sign that the company is trying to inflate its earnings.

Current Liabilities

Current liabilities are debts owed by a company that must be paid within a year. A key item that short sellers analyze is accounts payable. This is what a company owes to its suppliers, partners, and employees. It is common to pay these outstanding bills within a month or so. If accounts payables are increasing faster than sales, then a company may be having trouble paying its bills.

Debt

Debt creates so-called entity risk. That is, if the company cannot pay its debt, it enters bankruptcy. In many cases, the shareholders wind up losing all or a substantial amount of their investment.

This is not to imply that debt is bad. It can be a very useful way to provide needed capital for a company to expand. A company with a strong balance sheet—such as Merck or Coca-Cola—faces little risk in taking on debt. These companies generate more than sufficient cash flows.

But just like anything, if debt is used excessively, the risks can be high—and this could mean a plunge in the stock price.

To understand the implications of debt, we need to look at the concept of bankruptcy. As stated above, this is when a company cannot pay its current bills or violates covenants in its lending agreements (for example, a covenant may require that a company have a debt to equity ratio of no less than 30 percent). A company can declare bankruptcy or a creditor can force a company into bankruptcy.

However, bankruptcy does not mean that a company shuts down. Rather, the main goal of bankruptcy is to attempt to reorganize the company. Interestingly enough, some companies, such as LTV, have been in bankruptcy several times.

Bankruptcy is governed by federal law and, as a result, a federal court will oversee the process. There are several types of bankruptcy filings. The most common include:

- *Chapter 7.* This is when a company has little hope of surviving. With a Chapter 7 filing, a company will liquidate all its assets at the best prices possible. However, when there is a "fire sale," it is often the case that the company does sell the assets at steep discounts. Typically, a company will file a Chapter 11 filing. If there is no success in reviving the company, the next step is a Chapter 7 filing. This is what happened with MarchFirst, a high-flying Internet consulting company, in which shareholders lost everything. Actually, a Chapter 7 filing is rare for public companies.

- *Chapter 11.* With this filing, a company still has hope. Operations can potentially be turned around. That is why Chapter 11 is called a "reorganization." The debtor files a plan to turn around the company, as well as to discuss repayment of existing debts. A majority of the creditors must approve the plan. After this, the bankruptcy court will either approve or reject the plan.

Regardless of the type of bankruptcy filed, there is a "priority of claims." This is set forth under federal law and indicates the order in which creditors and shareholders get the proceeds from the bankruptcy.

Secured creditors get first claim. These are creditors that have debts backed by collateral, such as land, equipment, or buildings. If a company cannot pay off these debts, the secured creditor will take possession of the collateral. Next are the unsecured creditors. These include those having claims for wages and taxes. General unsecured creditors come next. These are creditors that have loans that are not backed by any collateral. And last in priority are the stockholders.

As you can see, stockholders are the last in line to get any proceeds from a bankruptcy filing. In a Chapter 7 filing, this means that, in most cases, stockholders get absolutely nothing. So, the stock price will go to zero. That's why bankruptcy is a great friend to short sellers. In terms of covering a short, there is no need to because there are no shares to buy. They are worthless. However, even in a Chapter 11 filing, there is a strong probability that the shareholders will get nothing. This is the case even if the company ultimately survives. How? The creditors will take the equity as part repayment of debts. For example, eToys was a leading-edge online retailer that went public during the heyday of the Internet craze. During the late 1990s, the company even had a higher value than Toys "R" Us. But eToys continued to lose huge sums of money and, by 2001, investors were not willing to provide the company with any more capital. By February, the company filed for Chapter 11 bankruptcy. In early March, the company announced that its stock price was "worthless." Just a few years earlier, the stock price was over $100 per share. Note: When a company declares either Chapter 11 or Chapter 7, the ticker symbol will be appended with a "Q." Thus, the ticker symbol of eToys became ETYSQ. Because of the consequences of bankruptcy, a short seller will pay close attention to a company's debt levels. The main areas to analyzing include the debt to equity ratio, cash flows, corporate bond prices, and credit line draw downs.

Debt to Equity Ratio

One ominous sign of impending collapse is when early-stage companies use large amounts of debt. This was the case with many start-up telecom companies in the late 1990s. When the marketplace became glutted with capacity, many of these companies entered bankruptcy.

Also, short sellers will often look at the debt to equity ratio (debt/ equity) to get a sense of the level of the debt.

So what should the ratio be? There is no firm number. It really depends on the industry and the firm. If you see that the ratio is much higher than the industry standard, it is usually a warning sign. The company may be borrowing money to meet its current cash needs since its operations are weakening. Also, later in the chapter we will look at ways that companies try to take debts off their balance sheet and how this can affect the debt to equity ratio.

Cash Flows

A short seller will look at a company's cash flows and compare this to its interest payment requirements. If the cash flows are falling, a company may be in jeopardy of bankruptcy. In Chapter 9, we will look at how to analyze a company's cash flows.

A corporate debt agreement will typically have covenants. These are minimum requirements that a company must maintain so as not to be in default with its creditors. Thus, short sellers will read the footnotes in the financials to see what the covenants are and track them.

One of the most common is the interest coverage ratio, which is calculated as:

$$\frac{\text{Operating income}}{\text{Interest expense}}$$

It is typical that a covenant from a lender is to require a company to maintain an interest coverage ratio of 8.0 or better. Thus, if over the last year, the ratio goes below 9 or so, it is a sign that a company could violate the covenant and perhaps could be forced into bankruptcy by its lenders.

Corporate Bond Prices

Short sellers also look at the current market values of a company's bonds. *A bond* is debt that is issued to the public and is traded on a daily basis. There are two independent research firms—Standard & Poor's and Moody's—that analyze and give ratings on bonds. A company like Merck will have top-rated bonds; that is, the likelihood of default is quite low. However, emerging companies have lower-rated bonds. These are often classified as junk bonds.

If a company does have junk bonds, this does not mean it is going to enter bankruptcy. In fact, some of the fastest-growing companies in the last 30 years have used junk bonds for their growth, such as McCaw Cellular and MCI.

The two rating systems for bonds are shown in Tables 7.2 and 7.3.

Moody's has an additional scale—from 1 to 3—for each of the categories in Table 7.2. Level 1 is the highest for the category and 3 is the lowest. Thus, if a bond is rated Aaa1, it is considered the highest for the category (by the way, it is the highest quality a bond can achieve).

Like Moody's, S&P has an additional rating for each of the categories in Table 7.3. A plus or minus sign show relative standing.

A junk bond for Moody's is Ba or below and BB or below for S&P.

You can find quotes on a company's bonds by going to bonds. yahoo.com. See Table 7.4 for an example of a bond quote.

In Table 7.4 you can see Moody's and S&P ratings, as well as the volume (100 bonds traded).

The price of a bond is a percentage of $1000, where the $1000 is called the face value. When the bond matures (comes due), a company

TABLE 7.2 The Bond Rating System of Moody's Investors Services

Aaa	Highest quality bonds often referred to as "gilt edged."
Aa	These are considered to be of high quality and are known as "high grade bonds."
A	This is a bond that has upper-medium-grade quality, although the bond could be susceptible to impairment.
Baa	While the bond appears to be relatively safe currently, the future could prove difficult in terms of payment of interest and principal.
Ba	This is a speculative bond.
B	The chances of the bonds being paid off is small.
Caa	These are of poor quality and may already be in default.
Ca	These have a high degree of speculative quality. This may be a bond that is also in default.
C	This is the lowest quality bond and the prospects of viability are poor.

TABLE 7.3 The S&P Bond Rating System

AAA	The company has an extremely high capacity to meet its interest and principal payments.
AA	A company has a very strong capacity to pay its obligations. There is only a slight difference between AAA and AA.
A	A company has a strong capacity to meet its obligations but is somewhat vulnerable to adverse effects.
BBB	A company has an adequate capacity to pay its obligations. Anything below this level is considered speculative.
BB	A company faces ongoing uncertainties and may be unable to pay its obligations.
B	Again, there is uncertainty in meeting future obligation. There is only a slight difference between BB and B.
CCC	A company is currently vulnerable in paying its obligations.
CC	A company is currently highly vulnerable in paying its obligations.

will pay the bond investor the $1000 (this is the repayment of the initial loan). The price of a bond goes up and down based on the level of interest rates and market sentiment. Although, if investors believe a company will have trouble paying the interest and principal, you will see a fall in the price of the bond. As for Nextel, its bond is selling at $6275.00 (62.75% × $1000). Short sellers will often say, "The bond is selling 62.75 cents on the dollar."

So how do you analyze the quotes?

Henry Miller, a vice chairman of Dresdner Kleinwort Wasserstein, has studied the prices of corporate bonds. Miller argues that if you see the bond price fall, then consider this as negative sentiment from professional traders (in most cases, it is professionals that trade bonds). Here are his conclusions:

TABLE 7.4 Bond Ratings for Nextel Communications

Rating	B1/B
Volume	100
Price	62.750
Yield to maturity	18.664%

- 80 to 90 cents on the dollar: For Miller, a light goes on. This could be the first sign of a company experiencing problems.

- 60 cents to 80 cents: There are definitely major concerns from investors. Things could be getting much worse for the company.

- 40 to 60 cents: The chances of a company going bankrupt is very great.

- 40 cents or below: The company is likely to file for bankruptcy at any time.

Miller advises considering the company a short sale target when the bonds fall in the 40 to 60 cents range.

Credit Lines Drawn Down

Short sellers see opportunity if a company draws down most or all of its credit line. A credit line is a fixed amount that a bank allows a company to borrow at any time. A company will have a credit line just in case it runs into temporary problems.

However, sometimes a company will need to draw down on the credit line if the problems are very severe. In fact, Wall Street views this typically as an act of desperation for a company. Also, it is often the case that S&P and Moody's will downgrade a company's bonds if there is a significant draw down.

Off-Balance-Sheet Debts.   Companies can hide their debt. These debts are called *off-balance-sheet debts* or *contingent liabilities*. By hiding debt, a company will make itself look more solvent than it really is. This does not mean the debts are not disclosed; rather, they are mentioned in the footnotes. Areas in which you will find off-sheet debts include:

Pension Accounting.   Most public companies have some type of retirement plan. There are two types of plans. A defined contribution plan allows the employee to put his or her own salary into mutual funds or the stock of his employer.

In a defined benefit plan, a company sets aside money in a trust and promises to pay its retired employees a certain amount during retirement. In the trust fund, the company will invest the money—

hopefully at a rate of return that will meet the future liabilities. For accounting purposes, a company must estimate the rate of return of the pension plan.

Sometimes a company will increase the estimate to make the plan look stronger. For a short seller, this would look like a company that is being aggressive with its accounting if the industry peers have not been increasing their estimates and the general securities markets have been weak.

Also, a company can use accounting to understate the liabilities of the pension plan. Accounting expert Edward Ketz believes companies have too much latitude with pensions. Under GAAP, a company is generally not allowed to net assets and liabilities. But there is an exception for pensions.

Let's take an example: ABC has a pension fund. According to its projections, it has an obligation of $100 million in retirement benefits. This is a debt to ABC. But ABC has been investing the money in the pension trust and has accumulated assets of $90 million. On the balance sheet, the two amounts would be netted and the company would have a debt of $10 million.

On the surface, it does not look like much. But what if the company invested most of its trust money in its own stock and over the past year, the stock is down 90 percent? The debt is still there. It does not go away. Thus, a short seller will try to get a sense of where the pension money is invested. If it is heavily in the company stock, and the stock collapse, the company could face a substantial liability.

Equity Method.   Ketz is also skeptical of companies that use the equity method. Short sellers are, too. The equity method can be a way to hide debts from the balance sheet.

Let's take a look at the equity method of accounting: Some companies will invest in other companies. If the ownership is less than 20 percent, it is treated as a passive investment. But over this amount, the company will be able to exert more and more influence over the operations. In a sense, the investment could be a quasi subsidiary. A company has two ways to account for this on its balance sheet. First, it can use the consolidation method. For example, suppose a hypothetical ABC Corp. buys 80 percent of the stock of XYZ Corp. for $1 million. The consolidation method means that ABC will basically assume the assets and liabilities of XYZ.

Suppose that ABC has $2 million in debts and $5 million in assets. As for XYZ, it has $500,000 in debts and $1 million in assets. Under consolidation, ABC will now have $6 million in assets and $1.5 million in debts.

Next, ABC can elect to use the equity method. In this case, ABC adds the $1 million purchase on its balance sheet as an asset. Thus, ABC has assets of $6 million and debts of $1 million. In other words, the $500,000 in debts of ABC do not show up. As a result, debts are understated when using the equity method.

Leases. Suppose a retail store wants to build 300 stores, which will cost $100 million. A company could borrow the $100 million and construct the stores. Simple. But this is probably not what the company will do. Rather, it will probably lease the property. If a company uses a capital lease, then it must record this is a liability.

But there is an exception: an operating lease. The difference between this lease and a capital lease is that the former requires that the company return the asset when the lease expires. In other words, the company has no ownership rights.

Even though operating leases are not considered liabilities, they are likely to be a future liability for a company. For example, suppose ABC runs superstores similar to Wal-Mart. It does not own the buildings, but has operating leases. These superstores are huge, over 100,000 square feet. So, after the lease expires, will ABC abandon the store? Probably not. ABC will likely have to renegotiate the lease. In other words, these leases are ongoing liabilities of a company.

In terms of a short seller, he will read the footnotes and calculate the amount of the lease payments. He will then compare this amount to revenues. If this represents a big percentage compared to the rest of the industry, then the company may be too aggressive in using leases as off-balance-sheet items.

Special Purpose Entities (SPE). The most prominent case of using SPEs is Enron. With this accounting technique, the company was able to push billions of debts off its balance sheets.

In a way, an SPE is similar to a joint venture. For example, suppose ABC Corp. is in the airline industry and wants to buy 100 planes. It could create an SPE (which is a separate company) that would buy and own the 100 planes. The SPE would borrow money against these planes as collateral for the loan. The revenue generated from the planes will be used to pay off the loans.If ABC owns less than 50 percent of the voting stock of the SPE, it does not have to recognize the SPE's debt on its balance sheet. Interestingly enough, ABC can put up as much as 97 percent of the capital to establish an SPE.

Besides taking debts off of ABC's own balance sheet, there are also special tax advantages for SPEs that make them attractive.

Many companies use SPEs. However, some use quite a few. If a company establishes more than 10 or so, it may mean the company is being too aggressive in taking debts off its balance sheet. In fact, Enron had about 900 SPEs.

A short seller will tote up these off-balance-sheet debts and get a true understanding of what a company owes. Next, the short seller will use a variation of the debt to equity ratio, such as the following:

$$\frac{\text{(Balance sheet debt + Off balance sheet debt)}}{\text{Equity}}$$

The short seller will use this calculation for competitors in the industry and see if there are major divergences. Also, a short seller will look at the growth in off-sheet debts to balance sheet debts and see if the former is growing significantly faster.

Equity

Equity is ownership in a company. When you buy common stock in a company, you essentially become a part owner in the enterprise. For example, you buy 100,000 shares of ABC and the company has 10 million shares outstanding. You own 1 percent of the company (100,000 divided 10 million).

A useful ratio is the return on equity (ROI), which is calculated as:

$$\frac{\text{Net income}}{\text{Equity}}$$

A red flag is when a company has an ROI that is lower than its growth rate. Let's continue with the example of ABC. It has net income of $10 million and equity of $100 million, which translates into an ROI of 10 percent. But the company's market is growing at 20 percent. Basically, according to the company's ROI, it cannot generate sufficient resources to grow to meet the 20 percent demand rate. This means the company will need to raise money—either in debt or in equity.

Toxic Equity

On the face of it, equity is good. It represents an investment or retained earnings of a company. From this, a company can continue to grow its operations. But, in some cases, the price of equity can be very expensive. It could prove deadly for a company. Thus, whenever a company is considering a financing, look at the structure. If it is a toxic structure, it could be a good short sale candidate.

Let's take a real-life example: ICG Communications has its roots in the mid-1980s. Originally, the company developed satellite teleport facilities in south Denver. But it was the passage of the Telecom Act of 1996 that compelled the company to aggressively pursue the local telephone market. To do this, without question, would require huge sums of cash. But this seemed to be no obstacle. In 1996, for example, ICG signed a $1 billion equipment deal with Lucent. Interestingly enough, the company even spent $33 million to build a new headquarters, a building that points westward (apparently, this signifies that the company is pushing forward into the future).

ICG looked at all avenues to raise capital—from venture capital, an IPO in 1994, and the sale of junk bonds. There were also vendor financing deals, such as with Lucent. ICG sold off certain assets from its Netcom business and the satellite business was sold off.

Of course, the capital markets began to crumble in early 2000 and financing became extremely difficult. Unfortunately, ICG had a tremendous burn rate. Losses were $100 million for the fourth quarter of 1999. So, ICG pursued alternative financing mechanisms. That is, ICG used a PIPE, which stands for private investment in a public equity; that is, this is the process in which institutional investors place money in an already existing public company. The investment buyout firm Hicks Muse Tate and Liberty Media agreed to invest a stunning $750 million in a PIPE transaction with ICG in April 2000.

But it was not enough. By the end of 2000, ICG was in bankruptcy and the stock was delisted. The company had $2.7 billion in assets and $2.8 billion in debts.

PIPEs can be, in a sense, "pipe dreams." They can also be structured to be extremely destructive to you, the individual investor.

This is not to imply that PIPEs are consistently bad. In some cases, they can prove to be very useful. Consider, for example, the biotech industry. Since the early 1990s, the industry has had major difficulties raising money. PIPE investors were willing to structure deals. And, when biotech returned in 2000, investors and companies were certainly happy.

Actually, there are some inherent advantages to PIPEs. They take little time to set up—say a couple weeks. And, since the investors are sophisticated, there are few regulatory hurdles. Moreover, PIPEs are not required to be registered with the Securities and Exchange Commission, which helps to lower the overall costs. However, the odds for success for PIPEs are not good. According to a study from the University of California Los Angeles (UCLA), of the 500 PIPEs issued between 1995 to 1998, about 85 percent of the stocks fell an average of one-third within one year. Let's take a look at the structure of a PIPE deal: Suppose you are a savvy private investor, with $1 billion in management. You see a public telecom company, Telecom Bust Corp., that is struggling. The stock price is at $1 per share and the company needs at least $20 million to survive. You work out a deal with Telecom Bust to create a new type of security. It is a convertible preferred stock. By being preferred, you have higher priority in the event of a liquidation. There may be a full liquidation preference, which gives these security holders first priority. You are also likely to get dividend payments, say 10 percent per year. Convertible means that you can exchange your preferred shares into shares of common stock of Telecom Bust. This is expressed as a conversion ratio. For example, you might be able to convert one preferred stock for four shares of Telecom Bust if the stock hits $1.50.

Seems harmless? Of course, there are many twists that can severely affect the company and individual investors. Here are some considerations:

Trouble.   In most cases, a company does a PIPE because it is in deep trouble. The business model is questionable, the product line is inadequate, potential customers lack interest, and so on.

Perception. Since PIPEs have a tainted reputation, this can make it difficult for the company to get new deals or find analysts interested in coverage.

Complexity. PIPE deals are often exceedingly complex. In fact, the main reason is to confuse management and individual investors. After all, it is typically the case that management does not have much high finance expertise. As a result, they are vulnerable to questionable deals.

Expensive Capital. PIPE investors will likely impose a high price for the capital. One structure is participating preferred. Taking the example above, you invested $10 million in the company and get 10 percent per year in dividends. You own roughly 30 percent of the company. Then, the company returns to profitability and is sold for $100 million. You can claim your $10 million back and any unpaid dividends. But you will also get to have 30 percent of the purchase price, which is $30 million. A nice payday. Or, the preferred may be supercharged. This means that the repayment of the preferred can range from 1.5 to 3 times or even more.

What's more, these deals often involve warrants. A *warrant* is a security that allows the investor to buy a certain number of shares at a fixed price. If the stock price increases, the warrants will be valuable and investors will exercise them. But this means that existing shareholders will experience dilution (their percentage of ownership will decline).

Death Spiral. It's hard to believe, but this is an official term in finance. This can happen if there are toxic elements to the deal structure. Perhaps the most noxious death spiral is the floorless convertible. In fact, it's almost a "can't lose" proposition for the PIPE investors. Essentially, if the stock price goes down, then the PIPE investor gets more shares. On the surface, this makes sense. After all, the investor is seeking downside protection.

But the devil is in the details. Example: You invest $10 million in a PIPE for Telecom Bust. Currently, the stock price is $5 per share. There is a floorless provision that expresses the conversion not on a per share basis but in gross dollars. So, at $5 per share, you can convert your preferred for 2 million shares (this is your $10 million investment divided by $5 per share). If the stock price is $1, then you get 5 million shares ($10 million divided by $1 per share). As you see, as the stock price goes down, you own more and more of the company. If you want to make a quick buck, you should then short Telecom Bust stock. Okay, suppose you short 1 million shares of the stock. You will have $5 million placed in escrow. It is likely the stock will start to fall, perhaps to $3 per share. At that price, you have the right to convert your preferred into 6 million shares. You only convert 1 million shares to pay off your short sale. You now can keep the $5 million and you still have potentially 5 million more shares. And then you can short more stock and do the same process over and over again—making a huge killing in the market. In the meantime, the stock is obliterated. Some deals will have "no short" provisions. But this means very little. It takes little effort to set up offshore hedge funds to do the short sales. This is a very common technique.

Investor.   A key factor is knowing the PIPE investor. If the investor is an unknown hedge fund or based overseas, you should be concerned. It's important that the investor be strategic. This type of investor has little incentive to play any financial games.

Example: In June 2000, the online travel site, Expedia, needed to raise additional money. Their business model appeared to be solid and the prospects good. Expedia struck a deal with Technology Crossover Ventures and Microsoft for a $60 million PIPE. The stock price was at $16.60 and there were 723,000 warrants. The convertible was not floorless.

Microsoft definitely had much at stake. Expedia was the company's first spin-off and owned more than 70 percent of the equity. In April 2001, Expedia reported that it exceeded analysts' estimates and posted an operating profit of $4.4 million on sales of $110. The stock now trades at $80 per share.

Conclusion

When looking at a balance sheet, it is important for the short seller to get an accurate understanding of what a company owns and owes. An aggressive company will overstate the former and understate the latter. This is why some companies—which look like they have little debt and ample assets—may suddenly wind up in bankruptcy. A short seller's mission is to find these situations.

In the next chapter, we will take a look at the income statement.

CHAPTER 8

The Income Statement

Does the Company Really Make Money?

Y ou have been following Big Loss Corp. as a possible short, but the financials are confusing. On the one hand, the company reported a loss of $20 million based on GAAP. But then it reported a $10 million profit based on so-called pro forma accounting. What really happened? Is the company in good shape or is the company hiding problems?

This is the critical question a short seller must answer. And to help get at the right answers, you need to look at a company's income statement. Interestingly enough, the income statement is the most vulnerable to manipulation and creative accounting. This creative accounting is known as "gaming the income statement."

In September 1998, then-SEC Chairman Arthur Levitt gave a speech about his concerns regarding corporate accounting. He said that many companies were engaging in "earnings management." That is, companies would try to slant their financials to make things appear better than they actually are. He said, "Managing may be giving way to manipulation; integrity may be losing out to illusion."

As you will see, a company has a variety of ways to aggressively inflate its earnings and create an illusion of prosperity. But a company cannot do this indefinitely. And when the game stops, the stock price can fall precipitously. Let's see how short sellers look at the income statement.

Trend Analysis

Before we look in detail at income statements, it is important to look at the overall trends of any type of financial statement (such as the balance sheet and cash flow statements). So when investigating a company as a short sale target, it is important to make sure you have all the statements for at least 5 years back. With these statements, you can get a sense of the direction of a company.

When looking at the trends, keep in mind that some companies are seasonal. For example, retailers generate much of their business in the fourth quarter. Thus, you will see a spike in these numbers. So, when comparing quarterly numbers, it is a good idea to adjust for seasons. Comparing the first quarter (which is the lowest for retailers) with the fourth quarter will not work. It is equivalent to comparing apples to oranges. However, comparing this year's fourth quarter with last year's fourth quarter will provide you with much more information.

Revenues

Revenue is what a company generates from its business activities, such as the sale of its products or services, subscriptions, fees, commissions or rentals. This is known as the *top line*, since the revenue is reported at the top of an income statement.

However, not all the revenue will be cash. Rather, it could be a promise to pay from a customer. This is known as accounts receivable, which is an asset and recorded on the balance sheet (see Chapter 7 for more information).

There are different components to revenues. First, look at operating revenues. These are the revenues that derive from the core business. Intel, for example, gets a substantial amount of its revenues from its chip business; Microsoft, on the other hand, generates much of its revenues from licensing its software.

Some companies will break out the revenues into different categories. For example, suppose Tech Corp. has three revenue streams: software, hardware, and services. A good technique is to express these categories as percentages. See Table 8.1.

As you can see, 50 percent of the revenues come from hardware. This is clearly an important part of the business. Sometimes companies will

TABLE 8.1   Tech Corp. Revenue Categories

Hardware revenues	$50 million	50%
Software	$25 million	25%
Services	$25 million	25%

move away from the core business and show that their smaller divisions are performing well. This may be stated in the title of a press release or talked about in a conference call. In other words, a company is trying to deflect attention away from the deterioration in its core business.

For example, suppose software revenues grew from $12.5 million last year to $25 million this year for a hefty 100 percent increase. Yet the company's core business grew from $45 million to $50 million. While it is good that software is strong, the fact remains that there seems to be weakness in the core business. In other words, look at all segments of the revenues and see if the core business is lagging. This could mean the company is experiencing trouble. Short sellers are definitely attentive to this.

So far, we have been talking about operating revenues. But many companies have nonoperating revenue—which is, by definition, not part of the core business. Short sellers will analyze the nonoperating revenue portion of the income statement closely, as well.

Intel provides a good example of important nonoperating revenues. Let's take a look at its second quarter 2000 press release for its earnings, which was titled "Q2 Revenue a Record $8.3 Billion, Up 23 Percent." The first paragraph validates the strong revenue growth:

> Intel Corporation today announced second quarter revenue of $8.3 billion, a new quarterly record, up 23 percent from the second quarter of 1999 and 4 percent sequentially. The company also had record unit shipments of microprocessors and flash memory in the second quarter.

In the next paragraph, the company reports substantial growth in profits:

> For the second quarter, net income excluding acquisition-related costs was $3.5 billion, up 98 percent from the second

quarter of 1999 and up 16 percent sequentially. Second quarter earnings excluding acquisition-related costs were $0.50 per share, an increase of 92 percent from $0.26 in the second quarter of 1999, and up 16 percent sequentially.

Even if you look at earnings on GAAP, they were very impressive:

Including acquisition-related costs in accordance with generally accepted accounting principles, second quarter net income was $3.1 billion, up 79 percent from the second quarter of 1999 and up 16 percent sequentially. Earnings per share were $0.45, up 80 percent from $0.25 in the second quarter of 1999 and up 15 percent sequentially.

But were these earnings the result of the company's booming chip business? Not necessarily. If you read the press release (or the company's 10-Q), you would have noticed that almost half the company's profits were from the noncore business of the company. Actually, if you excluded the nonoperating profits, the earnings per share would have increased 8 percent, not 92 percent.

The big problem with relying on investment income is that the values can be volatile. If the stock market falls—which it did—the profits can quickly turn into losses. This was not an isolated event. It affected such highfliers as Cisco, Nortel, and Lucent.

It is important to note that financial statements will often refer to revenues as "net operating revenues." The use of the word *net* is to account for discounts, refunds, and allowances. For all intents and purposes, when a company talks about revenues, it is referring to net operating revenues.

Revenue Recognition

A big question about revenues involves when they are created. Generally, a company will recognize revenues when a product or service is sold to a customer. This is known as *the point-of-sale approach*.

However, some industries have special characteristics. For example, some service companies will use the completed contract method. This is when a company has a product or service that involves a long-term development cycle. In that case, recognizing the revenue up front or at the end of the contract would skew the company's financials. For example, suppose XYZ company is building a bridge for $10 million. The construction will take 3 years. Recognizing the $10 million on the signing of the deal or at the completion would result in a big spurt in the company's revenues. With the completed contract method, the value of the contract is spread over the time period of the construction.

If a company uses a method other than the point-of-sale approach, then it must be disclosed in a footnote in the financials.

If a company is using the completed contract method, compare its approach to the rest of the industry. Is a company recognizing revenues earlier than its peers? If so, the company may be inflating its revenues.

In fact, this is the key issue for the short seller to recognize in regard to revenues: Are revenues being recognized too aggressively? A company has different ways to do this. One approach is simply to fraudulently create fictitious sales. This is clearly illegal (some executives have served prison sentences because of this) and, fortunately, it is a rare occurrence.

There are, however, legal ways to aggressively inflate sales. A company, for instance, may be liberal in how it estimates customer's ability to pay their invoices (we look at this in more detail in Chapter 7).

Another technique is "stuffing the channel." Here's an example: Suppose ABC Corp. has sales of $30 million for the quarter. However, Wall Street is expecting the company to hit $35 million. The shortfall could be disastrous when reported, as investors will begin to wonder if the company is having problems.

ABC decides to ship $5 million in more product to its existing customers. By shipping extra product, ABC is able to record a total of $35 million in sales for the quarter—ABC is stuffing its sales channel. This is not fraudulent. Many companies record sales when the product is shipped.

Of course, the practice can have some bad consequences. The customers will likely wait to pay for the products (why pay right away if you are not expecting the shipment?)

Also, in the next quarter, when the ABC sales force attempts to sell more product, there is likely to be much lower demand, since customers already have an increased supply of product. Channel stuffing takes away future sales.

Some companies will stuff the channel through as many quarters as possible. But eventually, customers will have a bulging supply of the product and probably will send the excess items back. In the end, sales will suffer.

How can you detect channel stuffing? A short seller will:

- Read the footnotes in the financial statements to see if the company has a revenue recognition policy that allows for sales to be recorded when the product is shipped.

- Look for significant growth in the company's accounts receivable (explained in more detail in Chapter 7).

- Look for significant growth in the company's inventory (explained in more detail in Chapter 7).

- Look for a surge in deals done at the end of the quarter. You can spot this if you see a flurry of press releases announcing deals.

Sudden Changes in Revenue

A short seller is alerted if there is a sudden burst in a company's revenues. While this may mean that the company is showing progress in its operations or has recently launched a new product, it also may mean that a company is manipulating its revenues.

A case in point is Lernout & Hauspie, a company that developed voice recognition software. The company showed sales of a mere $97,000 in Korea in 1998, which was an insignificant percentage of sales at the time. Two years later, Korean sales were $58.9 million in the first quarter. In fact, these sales represented 52 percent of all the company's sales. How was it that Korea accounted for more sales than Europe or the United States?

The answer was that the sales in Korea were heavily inflated. Basically, Lenout & Hauspie created a variety of companies in Korea that bought product from the parent company. The scheme was uncovered. And in quick fashion, Lenout & Hauspie went bankrupt and the CEO was arrested for fraud.

In addition to spotting manipulated revenues, there is another important lesson from this episode: Try to verify claims of the CEO. As for Lernout & Hauspie, the CEO claimed (before the company went bankrupt) that the company was going to report lower than expected earnings. The reason given? The CEO said the company adopted the more conservative accounting principles of Dragon Systems, a company that Lernout & Hauspie had recently bought.

Actually, however, Dragon Systems had filed an S-1 document to go public. If you read the document, you would have realized that its accounting policy was in fact the same as Lernout & Hauspie's. There was no change! A simple exercise in cross-referencing would have uncovered the dupe.

Vendor Financing

Another red flag that indicates questionable revenue is vendor financing. For example, let's say that Equipment Corp. sells big ticket items for $1 million a piece. The company's customers, however, are smaller companies that do not have sufficient resources to make the purchases. In order to generate revenue, Equipment Corp. will essentially provide a loan to its customers to buy its products.

This is not necessarily bad. If the customer is successful with the product, then Equipment Corp. will not only have booked a sale, but will get interest payments on the loan. Besides, vendor financing can be a great way to keep customers. A customer is less likely to shop around for a better price. And, by the way, Equipment Corp. will get higher margins. The reason is that Equipment Corp. will typically charge higher prices for its equipment. This is the trade-off for a customer that gets vendor financing.

Then again, if the customers falter, the game can get ugly. Let's continue with Equipment Corp. Suppose it extends $100 million in vendor financing to Upstart Corp. So $100 million in product goes to Upstart, but the company is not required to pay back the loan for 2 years. Unfortunately, Upstart is a shaky company and goes bust and cannot pay the $100 million to Equipment Corp. In this case, Equipment Corp. will take a $100 million write-off for the account, since there really was no revenue in the transaction.

What makes vendor financing very questionable is that, in most cases, customers who take advantage of the financing cannot get loans from the bank (just as in our example above with an upstart company). Simply put, the customers are not good credit risks.

In the late 1990s, the telecom industry engaged in aggressive vendor financing. One of the biggest providers was Lucent, which had commitments that exceeded $7 billion. The company even said it was "like a bank." However, when the telecom industry slowed considerably, Lucent was caught with many bad loans and its stock price plunged.

Another big promoter of vendor financing was Cisco. In fact, it has a separate company called Cisco Capital. While Cisco did not extend as much credit as Lucent, the company nonetheless had to take write-offs for bankrupt customers and the stock price plunged.

Gross Profit Margins

Gross profit is the difference between a company's revenues and the cost of producing goods (known as cost of goods sold or COGS). For example, suppose Disaster Corp. has sales of $100 million and COGS of $60 million. The gross profit margin is $40 million. A short seller will also calculate the gross margin percentage, which is the gross profit as a percentage of the sales. For Disaster Corp., it is as follows:

$$\frac{\text{Gross profit}}{\text{Sales}} = \text{Gross margin percentage}$$

$$\frac{\$40 \text{ million}}{\$100 \text{ million}} = 40\%$$

Basically, gross profit margin looks at the profit made based on costs that are directly related to the manufacturing of the product line. Thus, gross profit does not include costs such as selling, general and administrative (SG&A) expenses, interest, and taxes. Rather, COGS includes the costs of labor, materials, and processes to generate the product.

As a general rule of thumb, a company with a profit margin of 50 percent or below would alert a short seller. It indicates that a company's products do not provide as much value to customers (that is, customers are not willing to pay a premium for the products) as does the competition's. It may also indicate that the product is in a competitive market and the company has little pricing power.

Another consideration for short sellers is that a low profit margin means a company has a lower margin for error. If sales decline precipitously, then a company may take a significant hit to its bottom line. The reason is that there are two types of costs: variable and fixed. Variable costs are essentially COGS. Thus, if sales fall 10 percent, COGS will fall about the same amount. However, this is not the case with fixed costs. These are the required costs for running the business regardless of whether the company has sales or not. This is often referred to as overhead. True, these costs can be cut—but it tends to take some time to do so.

To illustrate this, let's continue with our example from Disaster Corp. Let's assume that in the next year, sales fall by 50 percent to $50 million.

Suppose Disaster Corp.'s gross profit margin is still 40 percent. This means that COGS will be 60 percent or $30 million (60% × $50 million in sales). Basically, the sales and COGS have declined by the same amount. The result is that the company has the same gross profit margin at $100 million as it did at $50 million.

The problem is that Disaster Corp. has substantial fixed costs. In this case, the company had $40 million in SG&A, interest, and taxes (that is, the same fixed costs as when it generated $100 million). Now, when the company generated $50 million in sales, the fixed costs were still about $40 million. Consequently, the company is losing $20 million ($50 million in sales minus $70 million in total costs).

An interesting case for gross profit margins is Enron. From 1998 to 2000, the company grew its sales at an amazing rate of 220 percent to $100 billion. Looks like the company was very successful, right? This was not the case, of course. A short seller would have looked at the gross profit to see if the company was inherently making money from these sales. Actually, Enron had a very high COGS. So the gross profit margin percentage was a mere 4.4 percent in 1998 and even fell to 1.9 percent in 2000. See Table 8.2.

TABLE 8.2 Enron's Profit Margins

Item	1998	2000
Revenues	$31 billion	$100 billion
Operating income	$1.378 billion	$1.953 billion
Margins	4.4%	1.9%

Lowering SG&A Expenses

If a company has stagnant growth in its revenues, it can attempt to improve its earnings by lowering its SG&A expenses. Keep in mind that these reductions cannot go on forever. After all, there is only so much a company can cut. Every cut in expenses will have some sort of effect on future sales and profits. A short seller will be very mindful if a company is, in a sense, "mortgaging its future" by cutting on critical expenditures. For example, a company may cut its R&D, which could make it less competitive in the next few years. Or a company may reduce its marketing expenditures, which may mean lower sales in the future.

Moreover, a company can use aggressive accounting to help lower SG&A. One approach is by selling off a division. For example, let's say that Disaster Corp. has $20 billion in sales and $1 billion in net income. The company has been growing its sales at only 4 percent per year. Disaster sells a division for $500 million (after tax). Disaster could book this as a one-time gain.

However, it instead uses the $500 million to reduce is SG&A. This could result in a profit for Disaster of $1.5 billion, which would certainly delight shareholders. But, in reality, this was not a long-term reduction in SG&A; it was temporary.

You can find the SG&A reductions disclosed in the footnotes of a company's 10-K or 10-Q.

EBITDA

A company's income statement will also have a section for EBITDA, which stands for earnings before interest, taxes, depreciation, and amortization. In fact, companies like to focus on this number. After all, it excludes some major items and can give the impression a company is healthier than it really is. As for short sellers, they are attentive if a company focuses on this number and downplays net income.

Let's take an example: Winstar. This was a high-flying telecom company with a stock price of $11 per share when it published a press release for its earnings on February 2001. The title was "Winstar Reports Strong Fourth Quarter Results." The subtitles included:

Broadband Revenue: Double-Digit Sequential Increase—15th Straight Quarter

On-Net Percentage: Over 85 Percent for Quarter—Another Industry Record

Gross Margin: Sharp Increase—8th Consecutive Quarter

EBITDA: Strong Improvement—6th Consecutive Quarter

In the third paragraph, the press release stated:

> The combination of strong revenue growth and margin improvement enabled Winstar to narrow its EBITDA loss for the quarter to $19.9 million, a $41.9 million improvement from the year-ago quarter, and a $12.0 million, or 37.7 percent, improvement from the prior quarter. This is the company's sixth consecutive quarter of significant improvement since posting its peak EBITDA loss in the second quarter of 1999. Winstar expects its EBITDA losses to continue to decline until it reaches EBITDA breakeven, which is expected to occur during the second quarter of 2001.

Things sound great, right? Actually, within two months, the company filed for bankruptcy. The stock was halted at 14 cents per share.

The problem was that investors were confusing EBIDTA with cash flow. Simply put, they are not the same.

For EBIDTA, it is true that depreciation and amortization do not involve any outflow of cash. But if a company has taxes or interest, these are real outflows. With Winstar, the company had $5 billion in debt and had to come up with a $77 million interest payment. But there was not enough money in the bank. Basically, while EBIDTA was improving, the company's cash flows were hemorrhaging (we look in more detail at cash flow statements in Chapter 9).

Taxes

Businesses usually have two sets of books: those that are reported to shareholders and those that are reported to the IRS. While the company wants to show strength in the former, there is an incentive to do the opposite for the latter.

It behooves a short seller to look at reported earnings and what a company pays to the IRS. If a company is showing substantial earnings but the IRS bill is low, this is a sign that the company may be very aggressive with its reporting.

Ratio Analysis

When studying an income statement, a short seller will compute a variety of financial ratios. These can provide a snapshot of whether a company's position is improving or worsening.

The ratio we will focus on in this chapter is the Fool ratio (which is based on the research of www.fool.com). Simply stated, the Fool ratio compares a company's price to earnings (PE) ratio to the growth in its earnings per share (EPS). The resulting figure gives an indication of whether a company is overvalued or undervalued.

Let's take an example: Overvalued Corp. generated net income of $5 million in the last year and has 1 million shares outstanding. Thus, the company has a 12-month EPS of $1 per share ($5 million divided by 1 million shares). If the stock price is currently $20 per share, then the PE ratio is 20 ($20 divided by $1 per share in EPS).

A short seller may look only at the PE ratio as an indication that the stock is overvalued. Suppose that a short seller has tracked the PE ratios of a certain industry over the past 10 years. When the PE for the industry group hit 25, the stocks hit a high and fell from there. Or, a short seller may look at the Fool ratio. This is based on the idea that investors look to the future. If they believe a company will continue to show strong growth, then the PE ratio will expand. If the reverse is the belief, the PE will begin to contract.

Short sellers look for situations in which Wall Street has excessively optimistic expectations of growth. Once the growth slows down, investors will start to sell the stock and the price will begin to fall.

From any major financial Web site, you can get earnings forecasts. This is what you use to estimate the future growth rate. In the case of Overvalued Corp., let's say that analysts have the estimates shown in Table 8.3.

TABLE 8.3   Overvalued Corp. Earnings Forecast

2003	2004	2005
50 cents in EPS	75 cents in EPS	$1.00 in EPS

To calculate the growth rate, you use the following formula:

$$\frac{(\text{Earnings for 2005} - \text{Earnings for 2003})}{\text{Earnings for 2003} \times 100} = \text{Growth rate}$$

$$\frac{(\$1.00 - \$0.50)}{\$0.50 \times 100} = 100\% \text{ growth rate.}$$

However, this is the growth for a 2-year period. We need to look at the growth rate an annual basis (called annualizing the numbers). You do this by dividing the growth rate by the number of years, which is 2, or 100%/2 = 50% per year.

Now, you have the necessary information to calculate the Fool Ratio, which is:

$$\frac{\text{PE ratio}}{\text{Growth rate}}$$

So, if Overvalued Corp. has a PE of 100 and a growth rate of 50 percent, the Fool ratio is 2.0 (100 PE divided by 50). Basically, the higher the ratio, the more overvalued a company appears to be. See Table 8.4 for the Fool ratio guidelines.

Honey Pot Accounting

The former CEO of tech firm Network Associates, Bill Larson, is credited with the phrase "honey pot accounting." It described the process in which he essentially stored current earnings for a rainy day.

For example, suppose a company has a very strong quarter. It may

TABLE 8.4   Fool Ratio Guidelines

Fool Ratio	Recommendation
0.50 or less	Buy
0.50 to 0.65	Look to buy
0.65 to 1.00	Hold
1.00 to 1.30	Look to sell
1.30 to 1.70	Consider shorting
Over 1.70	Short

decide to not report all these revenues, but instead classify a certain percentage as deferred revenues. As the name implies, deferred revenues are revenues that a company will recognize over time.

These deferred revenues are set aside in a reserve. So, let's say in a year it appears the company will not meet Wall Street expectations. The company can dip into its honey pot and post the necessary revenues.

No doubt, a short seller will be alerted if it sees a company dipping into a honey pot to meet expectations. A short seller is even more interested if a company does not have enough reserves to meet the quarter. In other words, the company could be facing a serious deterioration in its business.

It is not easy to determine if a company is drawing down on its reserves. Most companies do not make it a habit of disclosing such information. However, some companies may disclose it in a press release or in a conference call.

Another sign that a company has revenues locked away in a honey pot may be that, while the rest of the industry is suffering, a company is continuing to show strength in its business.

Earnings Revisions

An analyst who follows a company will often develop an earnings estimate for the next quarter and possibly for the next few years. The analysis is based on looking at many factors, such as industry trends, a company's financials, product line, competition, and so on.

There are three main organizations that collect and publish earnings estimates: IBES, First Call, and Zack's. These firms take the earnings estimates from Wall Street analysts and come up with consensus estimates. These estimates can be very influential. For example, if a company beats Wall Street's estimate, then the stock can increase substantially. If it misses the estimate, the results can be harsh for the stock price.

As the economy and the industry change, analysts may revise their estimates—upward or downward. In fact, these revisions can be a useful way to gauge a possible short sale.

Generally, analysts tend to have a bullish bias with their ratings. However, their earnings estimates are a better indicator. For example, an analyst may still have a positive rating on the stock even though he is revising the earnings projections downward.

Generally, if analysts are revising estimates downward, there are likely to be more downward revisions over the next few quarters. By and large, analysts tend to be conservative. They do not want to call a big drop in earnings estimates—anything could happen to the company that could make earnings swing in the other direction. This is good for a short seller, since he has time to short a stock—that is, at a higher price—before more and more analysts publish negative ratings on the stock.

One-Time Charges

In the competitive global economy, it is not uncommon for companies to undergo a restructuring. Perhaps a company needs to sell off a division or lay off employees or discontinue a product line. In fact, this is a healthy part of the global economy.

To lessen the impact of this, a company will often call these changes either *one-time, special, unusual,* or *nonrecurring charges.* These charges appear on the company's income statement.

These charges can be substantial—often in the billions of dollars. However, a company will often try to concentrate as much of the losses as possible in one quarter. While this reduces the current earnings substantially, it will make future comparisons look very favorable. This is known as "big bath accounting."

For example, suppose Restructure Corp. lays off 10,000 people and closes down several manufacturing plants. For the second quarter of 2002, the company takes a one-time charge against earnings of $2.5 billion.

A year later, the company posts a $230 million profit. Obviously, this looks much better compared to the $2.5 billion loss and investors may get excited and bid up the stock price.

Short sellers, though, carefully analyze one-time restructuring charges. Here are signs that a company may be having serious long-term problems and that the stock price will ultimately fall:

Recurring Charges. A one-time charge may become a common occurrence for a company. A short seller will be alerted if a company has had three or more restructurings in the last 2 years. It is a sign that the underlying fundamentals of the company are deteriorating.

Write-Off of Deferred Tax Assets.   A company will write these off if they believe they will not likely be used in the future. Interestingly enough, deferred tax assets are only useful if a company posts a profit. Thus, by writing these assets off, a company is hinting that it will not make money any time soon.

Big Charges.   Multex.com conducted a study on companies that take substantial charges (as a percentage of their revenues). The conclusion was that those companies that reported the biggest charges—compared to their industry peers—have poorer returns.

Why this result? One theory is that a write-off is an admission that a company's assets are showing deteriorating and lower returns. Thus, the future of the company is likely to be less favorable.

Inventory Write Downs.   This is when a company considers all or a part of its inventory to be worthless. This means that the company did not accurately forecast its expected sales. Moreover, it is a sign that future sales are likely to be slow.

Accounts Receivable Write-Off.   If you see much of the accounts receivable of one customer being written off, then this may be an indication that the customer base is experiencing problems and that other customers will be unable to pay. This was the case in the telecom industry in 2000, when many upstart companies ran out of money.

Charges for Acquisition Targets.   It is not uncommon for there to be tremendous restructuring after an acquisition. There may be duplication in terms of product line or employee base. However, sometimes the target of an acquisition will take the charges before the acquisition is consummated. Thus, the acquirer does not have to report the charges, but will be able to take advantage of the benefits of the restructuring. This is certainly an aggressive accounting method and could be an indication that the acquirer is having trouble keeping its earnings pace intact.

Pro Forma Earnings

Earlier in this chapter, we looked at a company that had GAAP earnings and pro forma earnings. Basically, all public companies must publish earnings that are according to GAAP, but they do not necessarily need to provide pro forma earnings. However, in the late 1990s, it became very popular to provide pro forma earnings. Why? It was easier to inflate these numbers.

For many years, companies have complained about GAAP. They say it is not reflective of the real economics of the companies. For example, a biotech company in its early stages may not necessarily have the same characteristics as an established big pharmaceutical company. As a result, the biotech company will attempt to make certain adjustments to its GAAP profits. The upshot is what are called *pro forma earnings.*

Pro forma numbers are not new. They have been in existence for decades. Traditionally, they have been used for unusual events, such as a huge merger. The pro forma numbers would adjust the financials for the complex transaction. It was, for the most part, a nonevent.

This certainly changed in the 1990s, as companies focused more on pro forma numbers. A big reason was that it became tougher for companies to meet Wall Street's high expectations. Pro forma earnings, on the other hand, made it easier for companies to post better numbers.

When a company issued a press release, it would headline the pro forma results, not the GAAP numbers. The stock prices would continue to rise.

With the implosion of Enron, there was much more skepticism regarding pro forma numbers. A big problem with pro forma numbers is that there are no standards. The approach differs from one company to the next.

For example, Yahoo! was an early user of pro forma numbers, which could vary more than 30 percent from GAAP numbers. Yahoo! would routinely exclude from its reported earnings the costs of buying Internet companies and the payroll taxes on employee stock options (see Yahoo!'s stock chart in Figure 8.1).

In another example, Internet travel site Expedia reported that it had its first profit in the company's history in 2001—that is, if you

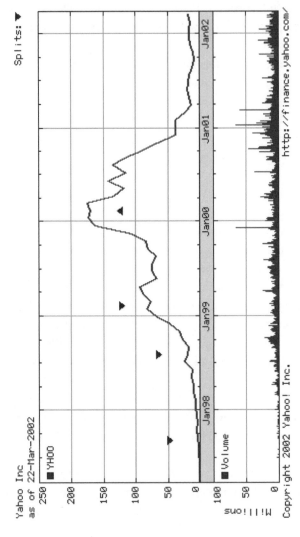

FIGURE 8.1.   Yahoo! would trumpet its pro forma earnings, but not its GAAP earnings, which were much lower.

looked at pro forma numbers. However, the company lost 37 cents per share if you looked at the GAAP numbers.

A short seller will study intently the pro forma numbers. Key areas to look for include:

Deflection.   A company's press release will have a headline that brags about the pro forma earnings but does not mention GAAP earnings. Moreover, in the fine print following the headline the company says that GAAP earnings are not what investors should focus on.

Variance.   Compare pro forma earnings to GAAP earnings. Is the difference more than 30 percent? If so, the company may be in worse shape than what appears on the surface.

Conclusion

Short sellers realize that a company can easily inflate the reported earnings on their income statement. In fact, a company can report strong earnings and yet still go bankrupt. Maybe the company is recognizing revenues too soon; perhaps the company is even making up revenues.

There are certain techniques to try to determine whether a company is playing fast and loose with its accounting. Your role will actually be similar to a detective. You will be collecting clues and building a case. Chances are you will not have 100 percent certainty, but you will be ahead of many other investors who believe whatever a company reports.

In the next chapter, we will look at the cash flow statement, which offers other important clues for determining short selling candidates.

The Cash Flow Statement

Cash Is King

ast quarter, Cash Poor, Inc. reported a nice jump in its earnings by 25 percent from the same quarter last year. You listened to the conference call and the CEO was upbeat about the business. By all indications, the company seemed to be in good shape. Yet, as you analyzed the financial statements, you looked at the Statement of Cash Flows and found that even though the company had reported profits, there was negative cash flow of $25 million for the past quarter. How can that be?

The answer: It happens quite often. The reason? Earnings and cash flow are not the same (we will look at why this is the case shortly). In fact, short sellers will often compare earnings with cash flows. If there is a disconnect between the two, a short seller is alerted. The company may be trying to hide problems.

Interestingly enough, chances are you haven't heard much about cash flow statements. A big reason for this is that companies usually do not like to talk about them; rather, they tend to focus on the income statement, which is easier to manage.

Essentially, a cash flow statement answers two big questions. It shows where a company is getting money and where it is spending money. While an income statement can be manipulated, this is difficult for a cash flow statement. There's an old saying: Income statements are opinion and cash flow statements are fact.

If net income is growing faster than cash flow, then the company is engaging in aggressive accounting, such as recognizing revenues too soon or understating expenses. If you see this gap grow bigger and bigger—and it is larger than the industry average—then this is a major red flag. It indicates that the company has potentially low quality of earnings.

Let's take a look at how you can use cash flow statements for short sale candidates.

The Difference

Why is there often a difference in the profits from the income statement and the statement of cash flows? As we learned in Chapter 6, public companies use accrual accounting. In most cases, a company will recognize a sale and collect the cash later.

To understand this concept, let's take a simple example. Let's take a look at Cash Flow Inc. The company's balance sheet is shown in Table 9.1. In the past quarter, the company showed a profit. The income statement is shown in Table 9.2.

However, only $5000 of the profit was cash from customers. The rest was for credit sales, which will be collected in the next month or so. Thus, while the company had a profit of $15,000, the actual cash coming into the company is only $5000. Of course, in the future, as the cash is collected, it will boost the cash position of the company—so long as the customers pay their bills.

TABLE 9.1   Balance Sheet for Cash Flow Inc.

Assets	
Cash	$10,000
Accounts receivable	$20,000
Inventory	$20,000
Total assets	$50,000
Liabilities & Equity	
Loan	$10,000
Equity	$40,000
Total liabilities & equity	$50,000

TABLE 9.2   Income Statement for Cash Flow Inc.

Sales	$100,000
Cost of goods sold	$40,000
Selling, marketing & general	$40,000
Total expenses	$80,000
Earnings before interest/taxes	$20,000
Interest	$1,000
Taxes	$4,000
Profit	$15,000

The $10,000 in profit becomes an asset of the company called accounts receivable, which is on the balance sheet.

Using Cash Flow Statements

You will find the cash flow statement in a company's 10-Q. But the statement is cumulative. For example, suppose Cash Flow Inc. reports its third quarter 10-Q. The cash flow statement will include the activities for the past 9 months (cumulative), not the last quarter.

If you want to look at only the third quarter, you need to filter out the first two quarters. To do this, subtract the prior 10-Q, which has cumulative figures for the first 6 months. This can be tedious, and a good idea is to use a spreadsheet to do this analysis (such as Microsoft Excel). To better understand the statement of cash flows, let's take the real-life example of high-tech company Nortel Networks. The filings (Figures 9.1, 9.2, and 9.3) are from the first and second quarter of 2001.

The cash flow statement is composed of three parts: operating activities, investing activities, and financing activities.

Operating Activities.   These are the inflows and outflows of cash in terms of the core business of the company.

In the second column of Figure 9.1, we see the data for the first quarter of 2001. The next column is the cumulative data for the first 6 months. In the last column, there is the adjustment for the first 3 months and first 6 months. That is, the fourth column shows the data for the second quarter.

	3 months ended Mar. 31, 2001	6 months ended June 30, 2001
Cash flows from operating activities		
Net loss applicable to common shares	$ (2,580)	$ (19,013)
Adjustments to reconcile net loss applicable to common shares to net cash used in operating activities, net of effects from acquisitions of businesses		
Amortization and depreciation	$ 2,175	$ 4,133
In-process research and development expense	$ 15	$ 15
Non-cash portion of special charges and related asset write downs	$ –	$ 12,901
Equity in net loss of associated companies	$ 28	$ 132
Stock option compensation	$ 36	$ 59
Tax benefit from stock options	$ 33	$ 34
Deferred income taxes	$ (130)	$ (1,090)
Other liabilities	$ (19)	$ (17)
Gain on sale of investments	$ (24)	$ (26)
Other - net	$ 14	$ (166)
Change in operating assets and liabilities		
Accounts receivable	$ 1,036	$ 2,359
Inventories	$ 34	$ 1,184
Income taxes	$ (454)	$ (882)
Accounts payable and accrued liabilities	$ (1,148)	$ (490)
Other operating and accrued liabilities	$ 121	$ 352
Net cash used in operating activities	$ (863)	$ (515)

Figure 9.1 Cash Flows Used in Operating Activities.

	3 months ended Mar. 31, 2001	6 months ended June 30, 2001
Cash flows from investing activities		
Expenditures for plant and equipment	-563	-854
Proceeds on disposals on plant and equipment		20
Increase in long-term receivables	-389	-502
Decrease in long-term receivables	61	93
Acquisitions of investments	-23	-73
Proceeds on sale of investments	44	66
Net cash from (used in) investing activities	-870	-1250

Figure 9.2 Cash Flows Used in Investing Activities.

	3 months ended Mar. 31, 2001	6 months ended June 30, 2001
Cash flow from financing activities		
Dividends on common shares	$ (60)	$ (123)
Increase in notes payable	$ 582	$ 1,421
Decrease in notes payable	$ (207)	$ -
Proceeds from long-term debt	$ 1,505	$ 1,500
Repayments of long-term debt	$ (37)	$ (407)
Increase (decrease) in capital leases payable	$ (9)	$ (24)
Issuance of common shares	$ 102	$ 133
Net cash from financing activities	$ 1,876	$ 2,500
Effect of foreign exchange rate changes on cash and cash equivalents	$ (15)	$ (17)
Net cash from continuing operations	$ -	$ 718
Net cash used in discontinued operations	$ -	$ (433)
Net increase in cash and cash equivalents	$ 128	$ 285
Cash and cash equivalents at beginning of period - net	$ 1,644	$ 1,644
Cash and cash equivalents at end of period - net	$ 1,772	$ 1,929

Figure 9.3 Cash fFows Used in Financing Activities.

The first item we want to look at is the net income. Then, there are a variety of adjustments to wash out the effects of accrual accounting. A positive number means cash is added; and a negative number means cash is reduced. The numbers are netted at the end to give the company's net cash from operations.

The most common adjustments include:

- *Depreciation.* This is added back since there is no actual cash outlay for depreciation (in fact, it is often called a *noncash expense*).

- *Inventory.* An increase in this column means that more cash is being used to invest in inventory.

- *Accounts Receivable.* An increase in this column results in the use of more cash by the company. The company is extending credit to the customer.

- *Accounts Payable.* A decrease here means an increase in cash (cash is required to pay down accounts payable, which is money owed to outside vendors).

After making these adjustments, you have the net operating cash flow. This represents a company's cash profits.

Investing Activities.   Figure 9.2 shows Nortel's Investing Activities. Most companies will use cash for capital investments (known as "cap ex" items). Capital investments are for long-term purposes, such as for plant, equipment, mergers and acquisitions, and perhaps even software. Investing in these capital assets uses up cash; selling the assets is a source of cash.

Moreover, a company may buy and sell stock or bonds for investment purposes. This was the case with big high-tech companies, which made venture capital investments in emerging start-ups.

After making these adjustments to the cash flow statement, you have the net cash provided (or used) by all investing activities.

Financing Activities.   Finally, a company may need to seek capital to pay for its operations. This is reported in the next section of the cash flow statement (see Figure 9-3). Companies have a variety of options in terms of raising capital: selling stock or bonds or borrowing from banks. The company can use its cash to buy back stock, pay dividends, and retire debt.

After the adjustments, you have the net cash provided (or used) by all financing activities. If a company is showing negative operating cash flow, it is probably the case that the company uses external financing sources to deal with the deficit.

You will notice there are three line items at the end of the cash flow statement. This section reconciles the cash balances from Nortel's balance sheet. Basically, it shows the increase or decrease in the cash balance from quarter to quarter from the company's balance sheet.

Free Cash Flow

Short sellers like to focus on free cash flow. In other words, this is cash that a company has available at the end of the quarter—free and clear. It can use the cash for many things, such as buying back stock, paying dividends, investing in operations, buying another business, and so on. Essentially, free cash flow gives a company options. That is why a company like Microsoft—which generates tremendous cash flow—is a darling for investors. Even if a new venture fails, the company is still generating new cash flow for something else to do.

Unfortunately, the cash flow statement does not indicate free cash flow. Thus, to find a company's free cash flow, you need to make some adjustments.

Keep in mind that there is no universal definition of free cash flow. Different short sellers may have their own variations. In this chapter, we will look at an approach used by Whitney Tilson, who is a Managing Partner of Tilson Capital Partners, a money management firm.

Tilson has written several articles on the subject. His studies have focused on the cash flows of Lucent during the first half of 2000 when the stock was trading in the $50s. Although he does not short sell for his fund, many of his articles provide a framework for finding good short sale candidates. And, of course, he likes to focus on free cash flow. His article on Lucent was certainly a good call, as Lucent eventually hit a bottom of $4.50 per share.

To find free cash flow, you need to make some adjustments to the statement of cash flows for the operations section. Let's look at the operations section of Lucent's cash flow in the first and second quarters of 2000 (see Table 9.3).

TABLE 9.3   Lucent Cash Flow Operating Activities

	Q1 2000	Q2 2000
Net cash provided by operating activities	$124 million	$344 million

On the face of it, Lucent appears to be showing positive cash flows, right? Not necessarily. Tilson wanted to know what the free cash flow was. To do this, he made three adjustments to the operating cash flow figures:

Tax Adjustment.   Tilson believes that there are certain tax items that should not be considered operating activities. One is the tax deduction a company receives from the exercise of employee stock options. He considers this a financing activity and places it in that statement. He also thinks this is the case for "deferred income taxes."

In this reorganization of the cash flow statement for Lucent, this resulted in a reduction of $456 million in the first quarter and $453 million in the second quarter. Also, for short selling purposes, Tilson made a $102 million adjustment for deferred income taxes in the first quarter and a $72 million adjustment for the second quarter. He did this because he believes deferred taxes are not a source of cash. A company will need to eventually pay these taxes.

Cap Ex.   As seen above in the investing activities section of the statement of cash flows, cap ex (capital expenditure) items are for investments in plant, equipment, mergers, and other major undertakings. To understand the cap ex adjustment, let's take a simple example: Cash Flow Corp. makes a purchase for a factory for $1,000,000, which should help produce future income for the next 10 years. Since the factory will last 10 years, the company will need to depreciate the value of this asset over time—allocating $100,000 per year in depreciation expense. This is a noncash expense, but is included on the income statement and thus reduces the profits of the company. Under accounting rules and regulations, Cash Flow Corp. is not allowed to allocate the $1 million price tag in one year.

For the statement of cash flows for operations, the $100,000 depreciation expenses is added back since it is not a cash outflow. However on the investing activities section, the full $1 million is specified as a cap ex item. For example, assuming the company paid $1 million in cash for the factory, then the following happens: On the balance sheet, the cash decreases by $1 million and the property, plant & equipment item increases by $1 million.

In other words, there was a $1 million cash outlay for the factory for this period. Tilson believes that all or a part of the $1 million must be adjusted against the cash flow section for operations.

Tilson sees two types of cap ex items. First, there are required expenditures (also called maintenance cap ex). Maintenance cap ex is what a company needs to spend to keep up its existing operations. These are expenditures that should be adjusted to arrive at free cash flow.

Next, there is growth cap ex. In this case, a company is spending more than it needs to. Essentially, the company is using free cash flow for expansion opportunities. Tilson believes these expenditures should not be adjusted.

Keep in mind that the cap ex adjustment is tricky. Often, it involves an in-depth understanding of the company as well as some guesswork. However, as a general rule, Tilson adjusts for most of the cap ex items. For Lucent, this meant a $585 million cap ex adjustment for the first quarter and a $634 million adjustment for the second quarter.

One-Time Charges. A company may make a one-time payment that does not reflect ongoing operations. An example would be a settlement for a lawsuit. This amount is subtracted from the operational cash flow. Table 9.4 shows the free cash flow for Lucent after the adjustments.

Interestingly enough, during the first quarter of 2000, Lucent reported pro forma net income of $1.25 billion and $818 million in the second quarter.

TABLE 9.4   Lucent's Free Cash Flow

	Quarter 1 2000	Quarter 2 2000
Net cash provided by operating activities	$124 million	$344 million
Adjustment for tax benefit from stock options	($456) million	($453) million
Adjustment for deferred income taxes	($102) million	$72 million
Adjustment for net cap ex	($585) million	($634) million
Free cash flow	($1,019) million	($671) million

Why the huge difference? There were many reasons:

- Large increases in cap ex items.

- The balance sheet was worsening. Accounts receivables increased from $5.4 billion to $11.7 billion and inventories increased from $2.9 billion to $5.7 billion.

- There was a substantial increase in the exercise of employee stock options. Interestingly enough, many short sellers consider a big jump in employee stock option exercises as a danger sign. Basically, employees are cashing out of their stock and (this could be an indication that employees consider the company to be overvalued. In Chapter 10, we will look in more detail at insider selling. As we will see, it is not foolproof. After all, there can be many reasons why someone wants to sell his or her stock other than the belief that the company is overvalued. But if there are large amounts of selling, it could be a red flag.

Quality of Earnings Ratio

After you have calculated free cash flow, you can then compare this to the company's earnings. It is essentially a gauge for the quality of earnings.

The quality of earnings ratio (which we will refer to as the *QE ratio*) is calculated as follows:

Step 1 : Net income – Cash from operations

Step 2: (Average total assets for quarter X + Average total Assets for quarter X + 1)/2 = Average total assets

Step 3: Divide the result from Step 1 by Step 2 to obtain the QE ratio

The QE ratio can be a good indicator of whether a company is in trouble. Studies have shown that if the ratio is 0.03 or higher, then the quality of earnings are suspect.

Suppose Cash Flow Corp. had net income of $50 million and has been growing at a strong pace in the past few years, as the stock price has soared. Let's also assume that the company was showing negative numbers in its operating cash flow of $100 million.

We make the calculations to determine quality of earnings, or the QE ratio:

- Step 1: $50 million – (–$100 million cash outflow) = $150 million (the two negatives make a positive for the $100 million cash flow)
- Step 2: Average assets were $500 million
- Step 3: $150 million/$500 million = 0.30

As you can see, this is off the charts in terms of the criteria for quality of earnings; it is well above the 0.03 benchmark. While this is not definitive evidence the company is in trouble, it is certainly a major red flag.

The source of trouble in quality of earnings for Cash Flow Corp is likely to be found in inventories and receivables. If one or both have soared, this may mean the company is having trouble selling its goods and could be in big trouble.

Debt and Free Cash Flow

Suppose you have a monthly income of $5000 and you spend $7000 each month. Also, you have no outside investments. What happens? Individuals who find themselves in such a situation typically borrow the money—often by using credit cards to finance their expenses.

A company is no different. If a company is showing negative free cash flows, it ultimately will need to finance this outflow by issuing stock or borrowing. If the company issues stock, then existing shareholders will see their ownership diluted. Example: let's assume Cash Flow Corp. has negative cash flow of $1 million per month and decides to sell 1 million shares at $10 each to finance the shortfall. Before this offering, the company had 10 million shares outstanding and you owned 100,000 shares. Thus, you own 1 percent of the company. After the 1 million new shares are offered, the company has 11 million shares outstanding and you now only own 0.9 percent of the company.

This is not necessarily bad. Many early-stage growth companies have negative cash flows and there is a need to get external financing. As long as the financial markets are healthy, this should not be a problem, provided that the company eventually starts to grow strongly and to generate good free cash flows.

If a company decides to borrow money, there is usually no risk of dilution (unless the debt can be converted into equity, which is known as a *convertible security*). However, there is a risk of default. That is, if a company cannot pay its debt, bankruptcy is the result. And, in many cases, shareholders get wiped out because they are last in priority to get any proceeds from a liquidation. (Owners of common stock are last in line when it comes to payment when a company goes under.)

As an example, let's take a look at Polaroid, which was a pioneer in photography. The company was founded in 1926 by Edwin Land, who left during his first year at Harvard to start the venture. He developed key innovations in photography, making Polaroid a fast-growing company and a leader in its industry. By the fall of 1999, the company hit record sales and the stock price reached $30. Prospects looked great.

Then there was a major shift in technology—toward digital cameras. Polaroid was unable to deal effectively with the transition. By 2001, the company was in bankruptcy and the stock was basically worthless at 6 cents per share. It now trades on the OTC Bulletin Board (see the stock chart for the company in Figure 9-4).

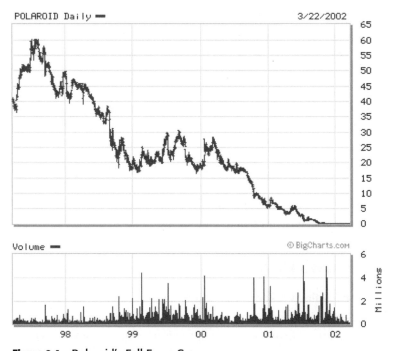

Figure 9.4   Polaroid's Fall From Grace.

Looking at the company's financials reveals that Polaroid had borrowed substantial amounts of money to continue its operations. By the middle of 2000, the company had interest payments of $77 million. True, the company had profits—before interest and taxes—of $107 million. It was a slim margin, but by this metric, the company could pay its bills. Or could it? Remember: A company's earnings are not cash; you need to look at the company's cash flow. If it cannot pay its current debts, bankruptcy could be imminent. As for Polaroid, the company had virtually no free cash flow, because of its heavy cap ex items.

Cash Flow Efficiency

Cash flow efficiency is how well a company manages its working capital (as seen in Chapter 7 on the balance sheet, working capital is the difference between current assets and current liabilities). Tom Gardner, cofounder of the Motley Fool, invented the flow ratio, which is a mathematical approach to measuring cash flow efficiency.

Basically, the flow ratio focuses on cash and those assets that can be readily converted into cash, such as marketable securities and short-term investments. It does not include inventory or accounts receivable in this category. Here is the formula:

$$\frac{(\text{Current assets} - \text{Cash \& cash alternatives})}{(\text{Current liabilities} - \text{Short-term debt})} = \text{Flow ratio}$$

Short-term debt includes notes payables and the part of long-term debt that has no more than a year to be paid off.

The lower the ratio, the better. If the ratio is below 1.0, then the company is not tying up its assets in inventory and receivables. If the ratio is 1.25 or above, then the company may be experiencing troubles and this would alert short sellers to an opportunity. There should be even more concern if the ratio deteriorates quarter by quarter.

Erratic Cash Flow

A major red flag for short sellers is when a company has erratic cash flow. This may indicate that a company is in a volatile industry or that it is having trouble managing its operations. A good example is Enron, which had the cash flows shown in Table 9.5.

TABLE 9.5　Enron's Cash Flow

Quarter	Operating Cash Flow
Q1 '00	−457 million
Q2 '00	−$90 million
Q3 '00	$674 million
Q4 '00	$4652 million
Q1 '01	−$464 million
Q2 '01	−$873 million

What is striking about Enron's cash flow is the wide swings from negative to positive figures and back to negative figures. What was particularly telling is when the company showed a substantial amount of cash flow in the fourth quarter of 2000 and then, in the next two quarters, lost $464 million and $873 million, respectively. This was the first time Enron showed such a precipitous decline in its history, displaying a major danger sign that put short sellers on alert.

Conclusion

The cash flow statement is often the first place a short seller will look to determine if a company is a good short sale opportunity. If a company has high debt and negative free cash flow, it is a major red flag and a good short sale candidate. There could be some big problems in the company, which makes its future questionable. In fact, the company could be on the verge of bankruptcy, as we saw with Polaroid. Also, look for any disconnect between reported earnings and free cash flows. A company may be trying to hide things.

In these chapters, we have taken a close look at the various aspects of financial statements that all investors, including short sellers, should investigate. From balance sheets to cash flow statements, clues are available as to when a company has taken on too much debt, when its cash flow isn't flowing, and when its balance sheet is out of balance. While there is, undoubtedly, a lot of information to be found in these statements, understanding them and using them as a weapon in your investment arsenal can only help improve the overall performance of your portfolio. Short sellers in particular should make it a common practice to use financial statements as a key tool when investigating short sale candidates.

In the next chapter, we will look at proxy statements. Like the cash flow statements, the proxies are also often overlooked. Of course, this can be a mistake. There can certainly be many danger signs in proxies, as we will see.

Proxy Statements and Insider Sales

Nepotism Inc. has been growing nicely over the past few years. But you are skeptical and think it could be a good short. As you read the company's filings with the SEC, you realize that there are some very interesting relationships among the officers. For example, one of the board members is the wife of the CEO. Another board member is the CEO of one of the company's biggest customers.

You should be concerned. According to Howard Schilit, an expert in accounting and the CEO of the Center for Financial Research and Analysis (CFRA), one of the biggest red flags is self-dealing in the company. It is important to ask yourself whether the officers and board members really are looking out for the interests of the firm or for their own interests.

Such issues come under the heading of "corporate governance." Essentially, corporate governance strives to make sure that the officers and the directors of a company are sincerely looking out for the interests of the company's shareholders. On the face of it, the subject is somewhat dull. But it can be revealing when trying to find a short sale candidate.

A main source for corporate governance can be found in a company's proxy statements. A proxy statement is a required report sent to all shareholders of record. The form is also called DEF-14A. The document is meant as a disclosure document for shareholders to make an informed vote at the shareholder's meeting.

An important part of the proxy is executive compensation, and the information in this section of the proxy can be a clue to problems with a company. For example, are the executive officers getting excessive compensation? Or, are the executives dumping their stock holdings?

In this chapter, we will analyze the proxy through the eyes of a short seller.

Worth the Big Bucks?

Every year, there are front-page stories on what major executives made last year. Some of the numbers can be staggering—exceeding $100 million or even more than $1 billion. The source of much of this information? It's the proxy statement.

If a company's performance has been strong, then a big pay package is not necessarily bad. However, it is important to compare the salaries of executives in the industry. Is the salary of the executives in the company you are investigating much higher, yet the performance below average? Were bonuses paid, even though the company was experiencing troubles? These are signs that management is looking mostly after its own interests, not shareholders.

This is especially the case if management does not have equity positions in the company that are above-average in the industry. Suppose the CEO of Nepotism Inc. is making $2 million per year in salary. Yet, in the industry, no CEO makes more than $500,000. Moreover, the CEO of Nepotism owns only 1000 shares of stock. Is there any incentive to make the stock go higher? Not really. The CEO certainly has a very comfortable arrangement.

Here are some other red flags in terms of executive compensation:

Repricing.   Many executives have large option packages to buy stock in the company. Suppose these packages were doled out when the stock was flying high at $50 to $60. After a year, the stock is at $10. The stock will need to go up at least $41 points for the options to have any value.

In response, management may attempt to reprice the employee stock options. That is, the exercise price of the stock options will be refigured at $10 so the stock does not have to increase much for the options to be valuable.

There are a couple criticisms against this. First of all, options are meant to motivate performance. However, if management fails to perform, why should they be given another chance to exercise their stock options with a repricing?

Next, a repricing has adverse accounting consequences. Basically, as the stock price increases, a company will take a bigger and bigger charge against earnings.

Restricted Stock.   There are certain restrictions on the ability of an executive to sell shares of restricted stock. There may be a restriction in terms of the number of shares that can be sold compared to the average volume for the stock. Or there may be time limits (say, the executive cannot sell any shares until at least 1 year of holding the stock).

But these restrictions tend not to be a big barrier. For an executive, waiting one year is not a long time. Besides, if the stock has sufficient volume, then the stock can be sold. Thus, if an executive has a grant of restricted stock, it is certainly a good deal and is likely to have some type of value. While an employee stock option will be worthless if the stock price falls below the exercise price, this is not the case with restricted stock. As long as the stock price is above zero, there will be value in the stock.

Deals That Can't Be Refused.   Certainly there are deals common in the corporate world that executives and management simply cannot ignore. To retain top talent companies may be required to offer some nice fringe benefits to their top executives. But in some cases, it can go too far and these fringe benefits are beyond the scope of reason or good financial management. Also, a company may spend huge amounts to get rid of former executives, which also can damage share price.

Compensation Committee Report.   This report, issued by the company, will indicate what the company's compensation approach is. If it is not based on performance, then be wary. Also, look who sits on the compensation committee. If the CEO or other officers are on the committee, this is a big problem since they likely are helping to set the guidelines for their own compensation packages. Will they also evaluate their own performance? If so, probably not as harshly as they should. In other words, the degree of incentive to enhance the stock price will not be as strong. Even moderate success will result in substantial compensation for the executives.

Besides showing compensation, the proxy statement will delve into the backgrounds of the executives and directors. Study these bios. Red flags include:

- Little experience in the industry (For instance, someone who was a CEO in a manufacturing company might not be the best leader for a retail group.)
- Prior run-ins with regulatory authorities, such as the SEC
- Prior failures, such as bankrupt companies
- Evidence of nepotism (Is the 23-year-old son the president of the company?)

"Related Parties"

Andrew Fastow, CFO of Enron, help to establish two partnerships in December 1999. These partnerships were LJM Cayman LP and LJM2 Co-Investment LP. In fact, the initials LJM were from the names of Fastow's wife and two sons.

As a general partner of these partnerships, Fastow signed a variety of deals with Enron. These deals clearly raise red flags, begging the question of whose interests he was looking out for— Enron's or his own.

Fastow made $30 million from the partnerships, which was much more than his salary at Enron. Actually, an internal partnership memo showed that the Enron deal had been renegotiated in favor of the partnership. This is a stark example of a related-party transaction. A related party transaction occurs when a company enters a contract with a third party that is an executive or board member—or the relative of an executive or board member. In such a transaction, the agreement is not at arm's length and there is an apparent conflict of interest.

While many related-party transactions are in the proxy statement, you will also see them in the company's 10-Ks and 10-Qs, filed with the SEC, and part of the public record. However, the details of such transactions are usually buried in the footnotes. That was the case with the Fastow/Enron situation. In fact, the situation points to the fact that although crucial information is disclosed by companies, many investors—

even savvy investors—fail to read the filings. True, some investors, including some short sellers, did take the time to read the filings and actually did profit from this information. But many did not.

One of the short sellers that did take the time to read the filings in late 2000 was Jim Chanos. He spotted the Enron limited partnerships in footnotes in the 10-K and 10-Q statements. But the footnotes did not disclose the name of the general partner. The participation of Fastow was not made public until October 2001, when the company had to write down its equity by $1.2 billion because of the partnerships. However, the footnote did say a top-level executive was a general manager of the limited partnerships. This certainly alerted Chanos. Who was this mysterious person?

Regardless of who the person was, it looked like a major conflict of interest. But this is not the only consideration a short seller has with related-party transactions. Another critical issue is: If your company's product is so good, why engage in related-party transactions? Shouldn't it sell on its own merits?

This was not the case with Enron (this was really a conflict-of-interest problem). Rather, this issue concerns a transaction that involves a company's product or service. For example, if the CEO makes a deal to sell a product at a 50 percent discount to another company that is run by his cousin, then this is a related-party transaction. A short seller would ask: Why the discount? Why the favor? Why give away value of the firm?

Here are some red flags regarding related-party transactions:

Vendor Financing.   This is when a company provides financing to its customers to buy its products. This can be in the form of a loan (we describe this in more detail in Chapter 8). The conflict of interest problem is: Were the terms of the loan too favorable for the customer? Was it meant as an aggressive way to get a new customer? Since the company will want to keep the customer, will it be vigilant in enforcing the loan?

Investment.   Often, a big company decides to invest in a smaller company. In many such deals, the smaller company agrees to buy the products of the big company as part of the agreement. This is similar to vendor financing, but it is not in the form of a loan. Rather, the company is getting a certain percentage of the equity of the customer.

In fact, these "investments" can be no-lose situations for the big company. Consider this example: Big Corp. decides to invest $5 million in Small Corp. In the deal, Small Corp. signs an exclusive agreement to sell the products of Big Corp. According to Big Corp.'s calculation, a conservative estimate is that it will make $10 million in profits on the deal. So even if the stock price of Small Corp. collapses, Big Corp. still makes money.

Propping Up a Business of a Friend or Relative. Let's take an example of Good Corp. and Bad Corp. Of course, Good Corp. is doing, well, very good and Bad Corp. is starting to show slow growth. It needs to find ways to improve its situation. The CEO of Good Corp. sits on the board of Bad Corp. In fact, it turns out that they are longtime friends, so the CEO of Bad Corp. pleads with him to do a deal. The CEO of Good Corp. agrees. No doubt, Bad Corp. announces the deal with great fanfare to the press and the stock rises. Yet, is it really a good deal? Perhaps so for Bad Corp. But what about the shareholders of Good Corp?

In this case, the board would not typically need to approve the deal. Rather, it is up to the discretion of senior management. But the details of the deal must be disclosed in the proxy or it may be disclosed in other financial documents, such as a 10-Q or 10-K. But as is usual, many investors gloss over these deals.

The Corporate Board

It is important to analyze very carefully the composition of the board. According to corporate law, the board represents the interests of the shareholders. However, as we have seen in this chapter, this is not always the case. Here are some things to consider regarding the board:

- Are there any conflicts of interest?
- Is there nepotism?
- Does the board consist mostly of company management?
- How does compensation of the board of directors compare with the industry?
- Are any of the board members consulting with the firm? If so, they may be reluctant to rock the boat, since it could potentially ruin

the consulting gig. For example, one Enron director received $72,000 in consulting fees from Enron.

In light of the Enron debacle, there are proposals for reforms of corporate governance. One proposal in Congress is that a company should be required to hire financial or industry analysts as board members so as to better understand the dynamics of the company and thus make more informed decisions.

Another proposal is to limit the number of boards a person may sit on. Simply put, a board member spread too thin among various companies may not have the time to participate as required in all board meetings. For example, one board member of Enron missed three-quarters of the meetings. This raises a variety of questions, including whether the board member is fulfilling his duties, and whether his pay is commensurate with his performance as a board member.

Insider Selling

An insider is a director, officer, or major shareholder of a company. If these persons decide to buy or sell stock in their company, it is called insider trading.

According to Section 16 of the Securities Exchange Act of 1934, insiders are required to disclose their transactions in public filings. The rationale is that it is presumed the insiders have in-depth information about their company and their purchase or sale of company stock would be a material event for investors.

There are a myriad of filings that an insider is required to make, such as a Form 3 or Form 4 and so on.

The filing that short sellers focus on is the Form 144. Basically, this is filed whenever an insider intends to sell restricted stock. This filing relinquishes the restricted nature of the securities. According to the SEC, a Form 144 is required if an insider desires to sell stock. By filing the form, the insider has a window of 90 days to do so. In some cases, an insider may actually decide not to sell the stock after making the filing; but this is rare.

Insiders tend to hold onto their shares for the long term. Why? This is actually encouraged by the so-called short-swing profit rule. This SEC rule stipulates that if an insider buys stock and within 6 months sells the shares at a profit, then the insider is disallowed the gain.

Insider selling is not necessarily always bad. There may be many reasons for the sales: divorce, buying a new house or car, funding a college education, and so on. Besides, in some cases insiders take cuts in salaries in exchange for stock options. By selling the stock options at a profit, the insiders are getting compensation for a good job.

In some cases, insiders will have an automatic selling program. For example, Bill Gates has billions of dollars in wealth in Microsoft stock that he wants to diversify into other investments. He also wants to set aside money for his charitable foundations. So he sells a certain number of shares every month. In a sense, this is like the reverse of the dollar-cost averaging method. And any insider can use it (you will notice this if an insider is selling a fixed amount every month or quarter).

While this in effect is not indicative of trouble in the company, there are some danger signs short sellers should be aware of:

- *Selling below 50 of the high.* If a stock is selling 50 percent or more from its high, and insiders are still selling their own positions, this is an indication that management has lost faith in the future. This was the case with Enron in 2001. If the stock is expected to rebound, it is important to question why insiders would sell at these levels.

- *Selling on small rallies:* Let's say a stock has fallen 30 percent. Then the stock has a 5 percent rally but soon starts to fall again. Also, during this time, insiders sold their positions. This can be an indication that insiders are trying to unload at any chance when there is a pop in the stock because they feel the long-term prospects are not good.

- *Cluster selling:* This is when three or more top executives start selling their holdings. Look to see if the amounts are higher than in the past. Selling 10 percent or more of one's overall holdings would certainly be a danger sign, because it would be an indication that the insider is attempting to bail out of the stock.

Conclusion

The proxy statement is often an overlooked tool investors and short sellers can use to find clues about the health of a company. Unfortunately, the proxy statement usually just goes straight into the trash.

While the proxy statement provides information for shareholders to cast well-informed votes pertaining to the board of directors, compensation, and mergers, it is not uncommon for a substantial amount of shareholders to not cast their votes, even though it is their right.

As we have seen, the proxy statement is extremely valuable, especially when analyzing conflicts of interest on the part of the board of directors. A thorough investigation of the proxy statement also can help you keep track of any insider selling. When conflicts of interest are present or when those in the know are "voting with their feet," it could be a strong indication of a good short opportunity.

CHAPTER 11

Technical Analysis

U p to this point we have been using fundamental analysis as a tool for investigating various stocks. But it's not the only tool. On CNBC, for example, you listen to a so-called technical analyst. On screen, you see different charts of a company. The analyst uses such unfamiliar terms as *resistance, consolidation,* and *trend lines.* Unfortunately, no explanation is given for these terms. Should you be listening?

The simple answer is: *Yes!* Keep in mind, though, that many academics believe that technical analysis is hogwash—some type of voodoo system. Rather, the academic world has focused on fundamental analysis. No doubt, fundamental analysis is extremely helpful. With it, you can spot deterioration in a company's finances, overvaluation relative to other industry players, and major industry trends.

Yet technical analysis has become a very important tool for Wall Street. Many top analysts use technical analysis. In a way, however, technical analysis becomes a self-fulfilling policy. That is, the more people that follow it, the higher the probability it will become a factor for future stock performance. For example, if investors look for a certain type of chart pattern—and it does appear on their screens—they are likely to buy or sell the stock. With enough volume, it can move the stock.

Thus, when analyzing a stock for a possible short, it is a good idea to use both fundamental and technical analysis.

So, what is technical analysis? In basic terms, it is when an investor looks at the patterns on a stock chart in terms of price and volume history. Sounds simple, huh?

As we will see, technical analysis can get complex. In fact, it is not uncommon for a stock chart to have two or more technical trends—one bullish and the other bearish!

Before the Internet, technical analysis was cumbersome. If you did not have the cash to buy sophisticated software systems, you had to draw the charts by hand. Of course, there are now a variety of good sites that help with charting, such as www.stockcharts.com and www.bigcharts.com.

Reading Stock Charts

A basic chart will have two axes. The vertical axis will show the price range and the horizontal axis shows the time period. In the stock chart for Microsoft in Figure 11.1, the price range is from $45 to $75 and the time is between March 2001 and March 2002. As you can see, there was quite a bit of activity during this time period. The activity can be charted in a variety of ways:

Line Charts.   This is the simplest chart used in technical analysis. Merely plot the closing price or average for any given time period. This can be done every day, or it can be weekly, monthly, and so on. Figure 11.1 shows a line chart.

What is meant by "plotting an average"? For technical analysts, this is known as a *moving average.* For example, a 10-moving average would take the average prices for the past 10 days and plot the result for today. The reason for this is to reduce the overall volatility in the chart and thereby to make it easier to see patterns. This is known as *smoothing.*

A common analytical technique is to track a stock's 200-day moving average. If the stock begins to fall below this support line, this signals loss of momentum and perhaps the trigger of a bear mode. In fact, the 200-day moving average can also be used to track the overall direction of the market (such as the Dow or S&P 500). Figure 11.2 shows the 200-day moving average for Microsoft.

For those with a shorter time horizon—say, less than six months—a 50-day moving average may be used or a 20-day moving average.

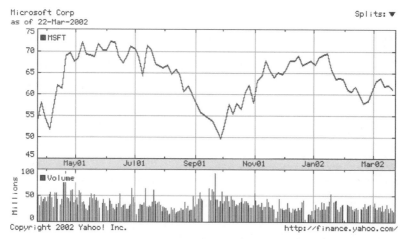

Figure 11.1   Stock Chart for Microsoft.

Then there is the *Bear Cross*. This is when the 50-day moving average falls below the 200-day moving average. This signals a bear mode.

Bar Chart.   The most common type of chart is the bar chart, which you see in Figure 11.3 for Microsoft. For each trading day, there is a vertical bar within the price activity chart. The length of each of these bars covers the high and low for the day. The small protruding bar to the left is the opening price and the small protruding bar to the right is the closing price.

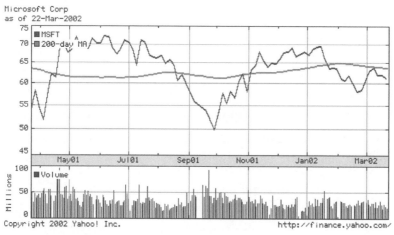

Figure 11.2   200-Day Moving Average.

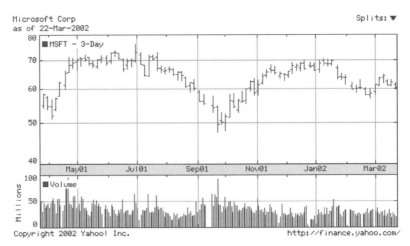

Figure 11.3 Bar Chart for Microsoft.

Below this chart, you will see the chart of volume for the stock. This is common for charting. The volume shows how many shares have traded for each day. The volume has a range from 20 million to nearly 100 million shares.

Candlestick Charts.   Figure 11.4 shows an example of a candlestick chart for Microsoft. However, we will look at these types of charts in detail later in this chapter.

What types of charts should short sellers use? It depends on your

Figure 11.4 Candlestick Chart for Microsoft.

time horizon. If you are a day trader—that is, you are looking for small gains over say several hours of time—then you should look at minute-by-minute bar or candlestick charts. If your holding period is between a day and a couple weeks, then use a daily bar or candlestick chart. If you are looking at 6 months to a year, then you might consider a weekly bar or candlestick chart. As you use charts more and more, you will develop your own preferences.

When analyzing a chart, try to determine the trends. The most common include:

Uptrend.   This is when a stock makes a series of higher lows and higher highs. To see if this is the case, get a ruler and draw a line that connects all the lows. If the line is going upward, then this is an upward trend.

Technicians look for breaks in the uptrend. A day trader may see this as a small change—even an intraday change of less than a 1 percent break in the uptrend. This could be enough for a day trader to go short on a stock. A short seller who has a longer-term horizon may look for a 5 percent change.

Keep in mind that there is no rule of thumb as to percentage. It is really a personal matter for investors.

Downtrend.   This is the opposite of an uptrend, in which there is a series of lower highs and lower lows. To see if this is the case, take a ruler and connect the highs. If the line is decreasing, then it is a downtrend.

Neutral Trend.   This means there are roughly equal highs and lows in price. That is, if the two lines are parallel, then the market is neutral.

There are two other key terms for technical analysis:

Resistance.   Suppose a stock reaches $50 per share and each time, falls back down. This price would represent the resistance level of the stock. That is, the market is not willing to buy the stock at this level. It is considered fully valued.

Some short sellers will short stocks that hit the resistance level. This can be a potentially dangerous move, though. Typically, when a stock breaks out of the resistance level, there can be a surge in the stock price, as other short sellers cover their positions in a short squeeze.

Support.   Suppose a stock hits $35 several times and does not break through. This is the support level. Whenever the stock does this, there are buyers who see opportunity.

As for short sellers, this may be an opportunity to cover a short position that is profitable. Or, if a support level is broken, a short seller may decide to short the stock. Breaking a support level is very negative for the stock price, especially if there is higher-than-average volume.

Traditional Bearish Chart Patterns

There are hundreds of different methods for technical analysis. However, there are some traditional methods that short sellers have used over the years. Let's take a look at the main ones:

Double Top.   As this implies, the stock has twice tried to pierce resistance, but has failed. This is usually on higher-than-average volume. After the second attempt, bulls are getting weary and bears are gaining the upper hand. This is usually indicated by lower-than-average volume. A sell-off may be in the offing and bulls move to take profits from the move. Figure 11.5 shows a double top for Gillette.

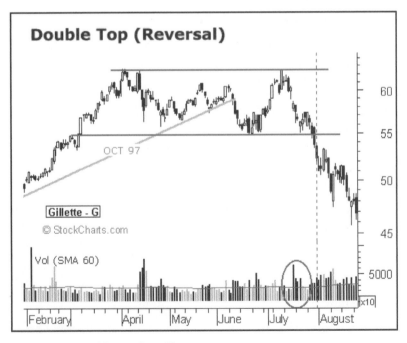

Figure 11.5   Double Top for Gillette.

Head and Shoulders Top.   This is similar to the double top, except that there is a higher formation between the left and right formations. As for the right shoulder, it should be lower than the left should and show lower-than-average volume. Just as with a double top, the bulls are running out of steam and the bears are getting the upper hand.

Figure 11.6 shows the head and shoulders top for C/Net, an Internet content company.

Volume

Volume is the amount of buying and selling for a security. Some technical analysts look at volume to help establish trends. The theory is that volume precedes price. If people are generally selling, then money is flowing out of a stock.

We will look at two indicators to help spot volume changes. These can be very effective when a security or market has been in a bull phase. If these volume indicators begin to fall, then it could be a sign that the security or market is poised for a fall as well.

Figure 11.6   Head & Shoulders Reversal for C/Net.

On Balance Volume (OBV).   Joe Granville presented this indicator in his 1963 book *New Strategy of Daily Stock Market Timing for Maximum Profits.* Here is the OBV formula: Add today's volume to a cumulative total when the security's price closes up and subtract the day's volume from the cumulative amount when the security's price closes down. This is graphed as a bar chart, such as that shown in Figure 11.7.

With the OBV, you want to look for a divergence. For example, if the price of the stock keeps increasing but the OBV is falling off, this is a sign that the stock will eventually fall. For example, in Figure 11.7 for Microsoft, the OBV was moving downward between May and June, after which the stock fell.

Accumulation/Distribution Line (ADL).   A top technician, Marc Chaikin, developed this indicator. While he thought the OBV indicator was a good step, Chaikin thought he could make some improvements. Here is one of the problems he had with the OBV indicator: Suppose XYZ stock closes at $50 per share. The next day, the stock opens at $45 per share. But by the end of trading, there is a huge rally and the stock closes at $49.90. According to OBV, this would be a negative day, even though the stock had a big rally.

Chaikin did not measure from one close to the next. Rather, he created a weighting system:

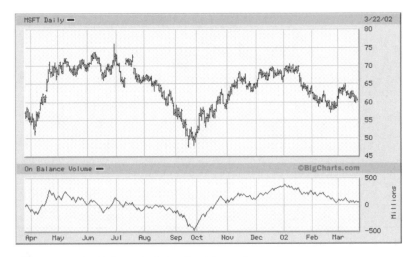

Figure 11.7   On Balance Volume for Microsoft.

- If the security closes at the high of its range, then add plus one.

- If the security closes between the high and low, then the value is zero.

- If the security closes above the halfway point of its range, but below the high, the value will range from zero to one.

- If the stock closes below the halfway point of its range, but above its low, the value will range from zero to negative one.

- If the security closes at the low of its range, then the value will be minus one.

The above number is multiplied by the volume and is either added to or subtracted from the cumulative total. The formula actually is somewhat complex, but most top financial sites will generate the graph for you.

A bearish signal would be if, after a bull run, the ADL begins to fall for a month or so. Figure 11.8 shows the Chaikin chart for Microsoft.

Figure 11.8 Chaikin Chart for Microsoft.

Stochastics

George C. Lane developed stochastics in the 1950s. Essentially, stochastics show momentum in stock prices—that is, whether a stock is overbought or oversold. A stochastic will range between 0 and 100 on the chart. There are two main types of stochastics: fast and slow. The fast stochastic will have two chart lines, the %K and the %D. The slow stochastic will take the fast stochastic and smooth it out. While the fast stochastic will give you bearish signs faster, it is subject to more false signals.

Generally, when a stochastic goes below 20, a stock is oversold and when a stock goes above 80, it is overbought. However, this does not mean you should necessarily short the stock when it has a reading above 80. It is not uncommon to see stocks—especially with strong momentum—continue to run up fast.

How do you play stochastics? One popular approach is to do the following: First, the stochastic goes above 80 and then it crosses below 80. But do not short here. Rather, wait until the indicator dips below 80 again and this is considered a sell signal.

Figure 11.9 shows the fast and slow stochastic for Microsoft.

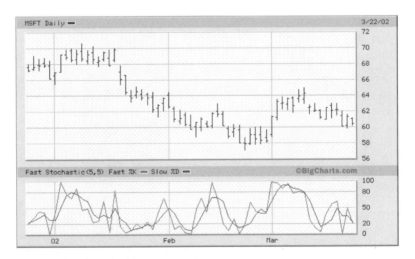

Figure 11.9 Fast and Slow Stochastic.

Bollinger Bands

John Bollinger developed the technical analysis tool called Bollinger Bands. He has his own newsletter, money management firm, and Web site (www.bollingerbands.com). He has been developing trading systems since 1977, when he bought his first PC. He is both a chartered financial analyst (CFA) and chartered market technician (CMT). The premise of Bollinger Bands is that stocks tend to trade in a certain range until there is a breakout. The Bollinger Bands work as follows: First, there is a 21-day moving average. Next, there is an upper band and a lower band. These are based on the standard deviation from the moving average. Talking about the theories of statistics and standard deviations are beyond the scope of this book, but the underlying idea of the Bollinger Band is that about 95 percent of the price volatility is contained within the bands. If the bands contract, then the volatility has lessened and vice versa.

Shorting strategies using Bollinger Bands include:

- Look for the bands to contract in a small range (compared to its chart history). Wait for the stock price to break below the lower band.

- Wait for the stock price to move above the upper band. Then wait for the stock price to fall below the upper band.

Figure 11.10 shows the Bollinger Band for Oracle. You can see

Figure 11.10 Bollinger Band for Oracle.

that in February and March the band started to shrink and the stock price broke below the lower band. After this, the stock continued to slide.

Moving Average Convergence–Divergence (MACD)

Technicians refer to moving average convergence–divergence as MACD. A common approach for the MACD is to calculate the 26-day and 12-day exponential moving averages (EMAs). The MACD subtracts the 26-day EMA from the 12-day EMA. This is the centerline, which oscillates above or below zero. If the centerline is above zero, then the 12-day EMA is trading above the 26-day EMA. If the centerline is negative, then the 26-day EMA is above the 12-day EMA.

Figure 11.11 shows the MACD for Microsoft.

There are three bearish MACD indicators:

Bearish Centerline Crossover. This is when the centerline moves below zero. It is important for the centerline to have been above zero

Figure 11.11   MACD for Microsoft.

for several weeks. Thus, a turn into negative territory would show there is strong bearish momentum.

Negative Divergence.   This does not happen as much as the other bearish indicators, but definitely shows strong bearishness. A negative divergence is when a stock increases in value or moves sideways, yet the MACD centerline declines.

Bearish Moving Average Crossover.   This is when the centerline goes below the 9-day EMA. This happens often and thus is not considered a very reliable indicator.

Relative Strength Indicator (RSI)

The relative strength indicator (RSI) shows the momentum of the stock—that is, whether it is overbought or oversold. The RSI ranges from 0 to 100. If a stock hits 30 or below, it is considered to be oversold. If the indicator reaches 70 or above, it is overbought. Figure 11.12 shows the RSI for Microsoft.

Figure 11.12   RSI Chart for Microsoft.

Short sellers have two main ways to play the RSI:

- The stock is in a downtrend and the RSI goes above 70 and then goes below 70.
- The stock price hits a new high, yet the RSI does not confirm. Instead, it makes a lower top. This is known as a bearish divergence.

Candlestick Charts

A popular technical analysis tool, candlestick analysis has its origins in sixteenth century Japan. The charts were used to predict the price for rice. In fact, some of the terms are quite colorful, such as the "Three Buddha Top" and the "Doji Star."

One of the first proponents of candlestick trading was Munehisa Homma, who built a fortune from rice trading. He even wrote two books on his investment techniques. For his achievements, he was named a Samurai.

Look at Figure 11.13 for an example of a candlestick chart for Microsoft. The thick vertical rectangle for each trading day is called *the real body*. This represents the range of the day's open and close. If the

Figure 11.13   Candlestick Chart for Microsoft.

real body is filled, it means that the close was lower than the open. This is a negative sign. And a white real body means that the close is higher than the open, which is a bullish sign. Moreover, if the real bar increases in size, this means the buying or selling is intensifying.

The thin vertical line at the top is the upper shadow and is the high for the day. The thin vertical line at the bottom is the lower shadow and is the day's low.

If a chart has a long upper shadow and small lower shadow, then this indicates that buyers were aggressive during the trading, but the sellers were able to reduce the price at the close. Then again, if a chart has a small upper shadow and a long lower shadow, sellers were aggressive, but the buyers were able to push the stock higher at the close.

Many traders like candlestick charts because it is easier to see trends as compared to bar charts. Actually, a candlestick chart has somewhat of a 3-d quality.

We'll take a look at the different bearish candlestick patterns. However, you should keep in mind the following for each bear pattern:

Bull Run. The market or stock should already have undergone a bull run. The bull run need not be long-term. It could, in fact, be a run lasting a few days. The bull run may be a security that is trading above its trendline or above a moving average (say 10 days or 20 days).

Confirmation. A sustained decline needs to have confirmation. This could be a security that has large volume, or has long black candlesticks. Another sign is a stock that has a gap down. This is a security that opens below the previous day's low and remains at or below this point until the close.

Let's take a look at some of methods to see when stocks turn bearish:

Doji Lines. There is no real body, since the open and close are the same price. There may be a shadow if the stock is up or down during the day's trading.

Although, traders may consider a Doji line to be present if the difference between the open and close is slight. For example, suppose a stock is trading at $50 per share. The stock opened at $50 and closed at $50.125. To many traders, this would be a Doji line.

A bearish Doji is one with a long shadow with the open and close at the low for the day.

Hangman.   This is where the chart shows a small upper real body and the lower shadow is long. It looks like a hangman. Basically, it is showing that the bears are getting the upper hand.

Engulfing Patterns.   This is when the real body is bigger (i.e., engulfs) than the prior real body. A bearish signal would be when a black real body engulfs a white body. The opposite—which is known as a *harami*—is also a bearish sign. Essentially, both show there has been a shift in momentum.

Dark Cloud Cover.   This is a long real black body that overshadows at least half of a prior long real white body.

Marubozu.   This is where the real body is long, but there are no shadows (essentially, the stock opened at the high and closed at the low). The word *marubozu* means "bald" in Japanese.

Shooting Star.   This chart shows a long upper shadow that is at least two times bigger than the lower real body.

There is a simple trading strategy that is fairly popular: Look at the color of the candlestick. If it is white, then do not short; if black, then short it.

Market Breadth

Keep in mind that many investors use technical analysis not only to help select stocks but also to predict the overall direction of the stock market. You can use all the technical analysis techniques discussed in this chapter to do just that.

However, there is a technical analysis technique that is used solely to predict the stock market; basically, it measures market breadth. *Market breadth* measures whether much of the market is participating in an advance. If not, the market may be weak and poised for a fall.

During the 1930s, Colonel Leonard Ayers, who worked at the Cleveland Trust Company, invented the advance-decline (A-D) line so as to measure market breadth. Simply put, this sums up the differences between the number of stock prices increasing and falling for a day.

This shows the breadth of the market. If the A-D line is increasing, the breadth is positive and vice versa.

The rule of thumb is that a market is poised to fall if the A-D line decreases for 3 to 6 months. This is called *negative divergence.*

A Talk with the Chartman

With an MBA and a job as a manager at IBM, Gary Smith was able to study a variety of industries because of his diverse customer base. One customer was Wal-Mart, which he thought was a good company in the mid-1980s. So, he started to invest. At first, he focused on fundamentals, but then transitioned to technical analysis gradually. Now, he completely focuses on technical analysis.

Smith believes that technical analysis is a "matter of pattern recognition. The more patterns you see, the better you will get at technical analysis." It's all about lots of practice.

He writes a column on technical analysis for TheStreet.com and has a daily premium newsletter. Known as "The Chartman," he is a regular on Fox News.

The following is an interview with the Chartman:

TAULLI: Why the transition to technical analysis?

SMITH: Through fundamental analysis, I was able to find good companies. But this does not mean they will automatically go up. I wanted to find the entry point. This is where technical analysis came in.

TAULLI: You are a trader, right?

SMITH: That's right. I don't want to tie up my money in positions for a long period of time. Instead, I will look for small gains. A successful trade may be a 2 percent gain or so for a week.

The way I look at it is that I'm compounding money. In fact, I think it is very important to have a short time horizon for short selling.

TAULLI: As you know, some think that technical analysis is voodoo.

SMITH: I look at technical analysis as pattern recognition. With it, I do not predict. I do not like to use that word. Technical analysis will not guarantee you anything. It is not a prophesy. It is saying that, given the pattern, the odds are that the stock will go up or down. I do not predict, I react.

TAULLI: Do you chart the overall market?

SMITH: I do. I will look at trends in the major indices. But I do not let this affect my decisions on individual stocks. If I see the S&P looks bullish, yet all my stocks are bearish, I will short these stocks.

TAULLI: Do you look at stochastics or the other complex technical analysis models?

SMITH: I keep things simple. Really, technical analysis can be boiled down to three things: price, volume, and time. All technical indicators are based on these three parts.

    What I look for are divergences. For example, suppose a stock has been trading between $95 to $100 in the past three weeks. Then, the stock closes at $92 on heavy volume. That is a divergence I take notice of. In other words, I try to keep things as simple as possible.

Conclusion

As you can tell by this chapter, there are many techniques for technical analysis, and you will eventually find those techniques that work for you. Even if you focus mostly on fundamental analysis, looking at a chart for confirmation can still be very helpful.

    In terms of short selling, technical analysis is something that can help in determining when is a good time to short. As we've seen in this book, it can take quite a lot of time for a stock to fall—even though there are many danger signs. Technical analysis, however, will show that investors are starting to get shaky. They are beginning to pull money out.

    Of course, technical analysis is a broad subject. And there are many good books on the subject, which we discuss in Appendix A. In this chapter, we were only able to scratch the surface and to point out what technical indicators short sellers look at.

    In the next chapter, we look at special-situation short sales. These are companies that are favorites of short sellers, such as tech and finance companies, as well as IPOs.

CHAPTER 12

Special Situation Shorts
Tech Companies, Finance Companies, and IPOS

You've followed the IPO market for the last few months, and yet it seems that every time you buy an IPO you lose money. You are now wondering if IPOs are actually good short sale candidates.

They could be. In this chapter, we will look at so-called special situation shorts. These are the kinds of companies that short sellers tend to focus on. They, of course, include IPOs and another form of IPO called tracking stocks. Other favorites of short sellers include tech and finance companies.

Tech Shorts

The core of technology is the binary system. Basically, it has two states: on or off. With this simple foundation, talented tech people can build quite sophisticated technology systems. In a way, tech stocks can be binary investments. Either they do very well or they flop. It is certainly an intensely competitive marketplace.

As an example, we will look at Palm. In March 2000, the company went public to much fanfare. The IPO was priced at $38 per share, and the company raised a hefty $874 million. The stock quickly hit nearly $170 per share.

As the name implies, Palm is an electronic handheld device to help organize information. Jeff Hawkins invented the technology in 1994 and had a hard time selling the devices. So, he sold the company to

3Com. With 3Com's distribution, Palm became the number 1 electronic organizer, with more than 90 percent market share.

No question, the Palm device was a great product and the IPO meant the company had substantial capital. However, the company faced a problem that all great tech companies face: transitioning from one technology to another.

In fact, tech companies typically have short product life cycles. A hot product can suddenly turn cold when a new innovation hits the marketplace. Thus, a tech company must be very nimble. But there are many problems a company can face in a technology transition, including:

- Competitors have noticed the success of the old product and have been developing their own.
- Users have high expectations and could be disappointed.
- Current users may be satisfied with the old product and do not want to spend the time and money for the new product.
- Users may put off buying the old products and wait for the new one to be released. Thus, a product delay could result in a falloff in revenues.

The above factors were certainly factors for Palm. First of all, Hawkins left Palm and created his own company, Handspring, which develops handheld products. He was able to raise large amounts of venture capital and took the company public, increasing Palm's competition. And, he was not the only competitor. Others included such major firms as Compaq, Sony, Casio, Microsoft, Sharp, Nokia, and Hewlett-Packard. These companies wanted to get a share of the profitable handheld market.

Next, Palm was primarily a consumer product. But the company wanted to enter the lucrative corporate market. After all, corporate customers typically have big budgets to make large orders. However, Microsoft had already developed the framework for a handheld device called the Pocket PC. Even though the cost was higher than a Palm, the Pocket PC integrated better with corporate information technology systems. Moreover, there was more functionality in the Pocket PC compared to the Palm system.

In addition, tech firm Research In Motion already had a large market share of the corporate market with its Blackberry product. The product was widely popular and worked quite well.

Another troubling sign was Palm's revenue streams. On the face of it, things looked bright for Palm, as it had three revenue streams—sales of handheld devices, wireless services, and licensing of its operating system software.

But under the surface, there were problems. Keep in mind that the basic Palm handheld device is a basic electronic organizer. You can store addresses, to-do lists, and calendars. The price can range from $100 to $200 for these models. While Palm was the clear market share leader in this market, by 2000, it still only had sold 7 million units since its launch in 1996. Actually, this is a low number for a consumer device. Apparently, the price point was too high to make the product mainstream.

To enhance the basic device, Palm created a wireless service called Palm.Net. With it, you can do e-mail, browse the Web, get access to news, and so on. The service ranges from $10 to $45 per month.

Again, the service may have had a high price point. Besides, Palm was competing against enhanced cell phones, which provided Internet access. Thus, these cell phones were more convenient for people than Palm's devices, since they had a dual purpose (no need to carry a cell phone and a handheld device).

Finally, Palm had a profitable business of selling its operating system software to other developers of handheld devices. Customers include: Handspring, Sony, and Nokia.

The problem? Microsoft. It has its own handheld operating system called Windows CE. By late 2000, Palm was coming under tremendous pressure. The demand for its products fell and the company was left with large amounts of inventory. There was also a brutal price war. Revenues fell by 65 percent from $471 million to $165 for the fourth quarter. The company had losses of $436.5 million. By 2001, the stock hit a low of $1.35. No doubt, it was a tremendous short for anyone who considered the many danger signs. Even as the news started coming out—such as when the company announced a shortfall in earnings and revenues—short sellers would have made more than 70 percent on their trades. See Figure 12.1 for the charting of Palm's stock decline.

Figure 12.1   Chart of Palm.

Talk to Experts

A key factor short sellers look for in tech companies is whether the technology is real or not. It is not uncommon for tech companies to promote a technology that is not innovative. Or, ironically enough, it may be too innovative. That is, the public is not ready for the innovation and the company is too far ahead of the curve.

Understanding a company's technology is no easy feat. First of all, it may be too expensive to even try to demo the technology (do you have the money to test a $100,000 enterprise software package?) Next, you then have to compare the technology to rivals.

How is an investor to do all this? Interestingly enough, even Wall Street analysts have difficulty. That is why they talk to experts in the field. You can too. And you should.

For example, Whitney Tilson, a portfolio manager, learned about competitive products to VISX from a talk with a doctor. "A few good questions can go a long way," said Tilson. "It meant that I did not buy any VISX when it was sky high."

Another example where outside experts were helpful to Tilson was with Sunrise Technologies. Like VISX, the company developed technology to improve eyesight. But Tilson saw many red flags:

• Its market segment was basically a niche.

- The company was taken public by a small underwriter (which was fined by the SEC and went bust).

- The company shifted its business model away from dental drills. The technology did not receive FDA approval because of safety issues.

- The company received a "going concern" opinion from its independent auditor.

- Some of the company's investors had been involved with pump-and-dump schemes.

- Of the 11 clinical investigators listed on the company's Web site for the company's eye laser, 9 were investors in the firm. It was a major conflict of interest and certainly cast doubts on the company's claims.

But Tilson went beyond this analysis. He also talked to experts in the field. He realized that the technology was not new, nor was it effective. He looked at the company's Web site and noticed that a chart of the product showed that after about 18 months, the procedure lost its effectiveness.

Thus, a company can hype its products for a few years. But eventually, investors will realize that a company is really nothing more than hype, and the stock will fall. Usually, the stock will collapse, giving short sellers an opportunity for substantial gains. Figure 12.2 shows the chart for Sunrise Technologies.

Figure 12.2   Chart of Sunrise Technologies.

Finance Companies

Some of the best shorts are finance companies. Tilson argues that finance companies are based on trust. If the trust is lost, investors and customers flee to the competition. The result can be a massive implosion. This is what happened to Enron. It also happened to savings and loans during the late 1980s.

One area to look for is finance companies that target less-creditworthy customers. When the economy is strong, these companies can do quite well, as their growth rates increase nicely. However, when the economy falters, it can be devastating for these companies.

This is what happened to the subprime finance companies in the late 1990s, as the economy went into recession. A variety of these companies saw their stock prices plunge and some went bust.

Despite all this, a subprime company, Providian, still had a strong stock price of between $40 and $50 per share in the middle of 2001. However, in the second quarter, Providian announced that it had to write off 10.3 percent of its customer base because they were essentially bad loans. Although the stock fell, it did not collapse. There were still believers.

Looking deeper at the financials, there were major red flags:

- The 10.3 percent was an increase from 7.4 percent from a year earlier. In other words, there was substantial erosion in the customer base. Loss rates for 1997, 1998, and 1999 were 6.3 percent, 7.6 percent, and 6.9 percent, respectively.

- As part of its business model, Providian gets customers and pools the loans. These loans are translated into stock (called *securitization*) that is sold to Wall Street. Providian attempts to make money on these sales. But with the significant increase in the customer base, it could be harder to sell these loans to Wall Street. Moreover, if the securitizations are lower, this means lower fees (a substantial part of the profits for Providian came from fee income).

- During the past year, the company had a marginal increase in its loss reserves. If losses continued, the company would eventually need to increase the loss reserve, which means pressure on growth.

- As the company was losing customers to default, it needed to increase its customer base to continue its overall growth rate. However, Providian had been decreasing its marketing expenditures. In the fourth quarter of 2000, marketing expenses were $180.4 million. By the second quarter, the expenses fell to $150.7 million.

- Providian was able to show strong growth because interest rates were falling. This meant that the cost of funds for Providian was falling. Meanwhile, Providian did not pass along these savings to customers. But then interest rates started to increase in the middle of 2001, putting pressure on the margins.

When the company reported its third quarter results, things were much worse. The company posted a 71 percent drop in earnings and warned that it would have a difficult fourth quarter. The company indicated that, because of increasing loan losses, it would stop lending to its riskiest customers. Moreover, the CEO resigned. Red flags abounded in the case of Providian, providing short sellers with ammunition to profit. Figure 12.3 shows the chart for Providian.

Providian's story is not unique. Another example of a shorting opportunity in the world of financial companies was NextCard. The

Figure 12.3   Chart of Providian Financial.

company was founded in late 1997 and used the Internet as its form of gaining new customers. In May 1999, the company had a red hot IPO at $20 per share.

In July 2000, it looked hopeful for the upstart company. The company announced that its breakeven date would be bumped up from the first quarter of 2002 to the fourth quarter of 2001. The company was upbeat about its loan growth and loan losses.

Interestingly enough, also in July 2000, CEO and cofounder Jeremy Lent, unexpectedly resigned. Lent had deep experience in the traditional credit card marketplace and was a visionary for the Internet approach. Sometimes a company will try to mute a bad press release with a good press release. Was this what NextCard was trying to do, that is, lessen the impact of the resignation? Was NextCard headed for trouble?

Red flags were flying:

- While Providian was able to increase its Internet customers by 1 million over a year period, NextCard only garnered 337,000 new customers.

- NextCard did not have much of a track record. Thus, looking at its historical loan loss rates was not an effective gauge. Were Internet customers good loan risks? Not necessarily. True, the company used sophisticated computer modeling to determine the credit worthiness of customers. Then again, NextCard's competitors did this, too. But would the models work when the economy tanked?

- Keep in mind that loan loss rates can be understated. For example, suppose XYZ has loan losses of $100 million. These losses are determined after the loans have been delinquent for 6 months. The total outstanding loans are $1 billion, so the loan loss is 10 percent. But this is misleading if the loan portfolio has been growing during this time. If during the 6 months, total outstanding loans increased from $700 million to $1 billion, then an argument can be made that the loan loss rate is really $100 million divided by $700 or 14 percent. As for NextCard, it posted loss rates below 10 percent but it was also showing strong growth in its loan portfolios.

- Compared to the industry, NextCard had a low loan yield. This is the difference between what NextCard charges its customers and its cost of money. Example: Suppose NextCard can borrow money at 5 percent and lend it at 10 percent. The difference is the loan yield, which is a 5 percent profit. The reason for the low yield rate was that the firm offered many teasers to get new customers (that is, lowered the cost of the cards).

- Even though NextCard claimed that its customer base had a relatively lower risk profile, this was not borne out in the loan loss rate. Rather, NextCard appeared to be similar to a subprime lender, such as Providian. But, while Providian had a high loan yield to compensate for the risk, NextCard did not.

Compared to the industry, NextCard had a high customer acquisition cost (it ranged from $80 to $100 per customer).

Customer acquisition is different on the Net. In general, if a customer is looking for a credit card, he or she is probably a higher risk as compared to someone who is solicited for business, such as through a phone call or direct mail.

NextCard had a high customer turnover rate of 25 to 30 percent . One reason for this was the teaser rate. After the teaser expired and the credit card interest rate increased, customers stopped using the card.

In late October 2001, NextCard announced that it suffered from substantial fraud losses and credit losses. It said that federal regulators wanted the company to increase its reserves, but there was not enough capital to do this. The stock fell by 84 percent in 1 day. Its investment banker, Goldman Sachs, was hired to sell the company. It did not happen. Instead, Nasdaq halted trading in the stock of NextCard at 14 cents per share pending an inquiry. Figure 12.4 shows a chart of NextCard.

With finance companies, you need to make industry comparisons. If the economy begins to falter, those finance companies that lend to higher credit risks can see rapid deterioration in their business. Also, if a finance company does well when the rest of the industry is not, then there is probably aggressive accounting. This can be a good short, as was the case with Providian.

Figure 12.4   Chart of NextCard.

Shorting IPOS

An IPO is initial public offering of a company's stock. It is the first time
a company offers its shares to the public. In most cases, there is much
fanfare and hype. In fact, it is not uncommon to see IPOs surge 20 percent or more on the first day of trading. Investors will usually sell into
the surge and take profits (this is known as flipping).

When the IPO market turns cold, there will likely be huge plunges
in many new issues and these plunges could be good short selling possibilities. This is what happened to the IPOs for 1999. For example, in
December 1999, the IPO of VA Linux skyrocketed 698 percent on its
first day of trading. It would be the highest point of the stock. By March
2001, it was trading below $2 per share. Figure 12.5 shows a chart of VA
Linux.

While IPOs can represent good shorting opportunities, keep in
mind that it is difficult to short stock within a few days of the IPO.
The reason is that a broker needs shares to lend to the short sellers
and these shares do not appear in accounts until a few days after the
IPO.

Despite this, there are several useful considerations in evaluating
IPOs:

Figure 12.5 Chart of VA Linux.

Who's Leading the Financing of the IPO?

The underwriter is the Wall Street firm that prepares a company to go public. If the underwriter is a small firm, then the IPO could be a good short sale candidate. Unlike the major underwriters—such as Morgan Stanley, Merrill Lynch, and so on—the small ones have difficulty providing a company with analyst support and aftermarket trading. In many cases, the stock becomes an orphan, as the small underwriter takes its fee and goes to the next deal. Moreover, small underwriters typically raise small amounts of offering, say under $50 million. In other words, the IPO company will not have sufficient capital to execute its business model.

Most underwriters will do firm commitment IPOs. For example, suppose XYZ company wants to go public. The underwriter will conduct due diligence on the company to see if it is appropriate for being a public company. If so, the underwriter will conduct a variety of presentations to investors (called road shows) to raise capital. Hopefully, there will be enough interest. Suppose there are commitments from institutional investors to raise $100 million. However, the company only wants to raise $80 million. This means the IPO is oversubscribed by $20 million.

The night before the IPO, the underwriter will write a check to XYZ for $80 million. This is a firm commitment. That is, if during the next day the market crashes and investors do not want to buy stock, the underwriter will be responsible for the $80 million payment.

This is rare, though. Most likely, the underwriter will be able to sell the $80 million in shares. But these shares will not be sold for $80. The underwriter may sell the shares to investors for a total of $85 million. The $5 million difference is the fee for the underwriter.

If an underwriter does the IPO on a "best efforts" basis, this means it will not write the check for $80 million. Instead, the underwriter will try to find enough investors for the $80 million. If no investors are interested, the underwriter is not obligated to the company. These tend to be lower-quality companies and short sale candidates.

Interestingly enough, some companies will not use the services of an underwriter. Instead, in what is termed a *self-underwritten IPO* or a *direct IPO,* the company will conduct its own IPO. These can be good short sale candidates. Reasons include:

- Most likely the company could not hire an investment bank.
- There is no outside due diligence.
- There is little analyst coverage.
- There is little aftermarket support.

Because of the reasons above, it is usually no surprise that these types of IPOs—direct IPOs or small IPOs—do not perform well in the aftermarket. Simply put, there is little support for the shares. In fact, there may be a lot of buyers in the IPO who flip their stock to make a quick profit. The stock then starts to fall, giving short sellers an opportunity for profit.

Lock-Up Expirations

The lock-up period is a clause found in most IPO deals that prevents employees of the company from selling any stock 6 months from after the time of the IPO. Without the lock-up agreement there may be a temptation to dump the stock to take a profit—which would put undue pressure on the price.

Then again, when the lock-up period expires, employees can dump their stock . And, yes, the stock price usually falls. Some investors will keep track of expiration periods and short the stocks when the appropriate amount of time elapses.

The underwriter has the discretion to shorten the lock-up for some or all of the insiders. If you see this happen, this is an indication that the company could be a good short. You can find the lock-up period in the company's prospectus or you can visit an IPO site, such as www.ipo.com, which tracks lock-up periods.

Analyzing the Prospectus

For a company to do an IPO, it must provide all investors with a prospectus. The prospectus is not fun reading, but it has crucial information. A company must disclose all material information.

A useful section to look at is Risk Factors. As you read various prospectuses, you will notice recurring risk factors (often they are the same word-for-word, regardless of the company). Basically, conservative corporate attorneys write risk factors and many of the clauses become boilerplate language.

But there are some risk factors outlined in the prospectus worth looking at that are specific to a company:

Litigation. Lawsuits can be expensive and drain a company's management. Moreover, litigation is inherently unpredictable. Who really knows what a jury is going to award? True, it is common for companies to be subject to litigation. However, for short sellers, focus on litigation that could result in a big judgment—such as a product liability case or environmental destruction. Even if a company ultimately prevails in the litigation, it will likely have been an expensive fight—in terms of legal fees and resources of management. While a company is fighting a lawsuit, the competitors can be focusing on their core business. Litigation distractions can be a favorite for short sellers.

Customer Concentration. If a company's sales come from a few customers, there is a big risk to the revenue base. For example, when the Internet bubble burst, many young IPO companies lost their customer bases as other Internet companies went bankrupt.

Changing Business Model.   Some companies will change their business model based on the latest fad. This is a major red flag. Will the company be positioned to take advantage of the new industry? What about the investments made to capitalize on the prior business model? Answers to questions such as these could indicate that the company is floundering.

Competition.   In many cases, a company will have tremendous competition. Be careful about those companies that are going head-to-head with huge competitors. This was the case with upstart telecom companies, many of which collapsed in the tech wreck of 2000–2001.

Take the example of Covad. The company provided high-speed Internet access called DSL (digital line subscriber). In January 1999, the company went public with much fanfare. The stock price went from $18 to $30.25. In all, the company raised $167.4 million.

Prior to this, the company had raised a staggering $152 million in venture capital. There were also key strategic agreements with AT&T, Qwest, and NEXTLINK. But an inquisitive investor would have found the following risk factor in the prospectus:

> All of the largest ILECs present in the Company's target markets are conducting technical and/or market trials or have entered into commercial deployment of DSL-based services. The Company recognizes that each ILEC has the potential to quickly overcome many of the issues that the Company believes have slowed wide deployment of DSL services by ILECs in the past. The ILECs currently represent and will in the future increasingly represent strong competition in all of the Company's target service areas. The ILECs have an established brand name and reputation for high quality in their service areas, possess sufficient capital to deploy DSL equipment rapidly, have their own copper lines and can bundle digital data services with their existing analog voice services to achieve economies of scale in serving customers. Certain of the ILECs have aggressively priced their consumer asymmetric digital subscriber line ("ADSL") services as low as $30-$40 per month, placing pricing pressure on the Company's TeleSpeed services. The ILECs are in a position to offer service from COs where the Company is unable to secure collocation space and

offer service because of asserted or actual space restrictions, which provides the ILECs with a potential competitive advantage compared with the Company. Accordingly, the Company may be unable to compete successfully against the ILECs, and any failure to do so would materially and adversely affect the Company's business, prospects, operating results and financial condition.

An ILEC is an incumbent local exchange carrier, which is a mega telecom carrier. Even though Covad raised a tremendous amount of money, the fact remained that the ILECs had even more money. They also had more branding and infrastructure. The ILECs also felt threatened and were not going to allow upstart companies like Covad take away a new industry. As a result, the ILECs used their resources to wage a price war against the DSL companies. The ILECs were no match and the DSL industry evaporated. By 2001, Covad was in bankruptcy. Figure 12.6 shows a graph of the Covad's stock.

Besides Risk Factors, there are some other enlightening sections to the prospectus:

Management Compensation. In this section, salaries and stock option compensation are disclosed. Does it look excessive compared

Figure 12.6 Chart of Covad.

to other companies in the industry? Also, there are management résumés. Do managers have strong experience in the industry? Do they have any notable prior success? Have they run public companies before?

In some cases, management may have questionable pasts. Have there been any securities violations or even criminal ones? Have there been prior bankrupt companies?

Look for nepotism. Is a son or daughter in an executive position or on the board of directors? If so, the company may not necessarily have weak points in its management structure. Decisions may be made based on personal reasons, not for business reasons. Also, is the company doing significant business with a family member? Such deals could ultimately be to the detriment of the company.

Going Concern. On the face of it, this seems like a harmless phrase. But it is not. This is a red flag and short sellers love it. A company's auditor will provide a "going concern" statement in a prospectus if it believes the company is in jeopardy of going bust.

Selling Stockholders. This lists all the major investors, directors, and officers that are selling stock at the time of the IPO. It is not unusual to see some selling. After all, the officers and founders have probably gone several years with low salaries. The IPO is a reward for their hard work.

However, if there is a large amount of selling—say the officers are dumping 20 percent or more of their stock—then this is a sign that the stock may fall.

Use of Proceeds. Usually this is a vague statement. The company will indicate that management will spend the money any way it wants. But sometimes there will be specific requirements for the cash. A common one is to pay down debt. While this will reduce overall interest costs, it still means a company has less money to grow its operations. If 40 percent or more of the proceeds goes to pay down debt, this is a danger sign.

A spin-off (which is explained below) also will have a use of proceeds section. In some cases, the parent company will take a substantial portion of the money for itself (say 40 percent or more). This could stunt the growth of the new company.

Spin-Offs and Tracking Stocks

Wall Street likes a story it can understand. However, as a company gets bigger, it becomes more difficult for analysts to really understand the focus of the company. In fact, the company may not have much of a focus.

To bring focus, a company might decide to spin off one or more divisions to shareholders. The theory is that the company is worth more separate than together.

There are certainly a variety of benefits for the spin-off:

- It will have its own stock that can be used to raise money or make acquisitions.

- The spin-off is often a great PR opportunity. The press likes to write about them.

- The spin-off may have an easier time striking deals with customers. For example, when Lucent was a division of AT&T, it had difficulty making deals with other telecom companies because of the fear of helping out a major competitor. When Lucent was a separate company, it was much easier.

Despite these benefits, spin-offs can be great short sale opportunities. To spot one, look for the following:

- Did the parent company take most of money raised in the spin-off transaction?

- Did the parent company place large amounts of debt on the balance sheet of the spin-off?

- Is the growth rate of the spin-off lagging? In other words, the spin-off may be an attempt by the parent to get rid of an underperforming division.

Also, look at the structure of the deal. If it is a so-called tracking stock, then it could be a good short sale candidate. As it does in a spin-off, the parent distributes shares of a subsidiary to existing shareholders when it creates a tracking stock. What's different?

Most importantly, the new shareholders of the tracking stock do not own anything. Rather, the company merely tracks the performance of a division of a bigger company. It's kind of a way for a parent company to have its "cake and eat it to." An example of a tracking stock was NBCi. It was essentially the consumer Internet operations for General Electric. Issued in 1999, NBCi zoomed like every other Internet company. At one point, the stock was over $100 per share. But that would quickly end. Even the legendary CEO of GE, Jack Welch, could not stop the slide. In April 2001, GE bought back NBCi for about $1.32 per share.

Here are other problems with tracking stocks:

- *Tracking stocks have no takeover value.* Typically, when one company buys another it is for a higher price. However, in the case with tracking stocks, a takeover is nearly impossible. Why? The main reason is that a tracking stock represents no ownership. So, an acquirer would not have control of the company. *No one is looking out for stockholder interests.* Theoretically, the board of directors is supposed to support the interests of the shareholders of the tracking stock. However, the tracking stock does not have its own board; rather, the board is from the parent company. So, is the board representing you or the interests of the parent? Chances are the board is looking out for the parent.

- *Tracking stocks have nutty valuations.* You typically see tracking stocks when the market is at excessive levels. In fact, this can be an indication that a market is poised for a fall. An example was in the late 1990s, when many brick-and-mortar companies attempted to spin off their online divisions. At first, the stocks did quite well, but it was a short. As seen above with NBCi and many others—such as Disney's Go.com—these Internet tracking stocks crashed.

Conclusion

Tech stocks, IPOs, and finance companies all offer investment opportunities, short or long, but, as always, be careful when shorting tech stocks. Even a company that is based on hype and little else can reach excessive levels. But when these companies begin to falter, the fall can be big. The same is the case with IPOs and finance companies.

If the risks seem too high or you do not have the time to engage in in-depth analysis, then it is a good idea to find someone who can. This can be done through a mutual fund or even a hedge fund that focuses on short selling. We will look at these types of investments in much more detail in the next chapter.

CHAPTER 13

Mutual Funds That Walk on the Bear Side

You have been investing aggressively over the past few years and have built up a substantial nest egg. But you are fearful. Will the stock market continue its rise? Or will it plunge, wiping out all your hard-earned appreciation? You really do not have an answer—in fact, no one can know for sure. However, you do not want to take any chances and decide to do some short selling to hedge your portfolio. But you simply do not have enough time to do your own research. Rather, you are looking for mutual fund that can help out.

Actually, there are mutual funds for virtually anything—including short selling. In this chapter, we will call these short funds. There are many types of short funds, as we will see shortly. Keep in mind that these funds are all new. The reason is that until the Taxpayer Relief Act of 1997, mutual funds were restricted by the "short-short" rule. This prevented mutual funds from generating more than 30 percent of gross income from gains from short sales.

The repeal of this rule does not mean that mutual funds have carte blanche to short sell. There are still important restrictions that are meant to protect investors from extreme volatility within a fund. For example, a fund may not invest more than 25 percent of its assets in any position, and margin may not exceed 30 percent of assets.

But for many investors, mutual funds are a great way to do short selling without the hard work of researching individual stocks. Despite this, it is important to do enough homework to find the funds that are right for you.

Background

Basically, a mutual fund is a pool of capital that is managed by one or more professional money managers. Key benefits for investors include:

- *Liquidity.* So long as the markets are open, you can sell your shares (these sales are known as redemptions).

- *Diversification.* A mutual fund will invest in at least 20 or more stocks. Thus, if some stocks go down, hopefully the others go up. However, of course, this does not always happen, especially when there is a bear market, in which case most stocks fall.

- *Affordability.* Mutual funds make it easy for most people to invest. The minimum range to enter, or buy, a mutual fund typically is from $1000 to $5000. Or, you can set up a periodic investment program in some mutual funds. That is, you can invest a fixed amount—say $100 or more—each month or quarter. These payments can come directly from your bank account.

- *Reinvestment.* You can reinvest dividends and capital gains from the fund back into more shares of the fund.

One crucial benefit of a mutual fund is its professional management. A professional manager spends full time in getting the best performance for the fund. Of course, just like anything else in the investment world, there are good and bad portfolio managers. So, before buying a short fund, try to do as much research as possible on the portfolio manager.

Look at the manager's years in the industry, finance degree and the Certified Financial Analyst designation, and investment philosophy.

In fact, before buying a mutual fund, the firm must send you a prospectus. Much of the document is dry, but there are key sections. For example, there are bios of the portfolio managers. Also, feel free to call the fund and ask any questions. Ask to see if they can send you any more information and perhaps even résumés of the portfolio managers.

There are also good Web resources for information on mutual

funds, such as Morningstar.com. The site has an incredible amount of information, covering almost every mutual fund. Morningstar is famous for its mutual fund rankings, which analyze both overall return and risk for a fund for a 3-, 5-, and 10-year time period. If the fund is in the top 10 percent of its class, then it receives a 5-star rating. A 1-star is a fund that is in the lowest 10 percent.

Morningstar even has a Bear Market Ranking. Essentially, this indicates how a fund performs in down markets. The ranking goes from 1 to 10. The lower the ranking, the better the performance in bear markets.

Fees

To get the benefits of mutual funds, you need to pay a variety of fees. These fees are expressed as a percentage of your investment. For example, suppose you invest $10,000 in a fund and the fees amount to 2.5 percent. In this case, your fees will be $250. In other words, the fund must increase by $250 before you start making money.

The fees are broken down as follows:

- *Management Fee.* As the name implies, this is the fee that compensates the money managers. The fee will typically range from 1 to 3 percent.

- *Administrative Fee.* This is the fee to cover the costs of mailings to shareholders, customer support, leases, and record keeping. This fee ranges from 0.2 to 0.5 percent.

- *12b-1 Fee.* This is a fee that helps with the costs of marketing and distribution of the fund. The fee ranges from 0.25 to 1 percent.

- *Expense Ratio.* This includes the fees for management, and administrative fees.

These types of fees cannot be avoided (although, some mutual funds do not charge 12b-1 fees). Despite this, it is a good idea to compare each fund's fees. If a fee seems to be out of line with the rest of the peer group, then you probably should avoid the fund. A high fee can certainly eat into your return.

Some funds may charge commissions. Try to avoid these if you can. This is especially the case if a broker is not helping you select the fund.

After all, the commission is meant as compensation for a broker or financial planner.

There are three types of commissions:

Load. This is a commission you pay when you buy the fund. The fee can be as high as 3 percent of your investment.

Level Loads. These are also called C shares. For example, the fund may charge a load of 3 percent, but spread it out over a certain amount of time (say five years).

Redemption Fees. If you sell a fund, you will pay a fee. This can range from 0.25 percent to 2 percent.

Hidden Costs

Keep in mind that there is a hidden cost with mutual funds: turnover. This is the percentage of the portfolio that has been sold over a 12-month period. If the turnover rate is high, a mutual fund will tend to incur higher costs. In regard to short funds, they usually have high turnover ratios, largely because these funds usually do not hold positions for the long term. Moreover, if a stock surges, the fund will likely cover the position.

A high turnover can mean higher taxes for the mutual fund investor. These tax distributions are done at the end of the year. So, before buying a bear fund, make sure it has already paid out its distributions.

In the rest of the chapter, we will look in depth at some specific short funds.

Choosing Short Funds

If you do not have the time to do extensive research, a mutual fund is the best approach. Basically, you are allowing professional money managers to do the homework.

There are many different types of short funds, and we will look at each. However, this book will not recommend any. Mutual funds can change quickly. A manager may leave or the direction of the firm may be different. Thus, even if you do go the route of mutual funds, there is still some homework required. Moreover, you will need to monitor the fund—say on a monthly basis. Is the fund doing well compared to its peers? Morningstar.com can be a great resource for this tracking.

A question arises: Why even buy a short fund? Why not just buy a regular mutual fund instead? Aren't there many good-performing mutual funds that provide diversification and good returns? True, there are good mutual funds that do not short. However, it is a good idea to have some percentage of your portfolio in short funds or short positions. This is not to say that you should have all your portfolio in short positions. This would be very risky. Besides, history has shown that markets tend to rise over time. Having 10 or 15 percent of your portfolio in short positions is a reasonable amount.

Bear Mutual Funds

As the name implies, bear funds really expect the worst. The portfolio managers believe that the markets will be in a prolonged bear phase. Accordingly, their portfolios will have many short positions. Or these funds may be invested in defensive stocks—such as food companies— that do well in any type of market (after all, we all need to buy food, right?)

Appendix B lists a variety of bear mutual funds.

Indexing

An index is a way for investors to measure their performance. If the Dow increased 10 percent in the past 6 months, but your portfolio is up 15 percent, then you are beating the market by 5 percentage points. However, over the years, it is difficult to beat the general markets. In fact, it is a well-known fact that many mutual fund managers wind up underperforming the market over time.

As a result, some mutual funds believe if you can't beat the market, why not join it? That is, these funds buy the same stocks as the indexes and, as a result, track the overall performance. This is known as indexing.

In the mid 1970s, the mutual fund leader Vanguard introduced the first indexed mutual fund for individual investors. Called the Vanguard 500 Index Fund, it tracks the performance of the S&P 500 Index. And it has been a wild success, becoming the world's largest mutual fund. No surprise, many other mutual funds have jumped on the indexing bandwagon.

Generally, an index fund requires minimal professional portfolio management. In other words, the job of the portfolio manager is not to pick winning stocks, but to mimic the performance of a given index. This type of portfolio management is called "passive" management. This usually translates into lower portfolio management fees.

Several investment companies have set up index funds to short markets. These are a relatively new phenomenon. However, these funds have performed quite well during the bear markets of the late 1990s and early 2000. Bear index funds come in two flavors:

> *Inverse Funds.* For every 1 percent decline in the index, the fund will increase by 1 percent and vice versa. For example, suppose the S&P falls 1.2 percent in today's trading. Since an inverse does the exact opposite of an index, the index fund will increase in value by 1.2 percent

> *Double Inverse Funds.* For every 1 percent decline in the index, the fund will increase by 2 percent and vice versa.

Appendix C has a list of the myriad of inverse index funds.

The following interview with Chuck Tennes, a portfolio manager at an inverse index fund called Rydex, should help you to better understand this new type of investment.

TAULLI: Give us some of the background of the funds.

TENNES: We started up in 1994 and started our Ursa fund to short the S&P 500. We followed that up with the Arktos fund that shorts the Nasdaq 100. As you can probably see, we use Greek words for our funds. Ursa and Arktos mean "bear."

We think we have fairly good coverage by having funds for the S&P 500, Nasdaq 100 and Treasury bonds.

TAULLI: What about performance?

TENNES: As you know, we started our short funds during the bull market of the 1990s. So, the performance does not look strong at all. Then again, the funds did what they were supposed to do, that is, track the benchmarks.

During the bear market, we had our time in the sun. In the fourth quarter of 2001, our fund was the top in the nation. However, in the next quarter, this was not the case.

TAULLI: Your advice is not to chase the latest fad?

TENNES: That's right. It is a mistake to go after the hottest funds. They tend to be overtaken the next few quarters by the next hottest funds. Rather, you should practice the principles of asset allocation.

TAULLI: How do investors use your funds?

TENNES: Our funds have no loads. Nor are there penalties for redeeming the shares. This makes it very easy to get in and get out of funds.

It is true that some of our investors are traders and are speculating. But the biggest part of our investor base uses our funds for hedging their portfolios.

TAULLI: How can you tell?

TENNES: Interestingly enough, when the markets are surging, we see a surge in our funds. In other words, people consider the markets to be overheated and want to protect their portfolios from a possible fall.

I like to say that the market is not binary. That is, it is not a matter of either being in the market or out of the market. With our index funds, you can protect the gains you have generated over time. However, many investors think that they have no choice but to sell. But this creates transaction costs, disrupts your asset allocation, and results in capital gains taxes. Much of this is avoided by hedging a portfolio with index funds.

TAULLI: You have mentioned that your funds can be useful for non-market factors.

TENNES: That's right. For example, suppose you have built up a nice portfolio from the bull market. But, you want to buy a car in the next several months. During this time, you want to make sure the market does not fall 40 percent. An index fund can hedge your portfolio for the next few months.

With index funds, you can essentially pitch the level of your overall comfort to the market.

Another example was Y2K. We had customers who thought there could be a disaster from malfunctioning computer systems. These investors hedged their portfolios a few days before Y2K. When there was no disaster, the investors sold off their funds.

TAULLI: So far, all your funds are passive index funds. Do you plan to offer actively managed funds?

TENNES: It's unlikely. With an actively managed fund, you have little transparency. You have little idea what your portfolio manager is buying or selling. It's very secret—until months after the fact.

An index fund is very transparent. You know exactly what the portfolio manager is investing in. There are no surprises.

Besides, we have leveraged funds. In a sense, this is like having an active portfolio manager. If you believe an index will fall or rise, you can emphasize this position by a factor of two.

TAULLI: Another advantage to index funds is lower costs.

TENNES: That is true. But we do not claim to be the lowest cost fund, like a Vanguard. Then again, we are not the highest cost fund, either. By allowing investors to get in or out quickly, we have additional costs. There are also extra costs for leveraged funds.

TAULLI: Are their strategies that investors can use with your funds?

TENNES: Certainly. We have realized that as we offered different funds, our investors have been creative in how they use them in combination. An interesting example is the S&P 500. The index has a good number of technology stocks. But what if you are bearish on tech, but bullish on the rest of the market? In this case, you can buy the S&P 500 fund, but then purchase the inverse fund for the Nasdaq 100, which is heavily weighted for tech stocks. By doing this, you tend to wash out much of the tech exposure.

Long–Short Funds

Even in bear markets, there are some stocks that go up. That is the philosophy of long–short funds. As the name implies, these funds will both buy stocks and short them. In fact, the strategy is very similar to the net-long hedge funds discussed in Chapter 1. But, unlike with most hedge funds, you do not have to be a wealthy investor to participate in long–short funds.

Essentially, long–short funds try to get healthy returns—such as 10 percent or so per year—without much volatility. Yet, so far such funds have had a difficult time doing this.

One argument is that the mutual fund structure is a hindrance. While hedge funds do not have the problems with dealing with redemptions, this is not the case with long–short mutual funds. During some periods, the fund may have too much money to invest; in other periods, the fund may be forced to sell positions in order to meet redemptions from its investors.

Another problem has been investment strategy. Many long–short funds will purchase value stocks and short growth stocks. But in the late 1990s, value stocks did not perform well and growth stocks soared.

Appendix D lists a variety of long–short funds.

HOLDRs

It was Merrill Lynch that invented the HOLDR. A HOLDR is a security that represents ownership in common stock or ADRs (American depository receipts) of a particular industry or sector group. This is a liquid investment that allows an investor to diversify among 20 or more stocks. Without a HOLDR, an investor would have to spend much more money buying these stocks, as well as incur the transaction costs.

As an investor in a HOLDR, you have the same rights as a shareholder that owns the stocks in the portfolio. You can vote your shares and receive dividends.

The fees are substantially lower than a mutual fund as a HOLDR has an 8 cents per share annual custody fee. You have to pay a regular brokerage commission for the transaction.

While you can only sell a mutual fund at the end of the trading day, you can purchase a HOLDR at any time when the market is open, although, you must buy in round lots of 100 shares (no odd lots are allowed).

You have the right to cancel your HOLDR. This means that you will receive the individual shares in your HOLDR security. There is a fee of up to $10. This is not a taxable event.

Another advantage is taxes. Unlike mutual funds, there are no surprise tax distributions at the end of the year. You are only taxed on the gains in the stocks in your portfolio.

HOLDR Sectors

Biotech	Oil Services
Broadband	Pharmaceuticals
B2B Internet	Regional Banks
Europe	Retail
Internet	Semiconductor
Internet Architecture	Software
Internet Infrastructure	Telecom

The first HOLDR was for the Internet sector, launched in September 1999. The HOLDR hit a high of $192.13 and eventually collapsed to $23.90.

Investors can short HOLDRs. Moreover, the short sales are exempt from the tick rules. Why the exception? The HOLDR is known as an exchange traded fund (ETF) and any ETF is exempt from the short sale rules.

With the success of the HOLDRs, there was a proliferation of ETF products in the marketplace. However, there are two main differences between a HOLDR and these ETFs. You can buy odd lots of an ETF, but cannot cancel it and get the shares in the portfolio. Here's a look at some of the more popular ETSs.

DIAMONDs: This tracks the Dow Industrial Average.

Qubes (NASDAQ: QQQ): This tracks the Nasdaq 100. This is the most heavily traded ETF.

SPDRs (Spiders): This stands for Standard & Poor's Depository Receipts. This is a group of ETFs that track the S&P and its different industry sectors.

StreetTracks: State Street Global Advisers manages these ETFs. The securities track different indexes, such as for technology and global markets.

VIPERs: This stands for Vanguard Index Participation Receipts. These are ETFs that are based on the Vanguard mutual funds.

Hedge Funds

A hedge fund is a form of investment that is geared mostly to wealthy individuals or institutions. Moreover, hedge funds can have steep minimum investments—say $1 million or more.

However, there are new types of hedge fund products that make it easier to in terms of minimum investments (some go as low as $25,000). These hedge funds are known as *fund of funds*. Basically, a portfolio manager will select a variety of other hedge funds for you. Thus, you do not need to do the extensive homework necessary to research the funds. Nor do you have to pay the high minimums to invest in a variety of funds. Also, the portfolio manager will monitor the funds for you.

Not all hedge funds short stocks. In fact, there are a myriad of hedge funds that pursue nonshort strategies. Some hedge funds focus on distressed securities; some will speculate on currencies; some will even do buyouts of companies. So, if you are interested in investing in a hedge fund, make sure you get the background of the fund strategy and the résumés of the portfolio managers. You are entitled to this information. Even if you belong to a fund of funds, you should still get information on the different funds the portfolio manager has invested in.

Morningstar.com does not cover hedge funds. But one site that provides a wealth of information on hedge funds is www.hedge-world.com. It is a good start if you are thinking of investing in hedge funds.

Conclusion

Short funds can be quite volatile. When markets crash, these funds do very well. When markets soar, they do terribly. As stated earlier in this chapter, it is not a good idea to put a substantial amount of your wealth in these types of funds. So what type of fund you should select? Really, this is a decision based on your research or even income (such as in the case with hedge funds). If you are a wealthy investor—with a portfolio exceeding $1 million—then considering a hedge fund makes sense. If not, an alternative would be an index fund that tracks broad indexes, such as the S&P 500. Having such an inverse index fund in your portfolio can help reduce to overall volatility.

14

Tax Strategies
Don't Get the Short End of the Stick

L et's say that during the past year, you have done a variety of short sale trades. As with typical investors, some trades were good and others were not so good. Your brokerage has sent you tax forms for your trading activity. You've read the forms but do not quite know what to make of them. Are there special things—in terms of taxes—that you should be aware for short selling?

Absolutely. In this chapter, we will take a look at some of the opportunities to reduce your taxes. We will also warn you of potential traps.

Capital Gains Taxes

The IRS divides income into two types: ordinary income and capital gains. Ordinary income includes wages, dividends, interest, rents, and even prizes. Capital gains, on the other hand, involve the purchase and sale of a security, such as a stock, mutual fund, or real estate.

Example: Suppose you buy 100 shares of Sky Rocket Corp. for $10 each. The stock price increases to $15 and you sell the stock. You have a capital gain of $500 ($5 gain times 100 shares). If the stock falls to $5, and you sell it at that price, you have a capital loss of $500.

There is no difference with a short sale transaction. However, in the above examples, we reverse everything. The first transaction is a capital loss of $500 and the other is a capital gain of $500.

Generally, you do not have to report capital gains or losses until you sell your shares (or, in the case of selling short, buying the shares). This is called *realizing your gain or loss.* That is, your paper gains or losses have become real. There is a difference with a short sale. You realize the trade by not selling stock; instead, you do this by delivering shares to close out the trade.

Note: If you generate a capital gain from a short sale transaction and then reinvest the proceeds into another stock, you still will be required to pay taxes.

For a short sale, you need to know the following to determine a capital gain or loss:

- The date of sale
- The amount realized from the sale (from this, you deduct the brokerage commission)
- The date of covering the stock
- The cost of covering the stock, which is known as the cost basis (to this, you add the commission)

Let's take an example: You short 100 shares of Collapse Corp. at $10 each on August 1, 2001. The commission on the trade is $10. The amount realized is $990.00 (100 shares × $10 each = $1,000, minus the $10 commission). In October 2002 (14 months later), you cover your short position by buying 100 shares of XYZ for $5 each. The commission is $10. The cost basis is $510 ($500 plus the $10 commission). The capital gain is calculated as follows:

$$\text{Amount realized} - \text{Cost basis} = \text{Capital gain or loss}$$
$$\$990 - \$510 = \$480$$

Your brokerage firm will send you a tax form known as a Form 1099-B, usually in January of the following year from when the trades were made (in 2003 for trades made in 2002). Most firms will report the amount realized on the short sale trades. If not, you or your CPA will need to make the calculation. Then again, it is a good idea to check the Form 1099-B anyway. Sometimes there are mistakes.

Suppose you shorted stock but did not cover during the tax year. You will still receive the Form 1099-B indicating the total proceeds from the sale. This does not mean you owe any taxes. Rather, you will indicate on your Schedule D (which reports any capital gains and losses) that this is an open short sale position. Moreover, the Schedule D has instructions on how to handle this.

Capital gains are classified as either short term or long term. This is a critical distinction, because it can have a big impact on the amount of taxes you pay.

If your trade is a short-term gain, you must pay taxes according to ordinary tax rates. Table 14.1 shows the tax rate for married couples for 2002 (keep in mind that these rates are subject to change depending on any changes in the tax law from Congress).

The capital gains tax rate is much better. If a person is in the 15 percent tax bracket, the capital gains are taxed at 10 percent. The capital gains rate is 20 percent for anything above this tax bracket.

To get this favorable tax treatment, an investor must hold onto the stock for at least 1 year and 1 day. This is classified as a long-term capital gain. If not, it is a short-term gain and the investor's gain is taxed at the ordinary income tax rates.

Why? The rationale is that Congress wants investors to hold onto their securities for the long term. So, it is no surprise that investors attempt to convert short-term gains into long-term gains.

The 1-year requirement is what Congress thought was appropriate. Of course, Congress could change this—or even eliminate it.

TABLE 14.1   Tax Table for Couples
Filing Jointly

Taxable Income	Tax Rate
$0–$12,000	10%
$12,001–$46,700	15%
$46,701–$112,850	27%
$112,851–$171,950	30%
$171,951–$307,050	35%
$307,051 and over	38.6%

Short Sale Gains and Losses

Unfortunately, when dealing with short sales, the distinction between short-term and long-term gains can be tricky. Here is a look at the different possibilities of computing gains:

Possibility 1.   You short 100 shares of Big Fall Corp., which is trading at $15 per share. You do not currently own any shares of Big Fall. About 14 months later, you cover the short at $10 per share, making a capital gain of $500. But this is not considered a long-term gain; rather, it is a short-term gain. Why? The IRS believes you have not *owned* the stock for more than 1 year. Instead, you have borrowed stock for more than 1 year.

On the other hand, if you covered the short when the stock price was at $20 per share, you would have a short-term loss of $500.

Possibility 2.   You short 100 shares of Big Fall Corp. for $10 each. Two months later, you buy 100 shares of Big Fall for $12 each. But you do not use the shares to cover the short.

More than a year elapses and you sell the 100 shares for $15. The IRS will deem this a short-term gain. So how does the IRS tell whether you've simply bought the stock or you have covered the short? When you cover a short, you must indicate this to your broker. This is placed on your trade confirmation, which is reportable to the IRS.

For the 100 shares that you bought, the holding period does not start until you cover the 100 shares of Big Fall.

Possibility 3.   You buy 100 shares of Big Fall Corp. for $10 each. Three months later, you short 100 shares of Big Fall for $10. You do not use the 100 share of XYZ to cover the short. In about 10 months, you use the 100 shares to cover the short at $5 per share. Even though you held on to these 100 shares for more than 1 year, the transaction is still considered a short-term gain.

Possibility 4.   You buy 100 shares of XYZ for $10 each. After 1 year, you short 100 shares of XYZ for $12. In 2 months, the stock falls to $8 and you buy 100 shares to use to cover the short. This is considered a long-term capital gain even though you used stock—which you held less than one year—to cover the short.

Note: The four possibilities above do not apply for so-called excess shares. To understand this, let's take a look at Possibility 2 and make a change. You short 100 shares of Big Fall Corp. for $10 each. Two months later, you buy 200 shares of Big Fall for $12. Basically, the excess shares are those shares that do not match the amount of shares that you have shorted. In this case, it is 100 shares that you purchased.

So, a year later, you do not use 100 shares that you bought to cover the 100 share short position. Rather, you sell the 100 shares for $15. This is considered a short-term gain. But, if you sold all 200 shares, the additional 100 shares would be considered a long-term capital gain.

Most likely, you will have both short-term capital gains and losses. For the tax year, you net out all these transactions. Suppose you have $20,000 in short-term gains and $10,000 in short-term losses. You will have a net capital gain of $10,000. Unfortunately, this will be taxed at ordinary income rates.

Suppose the reverse happens and you have a short-term capital loss of $10,000. Again, there is bad news. You can only deduct up to $3000 against your ordinary income, not the whole loss of $10,000. The remaining $7000 in losses can be used for future years. This is known as a *carryforward* (there is no expiration for these carryforward losses). If next year, you have a net short-term gain of $2000, you can offset this with $2000 from your $7000 carryforward and then use $3000 to deduct from your ordinary income. You now have a $2000 carryforward.

Just as with short-term capital gains, you will add up all the long-term capital gains and losses to find the net amount. If you have a positive amount, you pay either 10 or 20 percent. If there is no gain or a loss, there is no tax owed. You can deduct up to $3000 in net capital long-term losses against ordinary income and carry forward anything above this amount.

There are four tax scenarios:

Long-Term Gain; Short-Term Gain. This is fairly straightforward. The long-term gains are taxed at either 10 or 20 percent depending on your tax bracket, and the short-term capital gains are taxed at ordinary tax rates.

Long-Term Loss; Short-Term Loss. If the losses are $3000 or less, then you can deduct this amount against ordinary income. What if it is more? Is the carryforward long-term or short-term? The rule is that you must deduct your short-term losses first. Example: You have long-term losses of $4000 and short-term losses of $2000. You apply the $2000 in short-term losses and then $1000 in long-term losses to add up to the $3000 to deduct against ordinary income. Then the remaining $3000 in long-term losses will be the carryforward.

Long-Term Loss; Short-Term Gain or Long-Term Gain; Short-Term Loss.   The rule is that whatever amount is greater is how it is classified. For example, you have a short-term loss of $5000 and a long-term gain of $10,000. You take the difference of the two, which is $5000. Since the long-term is the higher amount, this would be a long-term capital gain of $5000.

Worthless Stock

Finally, let's say that you short 100 shares of XYZ at $10 each and within a year, the stock goes to zero. You should certainly be happy, since you do not have to cover your short. You get to keep the $1000.

Then again, why not delay the gain, so you do not have to pay taxes for many years? The IRS has caught onto this and now requires that, when a stock becomes worthless, you must recognize the gain immediately.

What is considered worthless? If a stock is still trading—even if it is selling below a penny—it is not worthless. The best approach is to call your broker. He or she should have the details on whether a stock is worthless or not. IRS Publication 550 has more information regarding worthless stock.

Dividends

Suppose you short 100 shares of XYZ at $100 per share. The company pays a dividend of $1 per share every year. Thus, since you are borrowing the 100 shares, you must pay $100 in dividends each year.

You can deduct the $100 payment so long as the following applies:

• You itemize your deductions

• You hold the short for at least 46 days

If you meet the above criteria, you can make this deduction on Schedule A of the 1040 (the deduction is known as an *investment interest expense*). This is a deduction against your ordinary income.

However, if you do not meet the two criteria above, you still have a tax benefit. That is, you can add the $100 to your cost basis of your investment. In this case, the cost basis would be the price at which you cover the short sale. If this is $5000, then you add the $100 to this and your cost basis is $5100.

Trading Expenses

If you have any investment-related expenses—such as for investment publications, newspapers, newsletters, and software—you might be able to deduct these on Schedule A. You can also deduct margin interest on Schedule A.

These would be considered miscellaneous expenses. However, these expense must exceed 2 percent of your adjust gross income (AGI) to be allowed. Example: You have investment expenses of $1000 and margin of $500. Your AGI is $100,000. You would not be able to deduct the $1500, since it is only 1.5 percent of your AGI.

The IRS allows for more tax benefits if you are considered a "trader." What is a trader? The IRS does not provide a concrete definition. As with any other aspect of taxes, it is important to have a qualified account help you make such determinations. Although, generally speaking, a trader has the following characteristics:

- Spends much time on trading (it's almost a job)
- The trading is done for short-term purposes, holding stock for less than 30 days

As you can see, this is quite vague. To be safe, it is best to get professional help from an accountant, tax attorney, or the like.

If you are considered a trader, your investment expenses and margin interest are reported on Schedule C. The advantage is that there is no 2 percent minimum requirement that is the case for miscellaneous expenses.

Constructive Sales

As seen above, for a short sale transaction to be taxable, a gain must be realized. In most cases, this happens when you buy back the underlying security at a gain.

What are the exceptions? Let's take an example. Suppose you own 100 shares of ABC Corp. You bought these shares 3 years ago at $10 each and now the stock trades for $40. You want to lock in the gain, yet not pay any taxes on the transaction. One approach is to "short against the box." This means you will short 100 shares of ABC at $40 per share. Thus, suppose the stock price falls $5. The 100 shares you own will fall $5 in value, but the short position will increase $5 in value. Basically, there is no way the value of your position can fall (nor increase, either).

Until 1997, this transaction did not result in a transaction that was considered realized, that is, taxable. Unfortunately, this changed with the Taxpayer Relief Act of 1997. In the above example, you would have a long-term capital gain of $30 per share or $3000. This is known as a constructive sale. The holding period on your 100 shares will restart and the cost basis will be the amount of the short sale or $4000.

In fact, it does not matter in what order the transaction is made. For example, 3 years ago, you shorted 100 shares of ABC Corp. at $20 per share. The stock falls to $10 per share. You do not cover the short, but instead buy 100 shares at $10 each. This is considered a constructive sale. The holding period for the 100 shares will begin now and the cost basis will be $1,000 (100 shares times $10).

To skirt the constructive sale rule, an investor may be tempted to have a family member or related person make the offsetting transaction. However, the IRS forbids this.

There are exceptions to constructive sales:

- There must be a gain in the stock.
- You cover the short position no more than 30 days after the end of the tax year and hold onto your long position for 60 days after. In fact, after the 60 days has elapsed, you can take another short position and start the same cycle again.

Wash Rule

You buy 100 shares of XYZ for $10 each and after 6 months, the stock falls to $5. You still like the prospects of the company, but want to use to the $500 loss against other gains from your portfolio. So, you sell the stock and a few days later, buy it back for $5 each. Can you take the gain? No. You have violated the "wash rule." Basically, you need to wait 30 days to buy back the stock.

The wash rule also applies to short sale transactions. Unfortunately, it is more complex (even the IRS has trouble with it). There are two ways the rule applies: a replacement purchase or a replacement sale.

Example: You buy 100 shares of XYZ for $10 each on January 1. By June 1, the stock is trading for $5 each and you decide to short 100 shares. Three days later, you then buy 100 shares for $5 each. On August 1, you cover the short sale by delivering the stock you bought on January 1.

In this case, the short sale is a losing transaction. The shares were purchased at $10 and the stock was shorted at $5. The loss is $500. And the time between the trades was more than 30 days. So the wash sale does not apply, right? No. It does.

The wash sale can occur on the day of the short sale, not on the day of the covering of the short sale, if both of the following requirements are satisfied:

- On the day of the short sale, you own identical stock.

- You later deliver the stock you already own to cover the short position.

These are both met in our example. Thus, we look at the transactions between June 1 and June 4. The purchase of 100 shares on June 4 is considered a replacement purchase and a violation of the wash rule. You will not be able to take the loss for the August transaction. Instead, you add the $500 loss to the basis of the replacement purchase.

Let's take an example of a replacement sale: You short 100 shares of XYZ at $10 each. After 2 months, the stock rises to $12. You cover the short position and take a $200 loss. But you still think the stock will fall and within a few days, you short another 100 shares at $12. This would be a violation of the wash rule and you would not be able to deduct the loss.

Another example: You buy 100 shares of XYZ and short 100 shares of XYZ. The current stock price is $10. The stock increases $2 and you decide to take a loss on your short position by covering it. Then, a few days later, you decide to sell your long position and make $200. This is a violation of the wash rule and you cannot deduct the $200 loss.

Learning More

Interestingly enough, there are few resources for understanding the complex tax rules for short selling. However, there is a good book on the subject called *Capital Gains, Minimum Taxes: The Essential Guide for Investors and Traders.* The author is Kaye Thomas, a Harvard-educated tax attorney. I had an opportunity to interview him:

TAULLI: What are some good resources for understanding tax strategies for short selling?

THOMAS: The rules for short selling are definitely arcane. It takes some time to orient yourself to the rules. In terms of resources, I would first look at the IRS Publication 550. The IRS generally has very good publications that are written in plain English. Keep in mind that the publications are not perfect. In some cases, there are inconsistencies. Also, IRS Publications are not meant for financial planning but instead for understanding the basics.

You can get the IRS Publications at a local office, by calling or going to the Web site www.irs.gov. I also like the publications from JK Lasser. Their books are comprehensive, easy to understand, and well-indexed.

TAULLI: Are there areas that investors slip up on?

THOMAS: There is a quirk in the tax law that many short sellers and even tax preparers do not know about. First of all, if you buy a stock long, the sale for tax purposes is the transaction date. That is, it is the date you submit the order. So, if you put in an order for December 31, 2001, the sale is for the tax year of 2001.

But this is not the case for short selling. Rather, the date is when the stock is settled. This is when you receive the actual shares. Currently, it takes 3 days for a trade to settle. Thus, if you cover your short on December 31, it will not settle until 3 business days and the sale is for 2002, not 2001.

TAULLI: Do you recommend a professional tax preparer for short sellers?

THOMAS: In general, I recommend a qualified tax professional. Unfortunately, many do not have a good understanding of short sale rules. And it is not easy finding one. In many cases, they are in areas that have large financial districts, such as Chicago or New York.

While I recommend that you get a professional, I think it is important that you do not take his work at face value. Ask many questions and try to learn as much as you can. It can be very helpful.

In fact, a good resource is to go to financial sites that have discussion boards on taxes. A good one is Motley Fool (www.fool.com). I also have my own discussion board, in which I answer the questions personally. The site is at www.fairmark.com.

Conclusion

As you can see from this chapter, the tax rules for short selling are not easy. No doubt, it will take some time to get a feel for them. But you should not feel intimidated. In fact, you might even teach your tax accountant a thing or two about the rules.

Basically, the IRS makes it harder on short sellers. While it is easy to get favorable long-term capital gains treatment when you buy a stock, it is almost impossible when you short a stock. True, the IRS claims that you really do not own the stock; rather, you have borrowed it, so this time period does not count in determining if you have a long-term capital gain. Then again, there is no reason this can be changed.

Another key tax issue is the constructive sale. It was quite common for investors to lock in gains. But this makes much less sense now, since it is considered a sale and is taxable.

In taxes, as in many other aspects of short selling, there are restrictions that you will not find with buying a stock. It's the nature of the game. For the most part, short selling does not have much support in Congress. So do not expect many changes in the taxes or the restrictions on short selling.

Short Selling Resources

Bear Journalists.   Simply put, there are but a handful of journalists who focus on troubled companies. In a way, it can be a tough profession. If a journalist writes a negative report on a company, it is likely to result in quite a bit of complaints from those that are long on the stock, which could make it difficult for financial journalists to maintain productive relationships with their sources. However, from popular financial media such as *Barron's* to TheStreet.com, there are many whose expertise can be relied on.

Short sellers may find it helpful to refer to the writings of the following top financial journalists:

Jonathan Laing.   *Barron's* is known for having a somewhat skeptical approach. One of their top writers is Jonathan Laing, who analyzes company financial statements deeply. Laing was one of the first journalists in 1997 to closely scrutinize Sunbeam's earnings.

Christopher Byron.   You can find Christopher Byron's columns on MSNBC, in the *New York Observer*, and even in *Playboy*. Byron has written about investing for more than 30 years. One of his most famous "calls" came in 2000 when he targeted Exodus Communications. Despite a high of $80 in March 2000, Exodus was poised to fall. But with the industry slowing and Exodus facing massive amounts of debt, the writing was on the wall. Shortly after Byron's story, the stock plummeted when Exodus announced it was filing for bankruptcy.

Whitney Tilson.   Portfolio manager of his namesake fund, Whitney Tilson is not a short seller. However, his articles, which appear on The Motley Fool (www.fool.com), can be very helpful in spotting short sale candidates. Tilson also has his own Web site http://*www.tilsonfunds.com/*.

Herb Greenberg.   Aside from a year as an analyst for an investment partnership, Greenberg has spent most of his career as a journalist.

For RealMoney.com (which is part of TheStreet.com), Greenberg writes a widely followed column about good short candidates. Greenberg also writes a monthly column for *Fortune*. His research and analysis is always thorough. Greenberg's tenaciousness paid off when in early 2000, his research indicated that the B2B software solutions firm AremisSoft was in trouble. Within months of the publication of Greenberg's expose, the SEC froze AremisSoft assets and its stock plunged to 69 cents per share.

Financial Newsletters.   Financial newsletters have been a part of Wall Street for many decades. While certainly there are plenty of respectable publications available to subscribers, there is a perception that the field consists of mostly market amateurs or snake oil salesmen who write investment newsletters. In fact, in the digital age, it is not hard to start an online market newsletter. Despite this, newsletters can be a great source of investment information. Actually, Forbes.com has a weekly column devoted to profiling newsletters.

Following is a roundup of newsletters that focus on the short side of the market. However, this is not an endorsement of the newsletters. It is a good idea to get a sample report and see the historical performance results before making a decision to subscribe.

Short on Value (http://www.shortonvalue.com).   Will Lyons has published *Short on Value* since 1992. This monthly newsletter provides an in-depth list of 30 stocks that are considered overvalued. The newsletter also establishes a model hedge portfolio.

Lyons also has a telephone hotline for subscribers (there is a new message each Monday). In some cases, he will provide an interim hotline if the markets are volatile.

Before starting the newsletter, Lyons was a commercial banker with Citizen & Southern for 11 years. He has a graduate degree in international business from the University of South Carolina.

For the most part, the focus is on financial statement analysis. However, Lyons does use some technical analysis. He recommends the www.stockcharts.com as a source for technical analysis charts.

There are some caveats from Lyons. He does not use put options for short sells. He thinks this is too risky and expensive. Moreover, he does not short biotech or medical products companies. First, he believes that you need an incredible understanding of medicine to make informed decisions. What's more, the Federal Drug Administration (FDA) can have an enormous impact on the stock price—whether the drug is rejected or adopted.

An annual subscription is $169, obtainable at this address:

Short On Value
2779 Claimont Road, Suite F-9
Atlanta, GA 30329
404-636-9092

Oxford Club Communiqué http://www.oxfordclub.com). Founded in 1984, Editor C. A. Green's *Oxford Club Communiqué* focuses on short sale candidates in global markets. Prior to 1984, Green was a Wall Street analyst for about 15 years.

Green focuses on companies that show "declining market share, lower earnings, severe losses, high debt levels, expensive litigation, and management incompetence."

Examples of some of his shorts:

- K-Mart from $40 to $1. He saw a troubling decline in market share in 2001.

- Daimler-Benz from $78 to below $40. He is a skeptic of mergers (Daimler-Benz merged with Chrysler.)

- Freeport Copper and Gold from $20 to $8. He thought that the industry had weak pricing power.

ShortBoy.com. The editor is Bill Ginsberg, who started his service in 1996 and only focuses on big-name companies that are highly liquid. This makes it much easier to borrow stock for short sales.

During every trading day at 11 a.m. Eastern time, he issues a short selling trading strategy on a particular stock. He indicates the price to short at (using a limit order) as well as at what price to cover. He also recommends using a buy-stop price for the trade (limit and buy-stop orders are explained in the Chapter 3).

An annual subscription to ShortBoy.com (obtainable online) is $119.

Grant's Interest Rate Observer (http://www.grantspub.com). James Grant started this newsletter in 1983. Despite the fact the title says "Interest Rate," it is really a comprehensive publication that covers not only the general economy but companies that look shaky. Of course, Grant takes a skeptical look at companies that take on large amounts of debt—which could signal a good short sale opportunity.

An annual subscription to Grant's newsletter is $725.

Grant's Financial Publishing
30 Wall Street
New York, NY 10005
(212) 809-7994

There are also several good newsletters that try to predict the overall market:

InvesTech Research. Jim Stack has published his InvesTech Research newsletter for more than 20 years. He does not like to follow the consensus.

Stack places a lot of emphasis on the actions of the Federal Reserve and has an extensive monetary database that goes back over 90 years.

Stack's was one of the few newsletters that anticipated the crash of 1987, and he called the bull market in 1991.

A one-year subscription costs $175. Contact: 1-800-955-8500.

InvesTech Research
2472 Birch Glen
Whitefish, MT 59937

Dow Theory Letter. This letter focuses on technical analysis.

The publisher of the Dow Theory Letter is Richard Russell, who started the newsletter in 1958. In 1998, he bought out Martin Zweig's newsletter, giving him a combined 7000 subscribers. An annual subscription is $250 and the website is http://www.dowtheoryletters.com.

Dow Theory Letters, Inc.
PO Box 1759
La Jolla, CA 92038-1759
858-454-0481

Institutional Research Services. There are a handful of firms that publish independent research on short sale candidates. These firms focus primarily on institutional clients and may charge $10,000 or more per year for the service.

While this is a price point that excludes many individual investors, these institutional services can be very influential. So, it is a good idea to pay attention to them (they are often quoted in the press). Also, these services provide Web sites where you can get sample reports (which can be good learning experiences).

Off Wall Street. Mark Roberts heads the operation and has seven analysts on staff. Since 1993, he has made 138 short recommendations, of which 118 were winners.

Roberts looks for the following:

- Companies that are poised for 50 percent drops
- Strong likelihood of negative earnings surprises
- Strong fundamental analysis calls to competitors, suppliers, and analysts

Off Wall Street
PO Box 2647
Cambridge, MA
617-868-7880
www.offwallstreet.com

Badger Consultants. The head of the operation is Tom Chanos, who is the brother of James Chanos, a well-known money manager of a short selling fund. Like his brother, Tom focuses heavily on a company's financial statements.

Asensio & Company (http://www.anensio.com). Manuel Asensio's firm develops in-depth research on short sale prospects and also manages portfolios for investors. Former CFO of a merchant bank and an analyst with Bear Stearns, he has more than 20 years experience in the financial industry. For the most part, he tries to uncover those companies he thinks are really frauds. And, in his reports, he is not afraid to mince words. If he thinks a company is a fraud, he will certainly say so. As a result, Asensio is often sued by the companies he targets.

Asensio publishes all his analysis on his Web site.

Behind the Numbers.   David Tice started the firm in 1988. The tag line is "quality of earnings, warnings, and sell recommendations."

Tice's philosophy is to:

- Find stocks that can plunge and rip apart a portfolio (he refers to these companies as "torpedo stocks")
- Try to anticipate events that disappoint investors
- Place heavy emphasis at analyzing quality of earnings
- Focus on "grassroots" securities analysis, such as discussions with customers, suppliers, competitors, and even governmental agencies
- Focus on mid- to large-capitalization stocks usually owned by institutions

Here is Tice's contact information:

Behind the Numbers
8140 Walnut Hill Lane, Suite 300
Dallas, TX 75231
214-696-5474
www.behindthenumbers.com

Center for Financial Research and Analysis (CFRA).   The founder of the firm is Howard Schilit. Some have called him the "Most Hated Man on Wall Street," since he publishes penetrating reports on companies that engage in aggressive accounting.

But Schilit has a big following. His fans call him the "fraud detective." According to Schilit: "We provide research to more than 400 investment firms. We are not recommending that a stock be sold. Rather, we look at the financials and try to determine if a company is hiding things."

In fact, Schilit's reports can be influential. When they hit the Street, it is not uncommon for stocks to fall. In some cases, he is the first person to blow the whistle on a suspect company. Examples include Microstrategy and Rite Aid.

In late 1999, CFRA transitioned its paper-based publications to appear only on the Net. The service has these components:

Daily Research. These are full-length reports, news reports, and updates based on extensive analysis of SEC filings.

Company Database. You can conduct searches of prior reports.

Customized Research Projects. If you want research conducted on a company not covered by CFRA, you can request a custom report.

Portfolio Monitoring. CFRA has sophisticated modeling software that helps to detect early warning signs of problems.

Center for Financial Research & Analysis, Inc.
6001 Montrose Road, Suite 902
Rockville, MD 20852
(301) 984-1001

Web Sites

There are a variety of short-oriented Web sites. Unfortunately, many are sub-par. For example, the sites may just be a place to link to other sites. Or the site may talk about conspiracy theories and the end of the world. Short sellers should be skeptical when searching for financial information on Web sites. However, there are some good sites:

ComstockFunds.com.   This is the Web site for the bearish mutual fund Comstock Partners (the fund is discussed in detail in Chapter 13). Portfolio managers Marty Weiner and Charlie Minter provide engaging daily commentary on their views of the markets.

PrudentBear.com.   This is the Web site of David Tice, who is the portfolio manager of the Prudent Bear Fund and the editor of the publication *Behind the Numbers.*

The site includes:

- Links to short-related stories from the Web
- Anecdote of the week

- Quote of the day

- Commentary articles

- Book reviews

- Research reports

- Bears' Den (an online chat room)

- Short Seller's Challenge (you can submit a short sale idea and see if yours is the best performer)

- Books

In this book, we have looked at technical analysis and financial statement analysis. Both subjects are quite extensive and this book obviously could not include everything. But there are good books on both subjects.

Here are top books for technical analysis:

Technical Analysis of Stock Trends (8th Edition) by Robert Edwards, John Magee, and WHC Bassetti. This is a classic in technical analysis. In fact, this was the first book that set out the modern concepts of technical analysis. The book has been updated for using the Net, new exchanges, and portfolio management.

The Visual Investor: How to Spot Market Trends by John Murphy. The book is not only easy to read, but even includes helpful software programs. As the title shows, the book takes a visual approach to charting, not complex mathematical models. According to the book: "They say a picture is worth a thousand words. Maybe they should have said a thousand dollars. After all, we're talking here about using pictures to make money." John Murphy is one of the top technical analysts. He is a regular on CNBC and has his own consulting firm.

As for financial statement analysis, a great book is Howard Schilit's *Financial Shenanigans: How to Detect Accounting and Fraud in Financial Statements*. Another good book is *Quality of Earnings* by Thornton L. O'glove. The book is engaging and easy to understand. The author provides many tips for uncovering red flags in a company's financials.

BEAR FUNDS

Gabelli Mathers (MATRX).   Henry Van der Eb is the portfolio manager. He has managed the fund for more than 20 years and is a CFA.

There is little doubt that Eb is very bearish. In his 2001 message to shareholders, he said the fund is "positioned to take advantage of a sustained stock market decline."

In fact, Eb was also very bearish before the crash of 1987. He was also positioned for a downturn in 1990 and 1998.

Contact Information

Gabelli Funds
One Corporate Center
Rye, NY 10580-1434
800-422-3554

Comstock Capital Value (DRCVX).   The comanagers are Charlie Minter and Marty Weiner. Minter has worked on Wall Street since 1966. Weiner has been in finance since 1959 (where he started as a securities analyst with the SEC). He has held the CFA designation since 1969.

The investment philosophy is to look at the long-term economic forces in the world. From there, the firm will either buy or short any type of asset class, such as foreign stock, bonds, and even real estate investment trusts. The portfolio managers will also use derivatives.

The managers believe that the stock markets are involved in the biggest bubble in the history of finance, and since 1996 they have not bought any stock.

Even as the markets continued to surge, the portfolio managers did not relent on their bearishness. And by 2000, the fund started to make money, as it shorted highfliers like Cisco, Oracle, and Amazon.com.

Contact Information

> Comstock Capital Value Fund
> One Corporate Center
> Rye, NY 10580-1422
> 800-422-3554

Prudent Bear Fund (BEARX).   David Tice has managed this fund since late 1995. He is a CFA and CPA. He has been a long-time bear on the market and believes that the market hit unsustainable valuation levels in the late 1990s.

He shorts those stocks that he believes are poised to drop. He also takes bets on the direction of the market, such as by shorting futures on such market indexes as the S&P 500 and Nasdaq 100.

Tice has his own Web site, PrudentBear.com, in which he writes his commentary on the market. For more information on this Web site, see the Appendix A.

Contact Information

> Prudent Bear Funds
> 8140 Walnut Hill Lane, Suite 405
> Dallas, TX 75231
> 888-778-2327

Grizzly Short Fund (GRZZX).   The coportfolio managers are Steven Leuthold and Charles Zender. Leuthold is the founder of this mutual fund and has more than 20 years experience on Wall Street. Zender has been with the Leuthold Fund since 1991.

There is little information on the fund since it was founded in June 2000.

Contact Information

1-800-273-6886

Robertson Stephens Contrarian (RSCOX).   The fund has three man-
agers. Paul Stephens is the founder of the investment bank of Robert-
son Stephens (which is now part of BancBoston). He has been
managing private portfolios since 1975. Andrew Pilara has been with
Robertson Stephens since 1993 after leaving his firm Pilara Associates.
Before this, he worked at Dean Witter Reynolds. Rick Barry worked at
Regal Asset Management and Merrill Lynch before joining Robertson
Stephens.

Contact Information

RS Funds
388 Market Street, Suite 200
San Francisco, CA 94111
1-800-766-3863

Inverse Index Funds

Potomac Funds

Contact Information

1-800-851-0511

Funds Offered

Name: OTC Short (POTSX)

Management: The portfolio manager is James Apple, who has managed the fund since 1997. Before this, he was a portfolio manager at Rydex and the Rushmore Funds.

Style: Inverse Correlation

Index: NASDAQ 100

Name: US Short (PSPSX)

Management: James Apple

Style: Inverse Correlation

Index: S&P 500

Name: Small Cap Short (POSSX)

Management: James Apple

Style: Inverse correlation

Index: Russell 2000

Name: Internet Short (PDISX)

Management: James Apple

Style: Inverse correlation

Index: Dow Jones Composite Internet

ProFunds

Contact Information

ProFunds
7900 Wisconsin Avenue, Suite 300
Bethesda, MD 20814
888-776-3636

Funds Offered

Name: ProFunds Bear (BRPIX)

Management: The fund has two portfolio managers. Louis Mayberg has over 14 years in the investment industry, with emphasis on hedge funds. Dr. William Seale has more than 30 years of experience in the financial industry. He was also a commissioner of the U.S. Commodity Futures Trading Commission. He is an Emeritus Professor of Finance at George Washington University.

Style: Inverse correlation

Index: S&P 500

Name: ProFunds UltraBear (URPIX)

Management: Same.

Style: Double inverse correlation

Index: S&P 500

Name: ProFunds UltraShort OTC

Management: Same.

Style: Double inverse correlation

Index: NASDAQ 100

ProFunds also has a variety of different specialized sector funds that have a double inverse style:

Banking (F081B)	Semiconductor (SMPIX)
Basic Materials (M$-GDBH)	Technology (TEPIX)
Biotechnology (BIPIX)	Telecommunications (TCPIX)
Energy (ENPIX)	Utilities (UTPIX)
Financial (FNPIX)	Wireless (WCPIX)
Healthcare (HCPIX)	Europe (M$-FGGH)
Internet (INPIX)	Japan (UMPIX)
Pharmaceuticals (PHPIX)	Mid Cap (UMPIX)
Real Estate (REPIX)	Small Cap (UAPIX)

Rydex Funds

Contact Information

301-468-8520

Funds Offered

Name: Tempest 500 Fund (RYTPX)

Management: All the funds are managed by teams. Skip Viragh is the founder of the Rydex fund and created the first leveraged index fund (called the Nova Fund). He came up with his ideas by asking financial advisers about what they wanted. Before starting the fund in 1993, he worked at Rushmore Funds.

Mike Byrum joined the Rydex Funds in 1993. Before this, he was a money manager with Rushmore Funds. He holds the CFA designation.

T. Daniel Gillespie manages the 17 Rydex sector funds. Before joining the fund in 1997, he was a portfolio manager at the Precious Metals Fund.

Charles Tennes joined Rydex in 1999. Before this, he was a money manager at GIT Investment Funds.

John "Buzz" Weidman is a specialist in derivatives trading. He has more than 20 years in the financial industry with such firms as the American Express. He was also a specialist on the American Stock Exchange.

Style: Double inverse correlation

Index: S&P 500

Name: Venture 100 Fund (RYVNX)

Management: Team.

Style: Double inverse correlation

Index: Nasdaq 100

Name: Arktos Fund (RYAIX)

Management: Team.

Style: Inverse correlation

Index: Nasdaq 100

Name: Ursa Fund (RYURX)

Management: Same.

Style: Inverse correlation

Index: S&P 500

Name: Juno Fund (RYJUX)

Management: Team

Style: Inverse correlation

Index: 30-year Treasury Bond

Long-Short Funds

Choice Long-Short Fund (CHLAX). This fund was started in early 2001. The portfolio manager is Patrick Adams, who has more than 15 years experience in the financial industry. Prior stints include Zurich Kemper and Founders Asset Management. He holds the CFA designation. Interestingly enough, this mutual fund is a clone of a long–short hedge fund that he manages.

Contact Information

Choice Funds
207 East Buffalo Street, Suite 400
Milwaukee, WI 53202
800-392-7107

Caldwell & Orkin Market Opportunity (COAGX). Michael Orkin manages the fund from Norcross, Georgia. In 1998, he shorted Internet stocks. But when these trades went against him, he instead became a buyer and rode the Internet wave. Then, when the Internet began to implode, Orkin started to short aggressively. For example, he shorted MotherNature.com at $10 and covered at $1½.

Orkin has managed his investment firm since 1985. Before this, he was an analyst with Pacific Equity Management, Oppenheimer Capital, and Ned Davis Research. He holds the CFA designation.

AXA Rosenberg Value Market Neutral Fund (BRMIX). The fund has three managers. Barr Rosenberg has a long history in finance. From 1968 to 1983, he was a professor of finance and economics at Berkeley. In 1975, he founded Barr Rosenberg Associates, a financial consulting firm. F. William Jump, a CFA, joined Rosenberg in 1990 and develops sophisticated computer models for the fund. As for Kenneth Reid, he joined in the firm in 1986 and is now the CEO.

The fund managers have developed a proprietary stock selection system called the Appraisal Model. It uses highly sophisticated computer models to pinpoint undervalued and overvalued stocks.

Contact Information

> Barr Rosenberg Series Trust
> 237 Park Avenue
> New York, NY 10017
> 800-447-3332

CGM Focus (CGMFX). The manager of the fund is Ken Heebner, whose nickname is "The Mad Bomber." The main reason is that, if a stock disappoints him, he will immediately dump everything. With his Focus Fund, though, he can not only dump the stock, but short it.

In fact, Heebner is one of the best fund manager's in the business. From 1980 to 1995, he was number 2 in overall performance (the one with the better record was the famed manager of Fidelity Magellan, Peter Lynch).

But Heebner's funds are not for the faint of heart. He invests in a small group of stocks, anywhere from 20 to 30. If he guesses right, the returns can be impressive; if he guesses wrong, it can be horrible for his fund investors. Although, one good bet was his shorting of tech stocks during 2000–2001. He targeted such stocks as Amazon.com and Global Crossing.

Heeber started as an economist in 1965 and entered the portfolio management world in 1971. He holds the CFA designation.

Contact Information

CGM Group
PO Box 449
Boston, MA 02117
800-345-4048

Quaker Aggressive Growth (QUAGX). The portfolio manager, Manu Daftary, began his career managing the portfolio of the University of Southern California in 1985. Several years later, he was a portfolio manager at an institutional investment firm, where he used short selling strategies. He holds the CFA designation.

Since late 1996, he has been managing the Quaker Aggressive Growth Fund. Daftary focuses on companies that have strong growth acceleration. But if he thinks the market is softening, he will put more money into cash and short stocks.

Daftary has made smart bets. In 1999, he invested heavily in optical networking stocks, such as Corning and Nortel Networks. But by 2000, he went out of tech stocks and put as much as 70 percent of the fund's assets into cash. He also made selective short bets on stocks. Interestingly enough, Daftary says he is not a market timer; rather, during 2000–2001, he was unable to find stocks that met his requirements for earnings growth.

Contact Information

Quaker Family of Funds
PO Box 844
Conshohocken, PA 19428-0844
800-220-8888

Needham Growth (NEEGX). Peter Trapp has managed the fund since 1995. He started his career in corporate finance in 1973 with First Boston. He also worked for Goldman Sachs.

Trapp does not want to overpay for stocks. In fact, he actively looks for companies that have reported bad news yet have long-term potential. However, if a company does not have long-term potential, he might short it.

Trapp has historically focused on technology stocks. While this was good for his portfolio when the sector was surging, it hurt the portfolio when the shares went into a tailspin. But Trapp was able to reduce the downfall because of his increased short selling. He made large sums from shorting Amazon.com, Yahoo, and PurchasePro.com. By March 2000, he had 25 percent in cash and 25 percent in shorts.

Contact Information

Needham Growth Fund
445 Park Avenue
New York, NY 10022
800-625-7071

Boston Partners Long/Short Equity Fund (BPLSX).   Portfolio manager Edmund Kellogg started his investment career in 1980, working at such mutual funds as the Keystone Group. He holds the CFA designation and has managed the Long/Short Fund since 1998.

He made a good bet in 2000 to short telecommunications and semiconductor stocks.

Contact Information

Boston Partners Family of Funds
400 Bellevue Parkway
Wilmington, DE 19809
800-261-4073

Phoenix-Euclid Market Neutral (EMNAX).   Carlton Neel has run the fund since 1995. Prior to this, he was a vice president of JP Morgan. His fund looks for value investments and will take short positions.

Contact Information

Phoenix Funds
C/O State Street Bank
PO Box 8301
Boston, MA 02266-8301
800-272-2700

Leuthold Core Investment (LCORX).   The fund has two managers, Steven Leuthold and James Floyd (this is the same Leuthold who manages the Grizzly Short Fund). As for Floyd, he has more than 20 years experience on Wall Street.

The fund will try just about anything if it will make money. For example, it has invested in biotech, junk bonds, and even emerging markets.

The comanagers use a sophisticated computer model to make their investment decisions. The model compares an investment sector to the interest rate on U.S. Treasury bonds and sees if the valuation is low or high. The theory is that eventually these sectors will revert to the mean.

The model worked very well in 2000. The comanagers anticipated a fall in the stock market and moved a substantial amount of money away from equities. What's more, the money was placed into biotech companies, which rallied. There was about 14 percent of the portfolio in short positions.

Contact Information

> Leuthold Funds
> 100 N. Sixth Street Suite 700A
> Minneapolis, MN 55403
> 800-273-6886

Calamos Market Neutral Fund (CVSIX).   The portfolio manager John Calamos has more than 20 years experience on Wall Street. He is the author of *Investing in Convertible Securities.* So, it is no surprise that his fund uses convertible bond arbitrage.

Contact Information

> Calamos Funds
> 1111 E. Warrenville Road
> Naperville, IL 60563-1448
> 800-823-7386

Lindner Market Neutral (LDNBX).   The fund has two portfolio managers. Jeff Fotta has 15 years experience in investment research and management. He holds the CFA designation. Thomas Lynch has been with Lindner since March 1999.

Originally, the fund was a pure bear fund. But in 2000, it shifted toward a long–short style of portfolio management.

Contact Information

> Lindner Group
> 7711 Carondelet
> PO Box 11208
> St. Louis, MO 63105
> 314-727-5305

Merger Fund (MERFX).   The coportfolio managers, Bonnie Smith and Frederick Green, have both run the fund since 1989. Smith has more than 15 years experience in Wall Street, starting her career at Westchester Capital. Green has been with Westchester Capital since 1980. Before this, he worked at a portfolio strategist at Goldman Sachs and Kidder Peabody.

The fund specializes in merger arbitrage (this is explained in more detail in Chapter 3). For each merger the fund targets, the goal is to make a 15 percent rate of return. The fund has arbitraged many high-profile mergers, such as the Texaco/Chevron combination.

During 2001, the fund had 35 percent of its assets in cash. The reason is that the M&A market slowed down considerably. In fact, the M&A market can be quite volatile. Yet, since inception, the fund has never had an annual loss.

Contact Information

> Merger Fund
> 100 Summit Lake Drive
> Valhalla, NY 10595
> 800-343-8959

GLOSSARY

accelerated depreciation   When a company depreciates more of an asset in the first few years. This is typical, for example, for high-tech assets (which can become obsolete quickly). See *depreciation.*

accounts payable   An amount that a company owes to a supplier, partners, or employees.

accounts receivable   Sales that are recognized but no cash has been collected yet. In other words, credit was extended for these sales and the accounts receivable is what customers owe the company. This is an asset of the company.

accredited investor   The SEC defines this person as having income of at least $200,000 per year or a net worth of $1 million or more. For example, it is mostly accredited investors that can invest in hedge funds. The reason for this classification is that the government assumes that wealthy investors have the sophistication to analyze investments or the resources to hire qualified advisers.

administrative fee   The fee to cover the costs of mailings to shareholders, customer support, leases, and record keeping for a mutual fund. This fee ranges from 0.2 to 0.5 percent.

advance–decline line   This compares the number of stocks going up with those going down. This essentially measure market breadth; that is, whether most stocks are participating in a rally or a decline. For example, if the market is advancing but there is little market breadth, the market could be poised for a fall.

after-hours trading   Trading that occurs after an exchange such as Nasdaq or NYSE closes. Short selling is allowed in after-hours trading.

allowance for doubtful accounts   This is an estimate by a company as to how much of the accounts receivable are unlikely to be collected. Short sellers are alerted if it looks like this item is under estimated.

amortization   Intangible assets—such as patents, copyright, trade names—have a limited life span. Amortization basically reduces the value of an intangible asset over time. It is similar to depreciation. See *depreciation.*

annual report   Typically this is a glossy publication that showcases a company to shareholders. Although, you will see the balance sheet, income statement, and cash flow statement.

arbitration   A clause in nearly every cash and margin account. This means that the investor agrees to handle all disputes with his broker not through the court system, but by a private system of arbitration panels. For the most part, arbitration tends to be quicker and less expensive.

assets   This is anything that the company owns, such as cash, inventory, land, equipment, and even patents.

auditor   An independent accounting firm that analyzes a company's financial disclosures to see if GAAP standards are being met. All public companies require audited financial statements.

balance sheet   A financial statement that shows a company's assets, liabilities, and equity.

bar chart   The most common type of chart is the bar chart. For each trading day, there is a vertical bar within the price activity chart. The length of each of these bars covers the high and low for the day. The small protruding bar to the left is the opening price and the small protruding bar to the right is the closing price.

bear fund   A mutual fund whose portfolio managers believe that the markets are headed for a prolonged bear market. As a result, they tend to have large amounts of short positions.

bear raid   An investor or group of investors short large amounts of stock to depress the stock value. After the stock price falls, the investor or investors then buy back the stock and try to boost the stock value (usually by manufacturing rumors). This is has been outlawed in the United States.

board of directors   Consists of officers and outside members. The role of the board is to represent the interests of shareholders. Also, the board usually is required to consent to major actions, such as dividends or mergers and acquisitions.

Bollinger bands   A technical analysis indicator that has the following parts: a 21-day moving average, and an upper and lower band that is based on a stock's standard deviation for the moving average. The idea is that stocks tend to trade in a certain range until there is a breakout.

bond   Debt that is issued to the public to raise money for a company. A bond must be paid off after a certain number of years. In the meantime, a bond pays interest to investors.

the borrow   An investor needs to borrow stock in order to short it. However, if there is no stock to borrow, then an investor cannot short. There are a variety of reasons for no borrow. Perhaps the stock cannot be margined or is not in street name. Or a broker may have a borrow, but wants to reserve it for major clients.

buy-in   In a margin account, the broker has the right for a buy-in. That is, the broker can demand that the investor cover a short position and no reason may be given. This is a major risk for short sellers.

call option   Gives an investor the right to buy 100 shares of stock for a certain period of time (usually 3 months).

candlestick charts   Developed centuries ago in Japan, this is a method for technical analysis. As the name implies, the prices tend to look like candles.

cap ex   See *investing activities.*

capital gain   The purchase and sale of a stock at a profit.

cash account   Allows an investor to buy and sell stock so long as stock or cash is in the account. An investor needs a cash and margin account to engage in short selling. See *margin account.*

cash flow statement   A financial statement that shows how much money a company is generating from operations, investment activities, and financing activities.

Chapter 7 bankruptcy   This is when a company has little hope of surviving. With a Chapter 7 filing, a company will liquidate all its assets at the best prices possible. Typically, shareholders are left with nothing.

Chapter 11 bankruptcy   Even though this is filed when a company is bankrupt (that is, cannot pay its creditors), this does not mean the company dissolves. Rather, this filing is known as reorganization and is meant to help a company survive. Despite this, shareholders are usually left with nothing.

common stock   Equity ownership in a company. It can receive dividends and appreciate in value if the company performs well. However, in the event of bankruptcy, common shareholders are last in line to get any proceeds of a liquidation.

conference call   After the release of an earnings report, a company will typically have a conference call with analysts and investors. These can be accessed by a 1-800 number or through the Internet.

confirmation   A broker will send the investor a written document (usually one page) that provides the details of a trade you made. A confirmation is also sent out for short sale trades.

consolidated tape   A high-speed electronic reporting system for quotes for major stock exchanges (such as Nasdaq and NYSE), as well as regional exchanges and ECNs (eletronic communications networks).

convertible preferred   A preferred share that can be converted into a certain number of common shares. See *preferred shares.*

corner   An investor or investor group continues to buy more and more of a company's stock. As the stock price increases to excessive levels, short sellers will build positions. However, the investors that mastermind the corner will have most of the stock and the short sellers will be unable to cover their positions. This causes a short squeeze. See *short squeeze.*

cost of goods sold (COGS)   These are the direct costs for producing the products that have been sold. These costs typically include inventories and salaries.

covering a short   The act of delivering the shares an investor shorts in a stock back to the person who lent the shares.

credit line   A fixed amount that a bank allows a company to borrow at any time. A company will have a credit line just in case it runs into temporary problems.

current assets   Assets that are short-term, expected to last no more than a year on the balance sheet. Current assets include cash and marketable securities, accounts receivable, inventory, restricted cash, and prepaid expenses.

current liabilities   Liabilities that must be paid by a company within a year.

current market value (CMV)   The current value of all the cash and securities in a margin account.

day order   This is a limit or stop order for a stock that is good for the rest of the trading day, unless cancelled.

days sales outstanding (DSO)   Shows how long it takes for a company to collect on its receivables. If it is taking longer, a company may be experiencing troubles.

day trader   According to the Nasdaq and NYSE definition, a trader who makes at least four trades per week (so long as these trades comprise more than 6 percent of all the trades during this period of time). If an investor is classified as a day trader, he has higher requirements when maintaining a margin account (such as a minimum $25,000 current market value).

debit balance   Outstanding loan from a broker in a margin account.

Dear Cross   When the 50-day moving average falls below the 200-day moving average. This signals a bear mode.

depreciation   Over time, the usefulness of assets tends to wear out or become obsolete. On financial statements, this is taken into account by reducing, or depreciating, the value of the asset (basically, depreciation is an expense item that occurs over the life of an existing asset).

dividend   The amount a company pays each quarter to shareholders. If a company announces it is cutting the dividend, this is a sign for short sellers that a company may be experiencing problems.

double inverse fund   A mutual fund that performs opposite of an index—but it is a 1-to-2 relationship. For example, if the S&P 500 decreases by 1 percent, the double inverse fund value will increase by 2 percent.

downtrend   When a stock has a series of lower highs and lower lows.

due diligence   When investment firm analyzes a company's financials and background before agreeing to raise money or provide financial services to the company.

earnings per share (EPS)   This is the company's net earnings divided by the number of shares outstanding. Thus, if the company earned $1 million and has 1 million shares outstanding, the EPS is $1 per share. The EPS is used to measure a company's price to earnings (PE) ratio. See *price to earnings ratio.*

8-K   Filing by a company for significant events, such as a merger, new director, or even bankruptcy.

electronic communications network (ECN)   A private system to trade stock listed on Nasdaq or NYSE. One of the most prominent ECNs is Instinet.

employee stock option plan   A plan set up by companies to motivate employees by offering them the right to buy shares in the company.

EPS   See *earnings per share.*

equity   After deducting for the margin loans, the equity shows an investor's right to ownership in an account.

exercise price   The price in which someone has the right to buy shares in accordance to a call or put option.

financing activities   A listing on a company's cash flow statement showing how a company is raising money, such as through selling stock, bonds, or borrowing from banks.

Financial Accounting Standards Board (FASB) Established in 1972, this organization established the Generally Accepted Accounting Principles (GAAP) for accounting and financial reporting.

first in, first out (FIFO) A method for calculating inventory by using the costs of the inventory that was purchased first.

float The number of shares of stock in a company that can be traded on the open market. If short interest represents 10 percent or more of the float, then a short seller could be in danger of a potential short squeeze. See *short squeeze.*

free cash flow The amount of money a company has to make new investments or distribute cash to shareholders. To determine free cash flow, you must make adjustments to a company's cash flow statement. See *cash flow statement.*

future A contract that gives an investor the ability to go long or short on a commodity, index, or even single stocks (known as a single stock future). To do this, an investor must put up a certain amount of margin against the total value of the contract (say, 3 to 5 percent).

Generally Accepted Accounting Principles (GAAP) Rules of accounting for financial statements.

going concern If an auditor believes a company will have much difficulty in staying solvent, then it will say it is a "going concern."

good till cancelled (GTC) A limit or stop order on a stock that is open until it is cancelled. Although, there are usually time limits for these orders, say a few weeks.

gross profit The difference between revenues and cost of goods sold (COGS). See *cost of goods sold.*

guidance What the company is projecting for the next few quarters. This can have a big impact on the stock.

hedge When investors use techniques—such as shorting stocks—to protect a portfolio if the markets fall.

hedge fund   A private pool of capital managed by professional portfolio managers. These funds typically buy long and short. Also, a hedge fund is typically geared for wealthy investors and institutions.

HOLDR   A security that represents ownership in common stock or ADRs of a particular industry or sector group. This is a liquid investment that allows an investor to diversify among 20 or more stocks.

hypothecation   A clause in a margin agreement that means you agree to pledge your securities as collateral for a margin loan. That is, if you fail to pay off the loan, the brokerage firm has the right to sell part or all of your securities.

income statement   A financial statement that shows a company's revenues, expenses, and earnings.

initial public offering (IPO)   The first time a company offers shares to the public to raise capital.

insider   An officer, director, or major shareholder of a company. An insider is not allowed to short the company's stock.

in the money   See *intrinsic value.*

intangible asset   An asset that has no physical form, such as a patent, copyright, trade name, or trademark.

intrinsic value   For call and put options. Intrinsic value is calculated as the current stock price minus the strike price of the option. If it is a positive number, then the stock option is considered to be "in the money." Thus, an investor is guaranteed to get this amount if he sells the option on the market. If there is no intrinsic value, then the option is "out of the money."

inventory   The value of a company's raw materials, work in progress, supplies to make products and finished products.

inventory turnover   Shows how many days it takes to sell existing inventory.

inverse fund   A mutual fund that performs the opposite of an index. For example, if the S&P 500 decreases 1 percent, the fund value will increase 1 percent.

investing activities   Found on a company's cash flow statement, this section shows what types of capital expenditures (also known as *cap ex items*) in such long-term things as plant, equipment, merger and acquisitions, and perhaps even software.

junk bond   A bond issued by a company that has a strong likelihood of not being paid off. See *bond.*

last in, first out (LIFO)   A method for calculating inventory by using the cost of the inventory that was purchased most recently.

liabilities   This is what a company owes. The debts can be accounts payables, notes, bonds, unpaid taxes, and so on.

limit order   With this order, an investor is basically haggling to get a better price. The investor will only get an order filled if it is at the price specified or above for a sale (or below if it is a buy).

line charts   This is the simplest chart used in technical analysis. It is the plotting of the closing price or average for any given time period. This can be every day, or it can be weekly, monthly, and so on.

load   A commission you pay when you buy a mutual fund. The fee can be as high as 3 percent of your investment.

lock-up agreement   A contract that prevents officers and employees from selling their shares after an initial public offering. The time period is usually 6 months. See *initial public offering.*

long   When an investor buys and holds onto a stock.

long–short fund   A mutual fund that shorts and buys stock.

management fee   The fee that compensates the money managers of a mutual fund. The fee will typically range from 1 to 3 percent.

margin account   A brokerage account that allows an investor to borrow against stock in the account. This is a loan and the investor must pay interest on the amount borrowed. To sell short, an investor needs to set up a margin account.

marginable stock   A stock that a brokerage firm will allow investors to borrow against. If a stock is not marginable, then investors are unable to short it.

market order   A broker will get an order filled at the current price. Thus, a market order tends to have fast execution and the commissions are usually lower. However, you may not necessarily get the best price.

market breadth   See *advance–decline line.*

marketable securities   These are short-term liquid assets, such as Treasury bills or commercial paper.

minimum maintenance requirement   The minimum amount that is required in current market value (CMV) of a margin account. If the CMV falls below the minimum, the brokerage can request that the investor deposit more cash or securities. If not, the broker has the right to liquidate part or all the securities in the account.

moving average   The plotting of an average price over time on a stock chart. For example, a 10-day moving average would take the average prices for the previous 10 days and plot the result for today. For the next day, it would use the average for the prior 10 days and so on. The moving average is used to reduce the overall volatility in a stock chart.

moving average convergence-divergence (MACD)   The most common approach for the MACD is to calculate the 26-day and 12-day exponential moving averages (EMAs). The MACD subtracts the 26-day EMA from the 12-day EMA. This is the centerline, which oscillates above or below zero. If the centerline is above zero, then the 12-day EMA is trading above the 26-day EMA. If the centerline is negative, then the 26-day EMA is above the 12-day EMA.

mutual fund   A pool of assets managed by professional investors. A mutual fund is an effective way to diversify assets while paying relatively low fees for the services provided.

National Association of Securities Dealers (NASD)   The self-regulatory agency for the securities industry. All stockbrokers are members of the NASD. If you go to the NASD's Web site at www.nasdr.com, you can do background checks on stockbrokers.

Off-balance-sheet debts or liabilities   When a company uses accounting measures to remove certain debts from the balance sheet. By doing this, a company will make itself look more solvent than it really is.

operating activities   Found on a company's cash flow statement, which shows the inflows and outflows of cash in terms of the core business of the company.

OTC Bulletin Board (also known as the OTCBB)   OTC stands for over the counter and this is basically any security that is not listed on the Nasdaq, NYSE, or AMEX. Typically, small companies are traded on the OTCBB. Also, there is no uptick rule in effect.

out of the money   See *intrinsic value.*

PE ratio   See *price to earnings ratio.*

price to earnings ratio (PE)   This is calculated by dividing the current stock price by the company's earnings per share (EPS). This is a calculation used by short sellers to see if a company is overvalued. For example, if the industry PE ratio is 10 and a company is selling for a 50 PE, then it might be overvalued. See *earnings per share.*

private investment in a public entity (PIPE)   An investment in an existing public company from high net worth individuals and institutions.

preferred stock   Represents equity ownership in a company. However, in the event of bankruptcy, the preferred stock holders are paid off before common stock holders.

premium   How much a put or call option costs. This is done by taking the price of option and multiplying it by 100 shares. So if the price of the option is $15, then the premium is $150 ($15 × 100 shares).

prepaid expenses   When a company has paid for something in advance, such as for rent, insurance, advertising, and supplies.

pro forma earnings   Earnings that are not according to the standards of GAAP (Generally Accepting Accounting Principles). For example, a company may adjust the earnings for a one-time restructuring charge or a merger.

prospectus   Filed by companies that are issuing securities to the public, such as through an initial public offering, a secondary offering, or even a mutual fund.

proxy statement   Document sent to all shareholders for important votes, such as for salaries, election of directors, and mergers.

put option   Gives the investor the right to sell 100 shares of a stock for a certain period of time (usually 3 months).

quarterly report   The financials for a company's prior quarter. The document is usually not long.

real body   Used in candlestick charts. A real body is a thick vertical rectangle that represents the range of a stock's open and close. If the real body is filled, it means that the close was lower than the open. A white real body means the close is higher than the open.

redemption fees   A fee paid when an investor sells shares in a mutual fund. This fee can range from 0.25 to 2 percent.

related-party transaction   Transactions in which one of the officers of the company has a conflict of interest. For example, the officer may strike a contract with a company that is owned by his brother. Such related-party transactions must be disclosed to the public.

relative strength indicator (RSI)   A technical analysis indicator that shows the momentum of the stock—that is, whether it is overbought or oversold. The RSI ranges from 0 to 100. If a stock hits 30 or below, it is considered to be oversold. If the indicator reaches 70 or above, it is overbought.

repricing   When a company lowers the exercise price of employee stock options. This is done because the stock price has plunged and the chances of the options making any money is unlikely.

restatement   When a company must adjust its prior revenue and earnings disclosures. In most cases, a company was too aggressive or even fraudulent. A short seller will often focus on companies that make restatements.

resistance   Suppose a stock reaches $50 per share and each time, falls back down. This price would represent the resistance level of the stock. That is, the market is not willing to buy the stock at this level. It is considered fully valued.

restricted cash/marketable securities   Cash or marketable securities that must be spent for a particular purpose, such as to fulfill a contract.

restricted stock   Stock that cannot be sold because of a restriction, such as by a contract or government regulation.

retained earnings   The profits a company maintains in its operations to continue to generate growth.

revenue   What a company generates from its business activities, such as the sale of its products or services, subscriptions, fees, commissions, or rentals. This is known as *the top line*, since the revenue is reported at the top of an income statement.

reverse split   When a company announces that it will reduce the number of shares outstanding. For example, if a company announces a 1 for 4 split, then for every four shares owned, the company will take away three. In this case, the stock price will be four times higher than its current price. Thus, companies use reverse stock splits to increase the stock price. However, short sellers see this as a sign that a company is having troubles.

risk factors   Risks that a company discloses to investors in its filings, such as the prospectus.

Securities Act of 1933   The first national law to regulate securities in the United States. The law requires complete disclosure of any offerings of securities to the public.

Securities Exchange Act of 1934   Another significant law passed by Congress to regulate the securities industry. The law established the Securities and Exchange Commission (SEC) and set forth rules on how securities are traded. The law also gave the Federal Reserve the power to regulate margin requirements. See *margin requirements.*

Securities and Exchange Commission (SEC)   The federal agency that enforces the securities laws in the United States. The SEC also regulates short selling.

sequential growth   A sales increase over a specific time period. Typically, a company's financials will compare the current quarter against the same quarter a year ago. However, some companies may compare the current quarter to the previous quarter.

short funds   Mutual funds that tend to use short selling in their portfolios.

shorting against the box   An investor buys and shorts the same amount of stock either at the same price or at different prices. For example, an investor shorts 100 shares at $50 and buys 100 shares at $40. The investor has locked in a profit of $10 per share. The reason is that if the stock price goes up, the short position falls by the same amount as the long position.

short interest   The total number of shares that have been shorted but not yet covered. On a monthly basis, both the NYSE and the Nasdaq publish short interest data. You also can find this data on popular finance sites, such as finance.yahoo.com.

short interest ratio   Calculated as the short interest divided by the average daily volume. This shows the number of days it would take to cover all the shorts. If the short interest is 1 million shares and the daily volume is 200,000 shares, then it would take 5 days to clear all the stock. If it would take more than a week to cover the shorts, short sellers could be vulnerable to a short squeeze. See *short squeeze.*

short selling   An investor borrows stock and immediately sells the shares on the open market. The investor promises to deliver the shares back to the person they were borrowed from. For example, an investor borrows 100 shares at $10 each and sells the stock, generating proceeds of $1000. The stock falls to $5 and the investor buys 100 shares for $500 and delivers the shares to the lender. The investor made $500 on the trade. If the stock went to $15, the investor would have lost $500.

short squeeze   When a stock begins to surge, short sellers will typically try to cover their positions. However, this creates even more demand for the stock and the price will increase even further.

special memorandum account (SMA)   As the value of a margin account increases, an investor will be able to borrow more money or withdraw cash from the account or buy more stock without putting up more cash.

spin-off   When a company sells all or a part of a division to shareholders in a public offering of shares.

stochastic   A technical analysis indicator that will range between 0 and 100 on the chart. There are two main types of stochastics, fast and slow. The fast stochastic will have two chart lines, the percent K and the percent D. The slow stochastic will take the fast stochastic and smooth it out. While the fast stochastic will give you bearish signs faster, it is subject to more false signals.

straight-line depreciation   When a company depreciates an asset in equal amounts over the life of an asset. For example, if the depreciation rate is 20 perent, then the depreciation will occur over 5 years (adding up to 100 percent of the asset).

street name   A brokerage firm will hold your certificates for the shares you own. To get a margin loan against stock, it must be in street name.

strike price   The price at which a person has the right to buy or sell a stock according to an option. See *call option* or *put option.*

stuffing the channel   When a company ships products that customers do not request. The company does this to inflate revenues. However, in many cases, the customers will have too many products and start to send them back.

support   When a stock hits a certain price several times and does not break through.

technical analysis   Using charts of historical prices and volume to make investment decisions.

10-K   A comprehensive financial document that includes the financial activities of a company for the year. In it, you will find the income statement, balance sheet, and statement of cash flows. There are also footnotes that can provide useful information.

10-Q   Provides financial information for a quarter of a company's history. These documents tend to have much more information than a company's quarterly report.

time value   In call and put options, the calculation of the difference between the premium of the option and the intrinsic value. However, as an option gets closer to expiration, the time value tends to fall in value. See *intrinsic value.*

top line   See *revenues.*

trading halt   This is when the NYSE, AMEX or Nasdaq suspend trading in a stock. Typically, a trading halt lasts for an hour or so. In many cases, a trading halt is a way for a company to better disseminate important announcements (such as a merger) so as not to create order imbalances.

trading suspension   The SEC has the authority to suspend trading in a stock for up to 10 trading days. This is done when the SEC believes that a public company is not providing current or accurate information to shareholders.

12b-1 fee   A fee that helps with the costs of marketing and distribution of a mutual fund. The fee ranges from 0.25 to 1 percent.

underwriter   The investment firm that manages a company's initial public offering (when the company issues stock to the public for the first time to raise capital).

uptick rule   Short selling is allowed only when done on an uptick or zero plus tick (the uptick rule does not apply to the OTC Bulletin Board market). An uptick is when the last reported stock price was an increase. If you look at a stock quote, an uptick would show a + sign. A zero plus tick, on the other hand, is when the current stock price is the same as the previous one, but is higher than the last different price.

uptrend   When a stock makes a series of higher lows and higher highs.

vendor financing   When a company lends money to its customers to buy its products. This can put a company in a precarious situation if the customer is unable to pay its future bills (in most cases, the products are purchased over time).

visibility   This describes the confidence a company has in its projects. If there is a lack of visibility, investors get concerned.

write-off   When a company decides to recognize that some or all of its inventory is worthless.

INDEX

Tom Taulli is the founder of Taulli Research, which provides research services to the financial industry. The author or coauthor of several books, including *Tapping into Wireless, Investing in IPOs,* and *Stock Options,* Taulli is a regular contributor to MSN Investor, *Bloomberg Personal Finance,* Forbes.com, and other national publications. An accomplished angel investor, his comments and insights have appeared in *The Wall Street Journal, Barron's, USA Today,* and TheStreet.com. He has his own site at *www.taulli.com.*